CHILD WELFARE PERSPECTIVES

Serving African American Children

edited by
Sondra Jackson &
Sheryl Brissett-Chapman

Transaction Publishers
New Brunswick (U.S.A.) and London (U.K.)

Copyright © 1999 by the Child Welfare League of America, Inc. Originally published as *Child Welfare,* vol. 76, no. 1, January/February 1997 © 1997 by the Child Welfare League of America, Inc.

All rights reserved under International and Pan-American Copyright Conventions. No part of this book may be reproduced or transmitted in any form or by any means, electronic or mechanical, including photocopy, recording, or any information storage and retrieval system, without prior permission in writing from the publisher. All inquiries should be addressed to Transaction Publishers, Rutgers—The State University, 35 Berrue Circle, Piscataway, New Jersey 08854-8042.

This book is printed on acid-free paper that meets the American National Standard for Permanence of Paper for Printed Library Materials.

Library of Congress Catalog Number: 98-9773
ISBN: 0-7658-0434-4
Printed in the United States of America

Library of Congress Cataloging-in-Publication Data

Serving African American children: child welfare perspectives /
    edited by Sondra Jackson and Sheryl Brissett-Chapman.
        p. cm.
    Originally published as v. 76, no. 1, Jan./Feb. 1997, of the
publication Child welfare.
    Includes bibliographical references.
    ISBN 0-7658-0434-4
    1. Social work with Afro-American children. 2. Afro-American
children—Services for. 3. Child welfare—United States. 4. Family
social work—United States. 5. Social work with Afro-Americans.
I. Jackson, Sondra. II. Brissett-Chapman, Sheryl.
HV3181.S46   1998
362.7'089'96073—dc21   98-9773
                                                                 CIP

CONTENTS

INTRODUCTION

Serving African American Children brings together articles by African American authors who are committed to research, policies, and programs affecting African American families and children. It was initiated by the Black Administrators in Child Welfare, Inc. (BACW) to present an African American perspective on child welfare issues affecting African American children. Endorsed and supported initially by the Child Welfare League of America (CWLA), BACW has continued to refine its role within the American child welfare system since the historic first meeting of its founding members in 1971.

BACW's mission is to have a positive impact on national, state, and local policies, legislation, and practices that affect African American children, youths, and families. Our goals are to (1) ensure that the African American experience becomes a part of the awareness, understanding, and service delivery of child welfare agencies; (2) ensure that African American clients are served in a manner that enriches their lives and supports their cultural heritage; (3) establish a support network for African American administrators that will enrich and expand their skills, experience, and administrative potential; and (4) advocate for the employment of African American administrative staff members in all public and private health and human services agencies involved with the African American child and family.

Through the years, BACW has issued position papers and policy statements on child welfare matters such as kinship care, day care, group care, in-home services, child protective services, transracial adoption, and out-of-home care. These have served as guides for BACW members in their roles as practitioners and administrators and as presenters and participants on national and local task forces. Through its annual conference, BACW shares with the child welfare community its position on various child welfare policy and practice issues. Throughout its history, BACW has had dedicated leaders who have contributed to the progress of the organization. As we come together out of love for our people and with a desire to better the conditions of African American children and families who are involved with the American child welfare system, our aim is to build, not destroy . . . to create, not tear down.

The articles in this special volume challenge the child welfare community to (1) ensure that all African American children will receive protection, nurturing, and an improved quality of life; (2) create and sustain mutual communication and support through program development; (3) ensure that African American consultants are involved in the evaluation of agencies where African American populations represent a significant proportion of the service population; and (4) increase African American leadership through education and training opportunities in preparation for executive level positions.

The chapters in this volume, originally published as a special edition of *Child Welfare* (vol. 76, no. 1, January/February 1997), can be grouped into three sections that reflect a variety of policy, research, and practice issues; clinical techniques and treatment models; and new perspectives in child welfare. The theme that runs throughout all of the articles is our grave concern about the overrepresentation of African American children and families in the child welfare system and about the limited—if not missing—influence of the African American perspective on policy and practice.

Policy, Research, and Practice Issues

In "African American Children in the Modern Child Welfare System: A Legacy of the Flemming Rule," Claudia Lawrence Webb links the overrepresentation of African American children in the current child welfare system to a significant historical development in child welfare known as the Flemming Rule. She states that "the Flemming Rule . . . a positive piece of welfare legislation which was negatively implemented . . . has had a profound effect on the modern U.S. child welfare system." Her article sets the stage for the possible consequences of current welfare reforms on the child welfare system today.

In "Family Preservation and Support Services: A Missed Opportunity for Kinship Care," Julia Danzy and Sondra Jackson discuss the importance of understanding "the natural relationship between kinship care and family preservation services to African American children and families." The authors present findings of a survey of state plans for providing family preservation and support services that suggest that most states missed an opportunity to plan for children in kinship care placements.

Sheryl Brissett-Chapman, in "Child Protection Risk Assessment and African American Children: Cultural Ramifications for Families and Communities," argues for urgency in pursuit of a dialogue that examines varied definitions of harm and risk for children, and the implications of those definitions for cuttural conflict, screening and intake, and resource allocation. She states that as outmoded and antiquated bureaucratic child caring systems fail to respond effectively to African American chitdren who come to the attention of child protective services, one can observe a frightening effect.

The overrepresentation of children and families in the out-of-home care system is discussed in "An Out-of-Home Care System in Crisis: Implications for African American Children in the Child Welfare System." Using current child welfare data and a review of the literature, Annie Woodley Brown and Barbara Bailey-Etta examine the nature of the crisis in child welfare and the relationship of poverty and social conditions to an increase in placements of African Americans.

Ruth G. McRoy, Zena Oglesby, and Helen Grape, in "Achieving Same-Race Adoptive Placements for African American Children: Culturally Sensitive Practice Approaches," analyze state and federal policies that limit the consideration of race as a factor in the selection of adoptive families, and describe successful placement practices of a public and a private agency, elaborating on culturally competent practice.

In the final article in this group, "African American Families and HIV/AIDS: Caring for Surviving Children," Alma J. Carten and Ilene Fennoy present the preliminary findings of a national research project to examine the health, social service, and legal needs of African American children who experience the death of one or both parents as a result of HIV/AIDS. The project seeks to guide the development of culturally competent policies and practices across service delivery systems managing the needs of African American families and children affected by HIV/AIDS.

Clinical Techniques and Treatment Models

The four articles in this section describe unique clinical techniques and treatment models. Shawan D. P. Gregory and Frederick B. Phillips, in "Of Mind, Body, and Spirit: Therapeutic Foster Care—An Innovative Approach to Healing from an NTU Perspective," describe an innovative therapeutic foster care program. The program incorporates a unique clinical approach, NTU psychotherapy, into its treatment approach. Through culturally competent therapeutic techniques, the community-based agency strives to improve the delivery of mental health services.

In "African American Female Adolescent Identity Development: A Three-Dimensional Perspective," Joyce West Stevens utilizes qualitative data from a longitudinal pregnancy-prevention research project to conceptualize a model of identity development in African American female adolescents, and presents implications for clinical practice in child welfare.

A treatment model for addicted African American women is presented in "A Rite of Passage Approach Designed to Preserve the Families of Substance-Abusing African American Women." Vanesta L. Poitier, Makini Niliwaambieni, and Cyprian Lamar Rowe describe an innovative approach to treatment for African American women and their families whose existence has been marked by family dysfunction and substance abuse. The model is rich in African culture and tradition and aims to make families self-sustaining.

Aminifu R. Harvey and Antoinette A. Coleman, in "An Afrocentric Program for African American Males in the Juvenile Justice System," set forth a range of social and psychological services for high-risk African American adolescent males and their families. Their model is based on an Afrocentric approach that incorporates the principles of spirituality and collectivity.

New Perspective in Child Welfare

The final three articles in this volume provide new perspectives and ask critical questions about culturally competent services with diverse client groups. In "Same-Race Practice: Do We Expect Too Much or Too Little?," Bernadette Jeffrey Fletcher explores practitioners' perceptions, expectations, and service recommendations for troubled youths along racial, gender, and age dimensions.

Geraldine Jackson-White, Cheryl Davenport Dozier, J. Toni Oliver, and Lydia Barnwell Gardner, in "Why African American Adoption Agencies Succeed: A New Perspective on Self-Help," present self-help activities specific to one adoption agency to illustrate contemporary models of self-help in the African American community.

Finally, Anna McPhatter, in "Cultural Competence in Child Welfare: What Is It? How Do We Achieve It? What Happens Without It?," challenges the child welfare system to explore the benefits of authentic commitment to achieving cultural competence. She describes a model comprising a grounded knowledge base, affective dimensions, and cumulative skills proficiency.

Acknowledgments

Although we have encountered many obstacles and disappointments in our struggle to influence the child welfare agenda, we are encouraged by this opportunity to share information on child welfare research, policy, and practice from an African American perspective. Our special thanks go to CWLA Executive Director David Liederman, BACW President Jestina Richardson, the CWLA publications staff, and Joyce Johnson, BACW Staff Director, who works tirelessly with our organization.

We also wish to thank the distinguished members of the special issue peer review panel: Charlene Ingram, Philadelphia Department of Human Services; Robert B. Hill, Institute for Urban Research, Morgan State University; Mark G. Battle, Community Outreach Services, University of Maryland at Baltimore School of Social Work; Joseph Crumbley, Therapist; Gladys Walton Hall, Howard University School of Social Work; Christine Diggs, Virginia State, School of Social Work; Muriel Gray, University of Maryland at Baltimore School of Social Work; Barbara Dorsey, University of Maryland at Baltimore School of Social Work; Llewellyn Cornelius, University of Maryland at Baltimore School of Social Work; E. Aracelis Francis, Minority Fellowship Programs, Council on Social Work Education; Otis Johnson, Chatham Savannah Youth Futures Authority; Jean Hyche-Williams, Coppin State College, Social Services Department; and Dee Kilpatrick, Jane Addams College of Social Work.

Special thanks go to Julia Danzy for her encouragement, commitment, and contributions to *Serving African American Children*. The editors are also grateful to Charlotte Anderson for handling the administrative and coordinating tasks involved in bringing this publication together. This volume was derived from a special edition of *Child Welfare* that for the first time brought together scholarly articles from an African American perspective. It is our sincere hope that this book will add to the knowledge in the field of child welfare and will be a beginning step in encouraging the publishing of African American perspectives on issues affecting African American children, youths, and families.

SONDRA M. JACKSON
Director of Training
University of Maryland
   School of Social Work
Baltimore, MD

SHERYL BRISSETT-CHAPMAN
Executive Director
Baptist Home for Children
   and Families
Bethesda, MD

1
African American Children in the Modern Child Welfare System: A Legacy of the Flemming Rule

Claudia Lawrence-Webb

Children of color throughout America—and especially those who are African American—are disproportionately represented in the child welfare system. This article links this current child welfare condition to the most significant but little known ruling in the historical development of the modern child welfare system—the Flemming Rule. The Flemming Rule, although intended to be constructive, was negatively implemented in a way that has had long-term serious consequences for African American children and their families. Implications for future policies are discussed.

Claudia Lawrence-Webb, D.S.W., is Assistant Professor, East Tennessee State University, Johnson City, TN.

Children of color throughout America, and especially African American children, are disproportionately represented in the child welfare system [Leashore et al. 1991; Children's Defense Fund 1990; National Black Child Development Institute 1990]. One explanation for this phenomenon may lie in the historical evolution and implementation of the Flemming Rule. This landmark administrative decision by Dr. Arthur Flemming, who was Secretary of the U.S. Department of Health, Education, and Welfare in the Eisenhower administration, had an enormous impact on the implementation of AFDC policies and child welfare services.

The Flemming Rule was an administrative response to discriminatory practices in the AFDC program under the Social Security Act of 1935, practices that resulted in mass expulsions of needy children from state welfare rolls.* The rule evolved as a result of widespread flagrant abuses of home suitability requirements by some states to deny AFDC benefits to African American children and their mothers. The evolution and implementation of this fundamentally important rule has been ignored in discussions and debates about AFDC and child welfare policies and the connection between these two vital aspects of social welfare.

Background

Racial oppression was built into the AFDC program when it was created as part of the 1935 Social Security Act [Mink 1990; Gordon 1990; Quadagno 1988; Skocpol 1988; Abramovitz 1988]. Rules regarding suitability of the home and other restrictions on the provision of AFDC were the creation of state governments and were implemented from 1935 to the early 1960s with the tacit approval of the federal Bureau of Public Assistance (BPA) [Skocpol 1988; Quadagno 1988; Bell 1965]. State AFDC programs were established with matching federal funds. In the

---

* The AFDC public assistance program (Aid to Families with Dependent Children) was originally known as the ADC program (Aid to Dependent Children). AFDC will be used in this text.

early years, there was a 50-50 match; over time, the federal share became larger. Despite the large federal role, states had great discretion in choosing policies in AFDC [Bell 1965]. These policies included "home suitability clauses," "substitute father rules," man-in-the-house rule," and "illegitimate child clauses" [Piven & Cloward 1971; Bell 1965]. The policies arbitrarily denied benefits to African Americans because their homes were seen as immoral, men other than biological fathers were identified by workers as assuming care of the recipients' children, the worker believed a man was living in the home, and/or the mother had children born out-of-wedlock.

For example, home suitability rules of the 1940s and 1950s evolved from the federal government's failure to provide clarity concerning a definition and specific criteria for determining the suitability of a home.[1] This led to variability at the state level and allowed public welfare agencies to become instruments of local interests and prejudices, a situation that ultimately led to debate about the usefulness of the policy and the real purpose it served.[2]

Ostensibly, home suitability requirements were created to ensure that public support was provided only to "moral" homes. States could reject at the point of application, or subsequently expel from the rolls, clients whose homes were labeled "immoral." Cases of expelled or rejected homes were closed without follow-up services under the rationalization that services to the children could not be provided because cases were no longer active [Bell 1965].

The records of the Children's Bureau,[3] the National Association for the Advancement of Colored People (NAACP),[4] and the National Urban League (NUL),[5] reflect the different application of AFDC eligibility standards for African Americans[6] in states such as Mississippi and Florida.[7] Prior to the Flemming Rule (1955–1959), the majority of African American families who lived in the South did not receive welfare benefits from the federal-state AFDC because they were arbitrarily denied.[8]

In 1960, states such as Louisiana overnight expelled thousands of clients from the AFDC rolls simply on the grounds that in these cases women had a child outside of marriage. This was taken as face value evidence of "unsuitability" and the expulsions took place without hearings for the clients and without any serious investigations or intervention by welfare agencies concerning the well-being of the child. The policies were immersed in the politics of racism, for the expulsions on the grounds of "unsuitability" were overwhelmingly applied to African American clients. The expulsion of clients and their children from the welfare rolls had extreme significance for the child welfare system because these children were then classified as being neglected due to a lack of adequate income to provide properly for them. This situation is known as the Louisiana Incident [Bell 1965].

The Flemming Rule

The Flemming Rule was implemented in response to the national publicity garnered by the 1960 actions of Louisiana and other states where mass expulsions took place. The public outcry that arose as a result of the actions of the Louisiana state government in its expulsion of 23,000 children from the welfare rolls in 1960 was overwhelming, although it was not the first time states had taken that kind of action.[9] Mississippi had engaged in this practice in the early 1950s and Florida had done so just a year earlier in 1959, when it expelled 14,000 children (over 90% of them African Americans) from the welfare rolls without any public outcry.[10]

The Flemming Rule declared that if a state believed a particular home was "unsuitable," that state had to (1) provide due process protections for the family, and (2) provide service interventions to families that were deemed to be "unsuitable." States could no longer simply apply a label of "unsuitable," expel the family from the AFDC rolls, and ignore the family. The rule was the first action taken against the arbitrary state home suitability policies.

It is possible to distinguish three distinct stages in these developments: (1) the pre-Flemming Rule stage;[11] (2) the transitional Flemming Rule stage,[12] and (3) the implementation of the Flemming Rule.[13]

Stages of Development

Initial Period: 1955–1959

The AFDC program had been initially perceived as a temporary program, one that people needed and deserved. Even so, it was fraught with issues of morality that had been inherited from its predecessor, the Widow's Pension Programs of the early 1900s [Quadagno 1988; Steiner 1966; Bell 1965]. It emphasized the morality and worthiness of its recipients as part of the means test for determining eligibility for assistance. The states' definitions of what constituted morality and immorality were highly variable and were shaped by local economics and politics. For example, Mississippi had as many as five different definitions for home suitability requirements in a five-year period (1958–1963). Initially, these definitions were broad in scope, although over time, they became increasingly specific and restrictive in nature. Definitions of unsuitability included cases of children born to the mother during the receipt of assistance;[14] agency guidelines that emphasized lowered expectations of parents accustomed to substandards of living and perceived them as devoid of ethical principles;[15] viewing "illegitimate" pregnancies or child(ren) as prima facia evidence of promiscuity;[16] substitute parent guidelines focusing on a parent's relationship with a person not the legal spouse;[17] and the parent's maintenance of a continuous relationship though not married.[18]

The federal government did not have a clear-cut definition for states to use in determining the suitability or morality of welfare recipients. The Social Security Administration (SSA) and its subunit, the Bureau of Public Assistance, often saw their roles as allowing states considerable discretion in setting policies regarding welfare eligibility. This was the case in home suitability requirements.[19]

From an early point in the history of the program, the federal government was aware of the fact that state governments established guidelines that focused in a punitive manner on the behavior of the parent as a determinant for AFDC benefits.[20] Nationwide, states that implemented the home suitability requirements most often referred to "illegitimacy" and illicit relationships on the part of the mother.[21] The expression of these behaviors by the mother determined the child's worthiness to receive benefits.

Clients who were rejected or expelled in most instances received no follow-up services for their children, despite the fact that an assessment had shown that the children were living in dangerous or highly negative environments.[22] Although state policies included formal guidelines for follow-up services,[23] the states followed highly discretionary, arbitrary, and discriminatory practices in implementing these guidelines.[24]

In simple terms, according to Dr. Flemming, in his memorandum dated January 16, 1961, to the Commissioner of Social Security, "The purpose behind the ADC title is to help the states meet the welfare needs of dependent children who are deprived of the support of a parent and are living in the home of a close relative."[25]

Transitional Period: January 1960–December 1962

In the second stage of the process, the transitional period of the development and announcement of the Flemming Rule, an attempt was made by the federal government to reshape the home suitability requirements and to correct the abuses of the first period.

In this period, BPA and SSA attempted to (1) set guidelines and provide clarification to states regarding the use of the home suitability requirement and limit its abuse; (2) ensure that children were not abandoned, unprotected, or left without a means of having their basic needs met once a state declared a home unsuitable; (3) emphasize to states the importance of service provision in conjunction with cash payments to welfare clients, and (4) use the power of the federal matching funds to implement these guidelines.

The state home suitability requirements at first "were limited in scope" in Flemming's words. In the early 1960s, when an increase and shift in the welfare population occurred, the definition of home suitability was expanded and states began to increase the number of conditions that could result in application denial or in expulsion from the program.[26] By 1961, the NAACP had accused certain states (Louisiana, Mississippi, Michigan) of expanding their definition of home suitability requirements while unfairly and arbitrarily interpreting and enforcing them to satisfy unjust and racist social, political, and economic purposes.[27] The denial of benefits on such a large scale to African Americans prompted the following statement from NAACP representatives in the Mississippi Delta: "The white landlords are being overheard to say now more and more when Negroes ask for assistance, 'Let the NAACP support you this winter.'"[28] NAACP representatives attributed the denial of welfare benefits to "the prevailing attitudes of state and other public officials."[29] Before the Flemming Rule, no formal determination was made that states using such policies were violating the Social Security Act of 1935. Thus, the concept of states' rights dominated AFDC programs before 1961, particularly as they applied to the treatment of African Americans. Overall, home suitability policies and practices were used to restrict public welfare's help to families in need by narrowly defining their needs in terms of financial assistance [Skocpol 1988; Quadagno 1988; Bell 1965]. The announcement and development of the Flemming Rule finally provided states with a federal definition of home suitability requirements and the limitations of its use by clearly stating that home suitability requirements could still be set by the state but the state could not use the conduct of the parent to deny financial assistance and services to a child.

In January 1961, Secretary Flemming wrote to the Commissioner of Social Security that the so-called "'suitable home' eligibility condition precluded any consideration of the child's need for food, clothing, and shelter if the home is thought by the assistance agency to be unsuitable...the purpose of the Aid to Dependent Children program cannot be carried out by an eligibility condition which denies the necessities of life to a child because of the conduct of the relative with whom he lives, however outrageous that conduct might be."[30] The Flemming Rule also made reference to the abandonment by the states of children to unprotected or unsafe situations when invoking state home suitability requirements. The Flemming Rule stated that:

> where for whatever reason the assistance agency determined that the mother or other relative has not mended her way...the result of the Aid to Dependent Children eligibility condition is to 'protect' the child by withholding from him the funds necessary for his food and clothing, yet to leave him in the very home conditions found by the state assistance agency to be 'unsuitable'. *The state owes this protection to all children*, whether or not they are in economic need, but it can scarcely provide that protection even to children within the Aid to Dependent Children category by withholding financial support and even continued social service, yet permit the child to continue to stay in the same environment.[31] [emphasis in original]

Secretary Flemming was adamant in his ruling that service and cash payment should be joined and that any states that did not meet the purpose and requirements of the federal grants under Title IV as delineated in section 401 of the Social Security Act should not be provided any monetary federal assistance by the federal government for their state grant-in-aid program.

Third Period: 1963–1965

The third period, occurring after the establishment and implementation of the Flemming Rule, involved a transformation from the goal of evaluating home suitability requirements to the goal of responding to neglect, including the establishment of such practices as (1) the use of public support to protect children from "neglectful" parents; (2) the provision of services to families in which "neglect" was found (particularly after the 1962 Service Amendments); (3) the replacing of the practice of expelling or rejecting recipients from the welfare roles with the offering of "services" that were often not "good" services, and (4) increasing the emphasis on services and service planning (service planning was designed to "correct" the neglectful home situation by either removing the child or improving the home). States no longer had the option of simply ignoring children and homes. Also, parents no longer had the option of withdrawing from services.

The shift from period one to period three involved a shift from the language of morality to the language of neglect in state and federal policy circles. This did not mean that in the 1960s the AFDC system stopped being concerned with immorality and "illegitimacy." The difference was that in period one it was not necessary for states to translate their concern about "immorality" into specific language and policies regarding child neglect. In period three, that translation had to take place because references to home suitability requirements under the Flemming Rule required states to go beyond simple labels of "immorality" and be specific about documenting neglect or abuse. The Flemming Rule discouraged the explicit use of morality terminology and immorality in terms of home suitability requirements for determining welfare eligibility because it perceived such behavior by state agencies as "punishing the child for the sins of its parent or other relative."[32]

This transformation of language was advanced by the passage of Public Law 87–31 in 1961, which became law after implementation of the Flemming Rule. P.L. 87–31 outlined service provisions and required their implementation by state caseworkers to address parents' inability to properly provide for their children.[33] It was the result of a collaboration between the Children's Bureau and BPA staff to deal with the expulsion of children from the welfare rolls.[34]

The new law incorporated aspects of the Flemming Rule with emphasis on service provision and the provision of federal financial help to states in the removal of children from unsuitable home conditions, or what was redefined as "neglectful" conditions. P.L. 87–31 connected aspects of protection, neglect, and relative foster care to the case support aspects of AFDC by promoting the concept of joint social service delivery and monetary payments to relatives designated as foster care placements for children removed from their "neglectful" or "abusive" parents.

The concept of service provision was strongly emphasized after the implementation of the Flemming Rule, and the passage of P.L. 87–31. The service provisions were further solidified after the passage of the 1962 Service Amendments, which combined P.L. 87–31's guidelines and Secretary Flemming's ruling, firmly fixing it into law.[35]

State AFDC workers began to emphasize removal of the child from the home as opposed to working with the family to correct the "neglectful" conditions, because the workers could not provide effective clinical intervention. This occurred because most AFDC-eligibility workers were not social workers and lacked training in the skills needed for understanding family dynamics and the complexity of case situations, and in clinical intervention techniques.[36]

With the passage of the 1962 Public Welfare Amendments [Bell 1965], the emphasis on services fed the escalating number of children identified as candidates for removal. Once a child was thought to be in a neglectful situation, state agencies were required by law to report the family to the court system, which was perceived as the appropriate channel for coping with child neglect. This was seen as a reform over the past practices. Previously, states simply expelled families from the welfare rolls and/or rejected applications for benefits without intervention to correct a living situation that had been identified by the public assistance worker as detrimental to the child. Under the old practices, families could remain together by simply dropping their AFDC application. Under the reformed system, however, families no longer had the option to refuse services and maintain the intactness of their family unit, and public welfare workers no longer could refuse to provide services to a welfare client deemed neglectful without follow-up services to deal with the neglectful situation.

Clients were forced into a judicial process that was insensitive and critical of welfare recipients due to negative societal perceptions of them. The adversarial relationship between clients and the child welfare agency was made worse by the federal monetary incentives being provided for states to place children in out-of-home care. These conditions contributed to the large number of children entering out-of-home care in the mid- to late-1960s [Billingsley & Giovannoni 1972].

A general desire to repeal the Flemming Rule pervaded the southern states and some northern states such as Michigan. In a February 1961 memorandum to NAACP executive director Roy Wilkins, Shad Polier (attorney for the Child Welfare League of America) stated that "the director of the Michigan Department of Social Welfare is planning to initiate action to reverse Secretary Flemming's historic ruling...even if Mr. Maxey is stopped, you can be certain that there will be extreme pressure from other states, including not only Louisiana, Mississippi, Florida and Texas, but possibly California...therefore it is essential that action be taken in anticipation of such a move."[37]

Although the Flemming Rule was promulgated in 1961, then permanently fixed into law in 1962, there was grave difficulty with its implementation from 1961 to 1965. States strongly resisted the implementation of the Flemming Rule and wanted to hold on to some aspects of the home suitability clause. They defined and implemented subversion strategies to circumvent the ruling, including the "illegitimate" child, man-in-the-house rule, and substitute parent requirements [Piven & Cloward 1971; Bell 1965]. Other strategies included residency requirements, farm policies, and employable mother rules.* It was not until 1970 that all state subversion strategies were put to rest by the U.S. Supreme Court decision of *Goldberg v. Kelley*, which prevented states from denying AFDC benefits and creating new strategies to circumvent the Flemming Rule [Levy 1992; Stier 1992; Doolittle 1982; Piven & Cloward 1971].[38]

---

* For a discussion of these strategies, see Chapter 10 of F. F. Piven & R. A. Cloward, *Regulating the Poor* (New York: Random House, 1971).

The Impact of the Flemming Rule on African American Children in the Modern Child Welfare System

The intent of the Flemming Rule was to ensure that children had their basic needs met along with their families and received equal services to rectify problems in order to safeguard them from neglect and to protect them. A major unexpected detrimental outcome arose from implementation of the Flemming Rule, however, because the services it mandated were often culturally insensitive. The workers serving African American families were often untrained Caucasian eligibility workers from lower working-class families who held entrenched negative racial stereotypes of African American clients and lacked professional social work education or skills. Clearly, the perception of the dominate elite, Caucasian eligibility workers was one of disdain for the African American clients [Bell 1965].

The home suitability requirements, both before and after the evolutionary process that included the Flemming Rule, placed African American mothers and children requesting AFDC benefits in impossible situations. These situations can be summarized as follows:

> In period one (1955–1959), if a mother requested aid she might be openly denied it due to the open flagrant system of segregation. If a mother had an "illegitimate" child, she was denied AFDC benefits abruptly.

> In the second period (January 1960–December 1962), if a mother openly had a relationship with a man outside marriage, she was denied assistance. If a mother had a relationship with a man in private outside marriage, she was denied assistance. If she requested services and her home was declared unsuitable, then benefits were denied. If she did not ask for services, however, and her home was reported as unsuitable, then benefits were not awarded. Clients could choose to not accept services to avoid trouble with an agency, but no assistance would be forthcoming.

By the third period (1963–1965), if the mother accepted service, her home might be declared unsuitable and her children removed, resulting in a loss of benefits. If she did not accept services, however, and her children were removed, benefits would be terminated. Period three saw a greater increase of case situations involved in the juvenile judicial process due to the following reasons: If the client requested assistance or was reported and the caseworker visited the home and declared the home unsuitable or neglectful, the family and children were forced into the juvenile judicial process based on child neglect. This was the foundation for redefining home suitability as neglect. Once the home situation was declared as child neglect, clients had no choice in the matter because the court process regarding neglected children was state legislated and supported by federal policy (P.L. 87–31). Once reported to the courts, African American families were locked into the Caucasian child welfare system because invariably their homes had been declared unsuitable or neglectful. As a consequence, the Caucasian child welfare system began to experience an increase in the number of protective service, foster care and adoption cases[39] (see figure 1).

Summary

In summary, the destructive social service provisions driven by AFDC policy and P.L. 87–31, which provided financial incentives for states to place children, the 1962 Public Service Amendments, and the Flemming Rule set up a situation in which African Americans were involved in a service system from which they could not withdraw once the neglect label was invoked. That system operated in an oppressive manner that can be described as constituting *oppressive inclusion* in that it contributed to the inappropriate removal of children in increasing numbers, especially African American children.[40]

FIGURE 1

Reason for Denial or Awarding of AFDC Benefits to African American Applicants

	DENIED	AWARDED
Initial Period (Pre-Flemming Rule) 1955–1959	• Generally Excluded • Openly Denied Due to Race (System of Segregation) • Illegitimate Child	• Home Suitable or Moral • Worker Discretion
Transitional Period (Flemming Rule) Jan. 1960– Dec. 1962	• Substitute Father • "Man-in-the-House" • Illegitimate Child • Open Illicit Relationship • Private Illicit Relationship • Service Request/Home Declared Unsuitable • No Service Request/Home Declared Unsuitable • Client Withdrawal of Application • Home Declared Unsuitable/ Issues of Morality and Neglect	• Home Suitable or Moral
Third Period (Post-Flemming Rule) 1963–1965	• Substitute Father • Accept Services/Home Declared Unsuitable and/or Neglectful • Decline Services/Home Declared Unsuitable • Client Reported/Home Declared Neglectful • Court Involvement/Child Removed/Home Declared Neglectful	• Home Suitable • No Neglect or Abuse

The number of children in out-of-home care began to rise in the late 1950s, a trend that escalated in the 1960s. In 1956, shortly after one of Mississippi's expulsion periods,[41] concern was expressed by Marshall Field of the Child Welfare League of America about the "number of families being pushed off AFDC through state action, especially illegitimate children...forcing many children into institutions and foster care."[42] Between 1959 and 1961, the proportion of non-Caucasian children served in the states, with few exceptions, increased. Statistics indicating slight decreases may be representative of a change in agency programs and structure, as in Kentucky [Jeter 1963] (see table 1).

In May 1961, according to the Children's Bureau, "reports from 20 states show that in general nearly 49% of the children receiving services in their own homes are children who came to the attention of the agency because of neglect or abuse in comparison to 44% in 1959."[43] Jeter's [1963] study conducted in cooperation with the Child Welfare League of America documents that by 1963, approximately "200,000 children, over 51% of those served by public agencies, were either in foster care or receiving some kind of foster care" [p. 4]. Most of the children in out-of-home care (81%) were placed because their parents were unmarried or because they came from broken homes.

According to the study, "in public agencies, the largest groups of children placed in foster care consisted of both Negro and American Indian children, 49% of the Negro children, and 53% of the American Indian children. In voluntary agencies the proportions were even higher, 57% and 59% in foster care" [p. 132]. These factors contributed to the further weakening of the African American family system[44] and the continuing disproportionate representation of African American children in the child welfare system. It established a system in which the delivery of services often was culturally inappropriate and insensitive.[45]

The Flemming Rule has had a profound effect on the modern U.S. child welfare system. Little did Secretary Flemming know the significance and far-reaching implications of a ruling that was intended to protect children. Instead, the ruling was used in an oppressive manner that proved to be detrimental to the very children whom he was attempting to protect.

Implications for Future Policies

Current welfare reform debates are again revisiting past destructive policies and reframing them as welfare reform. The promotion of family values is another way of redefining the concept

TABLE 1
Percentage of Children of Color, Nationally, Receiving Child Welfare Services from Public Child Welfare Agencies, 1961, 1959, and 1945. (Partial Table)

Census Region and State	% of Children of Color		
	1961	1959	1945
West South Central	32	29	13
Arkansas	22	18	15
Louisiana	39	38	23
Oklahoma	31	32	9
Texas	15	12	11
East North Central	24	22	15
Illinois	47	45	48
Indiana	21	17	10
Michigan	36	31	6
Ohio	24	23	25
Wisconsin	14	13	7
East South Central	36	32	18
Alabama	39	37	23
Kentucky	8	15	14
Mississippi	49	46	13
Tennessee	24	21	7
Outlying	(1)	(1)	(1)
Puerto Rico	21	31	22
Virgin Islands	92	(2)	(2)

(1) Percentage not computed. Data for region not comparable.
(2) Report not available.

Adapted from H. R. Jeter, and Child Welfare League of America, *Children, problems and services in child welfare programs* (Washington, DC: U.S. Department of Health, Education and Welfare, 1963).

of morality. Other terminology relating to out-of-wedlock child-bearing emphasizes the practice of controlling the sexual be-haviors of low-income women while blaming them and pun-ishing their children for what are perceived as parental inad-equacies. The current welfare reform policies will again force women into marital unions before they are ready. As in the past, the problem of poverty and the care of children remains cloaked in racial politics, as demonstrated by constant references to welfare as a service dominated by African Americans. As a result, African American children continue to be disproportionately represented in child welfare services and to receive fewer services than their Caucasian counterparts [National Black Child Development Institute 1990].

The new welfare reform policies have grave significance for African American families and their children. It is very likely that these policies may be arbitrarily applied to African Americans as was done in the past, which resulted in the Flemming Rule. If a similar situation of mass expulsions of children from the public welfare rolls occurs in the future, which is quite likely, America's families and children, especially African American families and children, face critical times. The present political climate may render it impossible to retrieve the situation.

The current policies in welfare reform are not new; they are just past discriminatory policies cloaked in the language of today. The importance of understanding the origin of past policies embedded in current rhetoric is necessary in terms of preventing past practices of mass expulsions of children from the welfare rolls without any means of support and the reestablishment of discriminatory practices that would deny assistance to those most in need—children. ◆

Notes

1. Brief submitted by Child Welfare League of America, Inc., represented by Shad Polier, Special Counsel for Child Welfare League of America, Inc., November 19, 1960 (Administrative File 1956–65, folder "Discrimination-Aid to Dependent Children Program, 1960–61," Box A–107, National Association for the Advancement of Colored People Records Collection, Record Group III, U.S. National Archives, Washington, DC) (hereafter Polier Brief), p. 2.

2. General Statement on *Operation: Feed the Babies* for Press Conference, 9/7/60 (*Operation: Feed the Babies*, folder "January October 1960," Part II, Series II, Box 9, National Urban League Records Collection, U.S. National Archives, Washington, DC) (hereafter General Statement).

3. Public Aid to Children in Their Own Homes, 1958–62, June 1956 (Central File 1953–57, Box 678, Children's Bureau Records Collection, Record Group 102, U.S. National Archives, Washington, DC) (hereafter Public Aid to Children).

4. Polier Brief.

5. General Statement.

6. Polier Brief, p. 2.

7. Public Aid to Children.

8. Suggested Draft of Letter to Branches, State Conferences, Youth Councils and College Chapter Re: Mississippi Relief Pressures, p. 2 (Administrative File 1956–1965, folder "Mississippi Pressures Relief-Fund 1956–63," Box A–233, National Association for the Advancement of Colored People Records Collection, Record Group III, U.S. National Archives, Washington, DC) (hereafter Suggested Draft of Letter to Branches).

9. Secretary Flemming's Memorandum to the Commissioner, January 16, 1961, pp. 4–5 (Administrative File 1956–65, folder "Discrimination-Aid to Dependent Children Program, 1960–61," Box A–107, National Association for the Advancement of Colored People Records Collection, Record Group III, U.S. National Archives, Washington, DC) (hereafter Flemming Memorandum).

10. Polier Brief, p. 5.

11. Memorandum from Dwight Ferguson to Mildred Arnold of Social Service Division of the Children's Bureau, 7/9/58 (Central File 1958–62, Box 885, Children's Bureau Records Collection, Record Group 102, U.S. National Archives, Washington, DC).

12. Flemming Memorandum.

13. *The New Public Welfare Legislation* by Wilbur Cohen, September 24, 1962 (AFDC Eligibility Review File, Box 1, Al Entry 26H.620.63 962, Bureau of Public Assistance Records Collection, Record Group 47, U.S. National Archives, Washington, DC) (hereafter New Public Welfare Legislation).

14. Decision of Commissioner of Social Security, Findings of Fact, January 16, 1961, p. 2 (Administrative File 1956–65, folder "Discrimination-Aid to Dependent Children Program, 1960–61," Box A–107, National Association for the Advancement of Colored People Records Collection, Record Group III, U.S. National Archives, Washington, DC) (hereafter Decision of Commissioner).

15. Inquiry on Methods Used By State Public Assistance Agencies in Determining Eligibility, FS–332, completed by State of Mississippi sent by Fred A. Ross,

Mississippi Commissioner of Public Welfare, to Wave L. Perry, Regional Representative of Bureau of Family Services, 1/25/63, p. 7 (folder "Mississippi" 620.63 1962, box 9, Bureau of Public Assistance Records Collection, Record Group 47, U.S. National Archives, Washington, DC) (hereafter Inquiry on Methods).

16. Inquiry on Methods, p. 11.

17. Complaint and Petition for a hearing pursuant to Section 404 of the Social Security Act, 2/1/66, March 65 (Central File 1963–66, folder "March 65 1963–1968," Central File 1963–66, Box 1034, Children's Bureau Records Collection, Record Group 102, U.S. National Archives, Washington, DC) (hereafter Complaint and Petition).

18. Summary of Major Findings: State of Mississippi, 7/1/63, p. 1 (folder "Unnumbered State Letters, 7/9/63—Summaries," AFDC Eligibility Review—Draft Summaries of State Findings by State—620.63/07, Subject File Box 2, Bureau of Public Assistance Records Collection, Record Group 47, U.S. National Archives, Washington, DC).

19. Commissioner William L. Mitchell's Findings after Louisiana Conformity Hearings (*Commissioner's Action Minutes*, January 16, 1961–January 25, 1963, No. 2945, Nos. 2943–3137, U.S. Social Security Administration, Baltimore, MD).

20. Decision of Commissioner.

21. Polier Brief, pp. 9–12.

22. Central File 1958–62, Box 885 (Children's Bureau Records Collection, Record Group 102, U.S. National Archives, Washington, DC).

23. Handbook of Public Assistance (folder "Public Aid to Children in Their Own Homes, Central file, 1958–62", Box 885, Children's Bureau Records Collection, Record Group 102, U.S. National Archives, Washington, DC).

24. Flemming Memorandum.

25. Flemming Memorandum, p. 1.

26. Flemming Memorandum, p. 6.

27. Polier Brief, pp. 1–2.

28. Suggested Draft of Letter to Branches, p. 1.

29. Suggested Draft of Letter to Branches, p. 6.

30. Flemming Memorandum, pp. 1–2.

31. Flemming Memorandum, p. 3.

32. Flemming Memorandum, p. 2.

33. Memorandum from Katherine B. Oettinger, Chief of Children's Bureau, to Mr. Joseph Myers, Deputy Commissioner, Re: P.L. 87–31, 10/5/61 (Central File 1958–62, folder "Public Aid to Children in Their Own Homes," Box 885, Children's Bureau Records Collection, Record Group 102, U.S. National Archives, Washington, DC).

34. Handbook of Public Assistance (folder "Public Aid to Children in Their Own Homes, 1958–62," November, 1961, p. 3, Central File 1958–62, Box 885, Children's Bureau Records Collection, Record Group 102, U.S. National Archives, Washington, DC).

35. New Public Welfare Legislation.

36. Hearings Before a Subcommittee of the Committee on Appropriations, House of Representatives, 88th Congress, First Session: Monday, 2/18/63, p. 4 (folder "Correspondence Jan. Jun. 1963," Box 1, Al, AFDC Eligibility Review 620.63 1962–64, Bureau of Public Assistance Records Collection, Record Group 47, U.S. National Archives, Washington DC).

37. Letter from Shad Polier, Special Counsel for Child Welfare League of America, Inc. to Roy Wilkins, Executive Director of the National Association for the Advancement of Colored People, 2/11/61, p. 1 (Administrative File 1956–65, folder "Discrimination-Aid to Dependent Children Program, 1960–61," Box A–107, National Association for the Advancement of Colored People Records Collection, Record Group III, U.S. National Archives, Washington, DC).

38. Complaint and Petition.

39. Background Paper on the Economic and Social Position of the Negro Family (Services to Children in Their Own Homes) from Annie Lee Sandusky of the Children's Bureau to Mr. Cray, 5/2/61 (Children's Bureau Records Collection, Record Group 102, U.S. National Archives, Washington, DC).

40. Memorandum from Annie Lee Sandusky to Ms. Hynnie, 3/20/61 (Children's Bureau Files 1019N, Central File 1958–62, Box 8854, Children's Bureau Records Collection, Record Group 102, U.S. National Archives, Washington, DC) (hereafter Memorandum from Annie Lee Sandusky).

41. Polier Brief, p. 5.

42. Public Aid to Children.

43. Background Paper on the Economic and Social Position of the Negro Family (Services to Children in Their Own Homes) from Annie Lee Sandusky of the Children's Bureau to Mr. Cray, 5/2/61 (Children's Bureau Records Collection, Record Group 102, U.S., National Archives, Washington, DC).

44. Polier Brief, p. 2.

45. Memorandum from Annie Lee Sandusky.

References

Abramovitz, M. (1988). *Regulating the lives of women: Social welfare policy from colonial times to the present.* Madison, WI: University of Wisconsin Press.

Bell, W. (1965). *Aid to dependent children.* New York: Columbia University Press.

Billingsley, A., & Giovannoni, J. M. (1972). *Children of the storm: Black children and American child welfare.* New York: Harcourt Brace Jovanovich, Inc.

Children's Defense Fund. (1990). *A report card briefing book and action primer.* Washington, DC: Author.

Doolittle, F. C. (1982). State-imposed nonfinancial eligibility conditions in AFDC: Confusion in supreme court decisions and a need for Congressional clarification. *Harvard Journal on Legislation, 19,* 1–48.

Gordon, L. (1990). *Women, the state, and welfare.* Madison, WI: University of Wisconsin Press.

Jeter, H. R., & Child Welfare League of America. (1963). *Children, problems and services in child welfare programs.* Washington, DC: U.S. Department of Health, Education and Welfare.

Leashore, B. R., Chipungu, S. S., & Everett, J. E. (1991). *Child welfare: An Africentric perspective.* New Brunswick, NJ: Rutgers University Press.

Levy, P. A. (1992). The durability of supreme court welfare reforms of the 1960s. *Social Service Review, 66,* 215–236.

Mink, G. (1990). The lady and the tramp: Gender, race, and the origins of the American welfare state. In L. Gordon (Ed.), *Women, the state and welfare* (pp. 92–122). Madison, WI: University of Wisconsin Press.

National Black Child Development Institute. (1990). The status of African-American children. Washington, DC: Author.

Piven, F. F., & Cloward, R. A. (1971). *Regulating the poor.* New York: Random House.

Quadagno, J. (1988). From old-age assistance to supplemental security income: The political economy of relief in the south, 1935–1972. In M. Weir, A. S. Orloff, & T. Skocpol (Eds.),

The politics of social policy in the United States (pp. 234–263). Princeton, NJ: Princeton University Press.

Skocpol, T. (1988). The limits of the new deal system and the roots of contemporary welfare dilemmas. In M. Weir, A. S. Orloff, & T. Skocpol (Eds.), *The politics of social policy in the United States* (pp. 293–311). Princeton, NJ: Princeton University Press.

Steiner, G. Y. (1966). *Social insecurity: The politics of welfare*. Chicago: Rand McNally and Company.

Stier, M. (1992). Corruption of blood and equal protection: Why the sins of the parents should not matter. *Stanford Law Review, 45,* 727–757.

2

Family Preservation and Support Services: A Missed Opportunity for Kinship Care

Julia Danzy and Sondra M. Jackson

This article discusses the historical significance of kinship care in preserving the African American family, the development of kinship care and family preservation programs, and the importance of the natural relationship between kinship care and family preservation services. Findings of a survey of states' use of kinship care in the development of plans for the Family Preservation and Support Services Act are presented. Whether child welfare agencies missed an opportunity to plan for kinship care in their family preservation plans is also explored.

Julia Danzy, M.S.W., ACSW, is Director of Social Service Planning, City Council, City of Philadelphia, PA. Sondra M. Jackson, M.S.W., LCSW, is Director of Training, University of Maryland School of Social Work, Baltimore, MD.

In 1993, the United States Congress enacted the Family Preservation and Support Services (FPSS) Act [P.L. 103–66]. This act offered states a unique opportunity to reform their child welfare systems. The U.S. Department of Health and Human Services (HHS) issued guidelines suggesting that states use the new act as a catalyst for establishing an integrated continuum of services that would be coordinated, family focused, and culturally relevant.

African American child welfare scholars and social workers "view kinship care (children placed with relatives) as a component of family preservation services as it gives children a chance to remain with their families" [Black Administrators in Child Welfare 1994]. To determine whether the federal FPSS guidelines specifically addressed kinship care, the authors examined the instructions to states for writing their plans. The federal guidelines listed kinship care among the elements that would ideally be a part of the service continuum. They did not, however, specifically encourage including children living with relatives in state plans for family preservation and support service programming [U.S. Department of Health and Human Services 1994].

Significance of Kinship Care for Child Welfare

African American children represent the largest percentage of children involved in the formal kinship care system [Berrick et al. 1994].* Therefore, it is appropriate that any program planning and development for this service category be cognizant of the historical concept of family from an African American perspective. African American child welfare professionals are concerned that a lack of cultural awareness may contribute to the failure of states to include kinship care in their Family Preservation and Support Services plans. To address this concern, the

---

* The formal kinship care system comprises the segment of children who are in the legal custody of the formal child welfare system and are living with relatives. Their relatives may be receiving foster care payments for their care and are governed by the formal child welfare system's foster care policies.

Black Administrators in Child Welfare, Inc. (BACW) sponsored a study that, in 1995, surveyed by questionnaire the state administrators who were contacts for the Family Preservation and Support Services programs in all 50 states and the District of Columbia. The goal was to gather information from each state about the use of kinship care on the continuum of child welfare services. The study was proposed from recommendations made by a kinship care work group formed by BACW, which had earlier issued a policy statement recognizing kinship care as the preferred and viable option for children in the child welfare system who cannot live with their parents, as a way for the children to retain their essential sense of cultural and family identity. BACW expressed its commitment to ensuring that child welfare agencies demonstrate an understanding of kinship care as an aspect of cultural strength within the African American family and as a form of family preservation [Black Administrators in Child Welfare 1994].

The Role of Kinship Care in Preserving African American Families

Although the use of relatives for the care of their young kin is a new practice for the child welfare system, it is not new for African American families. The extended family is one of the rich traditions of the African American community [Billingsley 1992; Stack 1974; Daley et al. 1995]. The African proverb, "It takes a whole village to raise a child," speaks to the collective role and sense of group responsibility held by the African community [Martin & Martin 1985]. During slavery, the African concept of extended family was responsible for the survival of the family. When the slave family was disrupted due to the selling of a member, the children were informally adopted by the slave community [Hill 1971]. Thus, the practice of defining kinship beyond blood ties and vesting nonkin with kin status helped sustain a sense of family despite slave conditions [Gutman 1976]. For the African American family, the extended family has been the support during times of crises [Ford et al. 1990].

After slavery ended, collective responsibility among extended family members continued to be a principal means by which the African American community responded to social and economic crisis [Foster 1983; Billingsley 1968]. This historical pattern of the extended family providing reassurance and the means for adaptation has been consistent and most prevalent in relation to the care of children. Given the African American history of extended family support, particularly in the arena of child care, kinship care is one of the best forms of family preservation.

The Development of Kinship Care in the Child Welfare System

In the mid-1980s, the public child welfare system began to experience an increase in child abuse reports and placements. By 1992, 2.9 million incidents of child abuse were reported. This statistic reflected a 100% increase since 1980 [National Committee for the Prevention of Child Abuse 1993; Children's Defense Fund 1994]. Thirty-one percent of this increase occurred during the period from 1985 to 1990 [National Committee for the Prevention of Child Abuse 1991]. While AIDS, violence, and poverty were contributing factors to the increase in out-of-home care placements [Scannapieco & Hegar 1995; Anderson 1990], substance abuse was one of the most influential factors [Berrick et al. 1994; Edmund S. Muskie Institute of Public Affairs 1995]. That substance abuse was an element contributing to child abuse was not new to the child welfare system, but the emergence of crack cocaine caused substance abuse to become a much more dominant factor. Crack, a smokable drug, was cheap, highly addictive, and caused severe mood swings from euphoria to depression and paranoia. Worst of all, crack, unlike heroin, became the favored drug for many females. Since the primary parent and, increasingly for many families, the sole parent in the home was female, this increased drug involvement increased the number of children at risk of abuse and neglect. Crack tended to consume the users' interest and made them less sensitive, responsive, and accessible to the children dependent upon them for their care [Child Welfare League of America 1992].

Unfortunately, for most child welfare agencies, the increased need for placement services followed one of the most significant periods of reduction in placements in out-of-home care. The enactment of P.L. 96–272 (The Adoption Assistance and Child Welfare Act of 1980) caused the child welfare system to focus directly on family preservation and reunifying children with their families. As a result, from 1980 to 1982, the number of children in out-of-home care declined sharply. In 1977, approximately 500,000 children were in out-of-home care; the number decreased to 262,000 by 1982 [Children's Defense Fund 1994; Barthel 1992].

This lowered number of placements also resulted in a decline in available out-of-home care settings. With the decreased need, child welfare systems actively encouraged the dismantling of out-of-home care services and directed funds to developing family preservation and family support services. Concurrent with the purposeful reduction in resources was a decline in the number of available foster parents. From 1984 to 1990, the supply of foster parents dropped from 147,000 to 100,000 [National Commission on Foster Family Care 1991]. Much of this decrease was also a result of the impact of economic conditions on families, which brought many women into the workforce. It was within this context that child welfare systems began to explore the use of nontraditional placement settings.

Several legal rulings sustained this willingness to change: *Miller v. Youakim* [1979], *Eugene F. v. Gross* [1986], *Reid v. Suter* [1992], and *L.J. v. Massinga* [1991]. These rulings clearly defined the right of relatives to be considered as placement resources for their young kin, and to receive the fiscal and service supports provided to all other foster parents. By the late 1980s, most child welfare agencies were making some placements with relatives. By the 1990s, urban metropolitan cities were seeing major increases in their kinship care placements. In 1990, New York City's kinship placements totaled 23,550, representing almost 50% of the total placement population. Illinois had 8,100 relative placements, representing 46% of all placements. By 1992, Philadelphia's child welfare kinship population had grown from 773 to 1,164, an increase of 50% [Congressional Research Services 1993; Dubowitz et al. 1993; Edmund S. Muskie Institute of Public Affairs 1995].

As the population in kinship care increases, states face the problem of accommodating the service into the established policies and practices of an out-of-home care system that was not designed for relative care. From an African American perspective, family preservation is the most appropriate approach to program planning in kinship care.

Family Preservation Program Development

The Family Preservation and Support Act established the federal government's formal recognition and creation of a discrete funding stream for family preservation programs. This federal action was preceded by many states having already initiated some form of family preservation service in their array of treatment programs. As of 1991, 12 states had implemented family preservation programs by statute, and 31 states had indicated that such programs were among their top legislative issues [Smith 1993].

While most child welfare agencies provide some type of services to children in their own homes, the use of home-based treatment programs as family preservation services increased with the development of the concept of intensive family preservation services. The distinctive characteristics of the intensive family preservation models are short-term, intensive services, provided because of an imminent risk of child placement; 24-hour worker accessibility; and low worker/caseload ratios [Barthel 1992]. The undergirding principle of all family preservation programs is the prevention of child placement and the amelioration of the problems that threaten the stability of the family.

The Relationship between Family Preservation and Kinship Care

The effort to fit a natural system of care into an unnatural system of child welfare services is the principal difficulty in kinship care programming. From an African American perspective, the care of a child by family members other than the biological parents is not child placement but rather family preservation. In the formal child welfare system, however, the transfer of the parenting role to a relative, that is, kinship care, is viewed as child placement. It is therefore not surprising that many child welfare agencies do not associate family preservation services with kinship care. In instances where family preservation services are viewed as an appropriate treatment strategy for this population, the relationship is within the context of reunification services.

In examining the growth trends of family preservation services and kinship care, one finds that each was being incorporated into the formal child welfare system during the same time period. Not only did their dramatic growth follow parallel lines, but many of their precipitating factors were the same, such as the dwindling supply of formal family foster homes and the major and minor protection principles of P.L. 96–272. The fact that family preservation and kinship care had these common elements would suggest that perhaps they had common grounds.

For the African American community, the terms *family preservation* and *kinship care* are interchangeable. Both are ways of sustaining and maintaining the family system. The failure of the child welfare system to be cognizant of this may contribute to the states' failure to incorporate the kinship care population in their state plans for the Family Preservation and Support Services Act.

The Survey

In October 1995, a questionnaire was mailed to the public child welfare administrators in each state and the District of Columbia who had been responsible for submitting the states' Family Preservation and Support Services plan earlier in the year. A list of contacts was obtained from the U.S. Department of Health and Human Services. States were required by HHS to submit five-year FPSS plans for funding by June 30, 1995. The questionnaire was reviewed by researchers and its questions were pilot-tested with state administrators and federal and private program managers before it was distributed. A second questionnaire and request for participation was sent a month after the initial contact to increase the response rate.

Sixty-eight percent of the state administrators returned the questionnaires. The responses were anonymous, but some state contacts requested the results in general and provided an opportunity to contact them for additional information. Some were contacted to clarify responses.

As a part of a larger study, the primary focus here is to (1) determine whether the state plan referenced kinship care specifically; (2) examine the context in which kin placements were referenced; (3) identify reasons that children living with kin were not referenced in the plans; and (4) identify the various program categories for the state's kinship care placement population.

Thirty-four respondents answered the question regarding whether kinship care was specifically referenced in their Family Preservation and Support Services Plan. More than two-thirds (68%) noted that kinship care was not specifically referenced in their Family Preservation and Support Services Plan. Only 31% responded that their plans specifically referenced children living with relatives. Several states explained that their plans did not differentiate kin placements from family foster care placements. Other states indicated that their definition of families included grandparents or other relatives.

As shown in table 1, 32% of the 11 states answering the

TABLE 1

Context in Which Kinship Care is Referenced in the FPSS Plan (*N* = 11 States)*

	n	%
Reunification Services	8	32%
Placement Prevention Services	6	24%
Family Support Services	6	24%
Other	5	20%

* Kinship care services were referenced in more than one service area by several states.

question reported the use of kinship care placements as a form of family reunification after a child has been in out-of-home care. Reunification with the relative in these cases achieved a permanent plan for the child. Fewer states (24%) used relatives to prevent placement in the regular out-of-home care system. Twenty-four percent chose to use their FPSS funding for community-based activities or family support services that would be made available to kinship placements. One state referenced the kinship population as a component of its out-of-home care reform initiative; another mentioned this population in its discussion of trends in out-of-home care. Several of the respondents stated that kinship placements could access any of the above service areas.

Of the 24 states not referencing kinship care in their FPSS plans, 29% had no formal kinship program (see table 2). Some of these states reported that they would be introducing kinship care legislation and would then add the kin population to their five-year plans. Sixteen percent of the 24 states reported that children in their child welfare system were living with relatives, but a place on the continuum of services for relative placements had not been decided in the state. The largest number of the 24 respondents (41%) reported that their states' FPSS plan did not reference kin placements due to the organization of services in the child welfare system. Several respondents also indicated that the exclusion of the kinship care population resulted from the

TABLE 2
Reasons States Did Not Reference Kinship Care in Their FPSS Plans
(*N* = 24 States)

Response	n	%
No formal kinship care program in the state	7	29%
No decision made in state about use of kin care	4	16%
Planners did not consider use of kinship care relevant due to the organization of services in the state	10	41%
Other	3	13%

lack of participation of persons viewed as involved in placement services. One respondent stated that the state plan was governed by the issues identified by community participants, and that their community members did not see kinship care as a problem.

The program categories serving relative placements yield some insights about the way the state views the program (see table 3). Forty percent of the respondents reported that kin placements are included services in the program traditionally known as foster care. To accommodate relative care, some states have defined the program as kinship foster care, indicating that it is a type of foster care.

Summary

Although formal kinship placements in the child welfare systems have become a primary placement alternative, they still present policy and practice conflicts for the child welfare system. As indicated by the responses to the survey completed by state child welfare administrators responsible for the Family Preservation and Support Services plans, there are differences in the states' programming for families in formal kinship care.

TABLE 3
Program Categories Used to Reference Kinship Placements
(N = 63 from 34 States)*

Program Categories	n	%
Foster Care	25	40%
Kinship Foster Care	6	10%
Kinship Care	7	11%
Extended Family Care	7	11%
Home of Relative Care	5	8%
Extended Family Care	2	3%
Independent Living	6	10%
Other	5	7%

*   Multiple responses were given

These differences involve inclusion or exclusion of the kinship population in the FPSS plans, program names for service intervention when children are placed with relatives, and the sources of the participants in plan development. The differences imply an intended or unavoidable admission by the public child welfare systems that the kinship placement population does not fit easily within the traditional child welfare system. The regulations and statutes that govern licensing, training, judicial reviews, foster care payments, and agency oversight are matters of concern and conflict for the formal child welfare system and the families it uses as kinship placements. In the few preliminary studies of children in formal kinship placements, findings show that these children stay in care for a longer period of time than the children in nonrelative family foster care placements and are less likely to be formally adopted by their relative caregiver [Gleeson & Craig 1994; Berrick et al. 1994; Edmund Muskie Institute 1995; Dubowitz et al. 1993]. African American administrators and practitioners must continue to ensure that the system recognizes kinship care as a resilient African American response to preserving the family [Scannapieco & Jackson 1996].

Child welfare agencies must be more supportive of kinship care in policy and practice and remove administrative obstacles [Black Administrators in Child Welfare 1993]. As child welfare agencies seek to understand kinship care as a cultural tradition, policy formation, program planning, and agency supports must reflect the intrinsic value of kin placements in preserving the African American family.

It is important for the national child welfare system to re-evaluate program development and service descriptions for its formal kinship care population. The fact that African Americans, as a group, constitute the largest percentage of the child welfare system's kinship care population, and the reality of the historical role of the African American extended family must not be ignored. This cultural dimension must be incorporated into any service model for the African American kinship triad—the biological parents, child, and relative caregiver. That a high percentage of child welfare systems missed the opportunity to include kinship families in the planning and the development of family preservation services may be a result of their lack of consideration of cultural factors in planning for this population. ♦

References

Administration on Children Youth and Families. (1994). *Implementation of New Legislation: Family preservation and support services, Title IV-B, subpart 2* (Log No. ACYF-Pl-94-01). Washington, DC: U.S. Department of Health and Human Services.

Anderson, G. R. (1990). *Courage to care.* Washington, DC: Child Welfare League of America.

Barthel, J. (1992). *For children's sake: The promise of family preservation services.* New York: Edna McConnell Clark Foundation.

Berrick, J. D., Barth, R. P., & Needell, B. (1994). A comparison of kinship foster homes and family foster homes: Implications for kinship as family preservation. *Children and Youth Services, 16,* 7–13.

Billingsley, A. (1968). *Black families in white America.* Englewood Cliffs, NJ: Prentice Hall.

Billingsley, A. (1992). *Climbing Jacob's ladder: The enduring legacy of African-American families.* New York: Simon & Schuster.

Black Administrators in Child Welfare, Inc. (1994). *Policy statement on kinship care.* Washington, DC: Author.

Black Community Crusade for Children. (1993). *Progress and peril: Black children in America.* Washington, DC: Children's Defense Fund.

Children's Defense Fund. (1994). *The state of America's children yearbook.* Washington, DC: Author.

Child Welfare League of America. (1992). *Children at the front: A different view of the war on alcohol and drugs.* Washington, DC: North American Commission on Chemical Dependency and Child Welfare.

Congressional Research Service. (1993). *"Kinship" foster care: An emerging federal issue.* Washington, DC: U.S. Government Printing Office.

Daley, A., Jennings, J., Beckett, J. O., & Leashore, S. (1995). Shared family care: Child protection and family preservation. *Social Work, 40,* 145–288.

Dubowitz, H., Feigelman, S., & Zuravin, S. (1993). A profile of kinship care. *Child Welfare, 72,* 153–169.

Edmund S. Muskie Institute of Public Affairs. (1995). *Kinship care in America: A national policy study.* Portland, ME: University of Southern Maine.

Ford, D. Y., Harris, J. M., & Turner, W. L. (1990). The extended African American family: A pragmatic strategy that blunts the blade of injustice. *The Urban League Review, 14*(2), 71–83.

Foster, H. J. (1983). African patterns in Afro-American families. *Journal of Black Studies, 14,* 201–232.

Gleeson, J. P., & Craig, L. C. (1994). Kinship care in child welfare: An analysis of state policies. *Children and Youth Services Review, 27,* 201–218.

Gutman, H. G. (1976). *The Black family in slavery and freedom, 1750–1952.* New York: Vintage Press.

Hill, R. (1971). *The strengths of Black families.* New York: Emerson Hall.

Martin, J. M., & Martin, E. P. (1985). *The helping tradition in the Black family and community.* Silver Spring, MD: NASW.

National Committee for the Prevention of Child Abuse. (1993). *The results of the 1992 annual fifty state survey.* Chicago: Author.

National Committee for the Prevention of Child Abuse. (1991). *The results of the 1990 annual fifty state survey.* Chicago: Author.

National Commission on Foster Care. (1991). *A blueprint for fostering infants, children & youth in the 1990s.* Washington, DC: Child Welfare League of America.

Scannapieco, M., & Hegar, R. (1995). From family duty to family policy: The evolution of kinship care. *Child Welfare, 74,* 200–216.

Scannapieco, M., & Jackson, S. (1996). Kinship care: The African American resilient response to family preservation. *Social Work, 41,* 190–196.

Smith, S. L. (1993). *Family preservation services: State legislative initiatives.* Washington, DC: National Conference of State Legislatures.

Stack, C. (1974). *All our kin: Strategies for survival in a Black community.* New York: Harper and Row.

3

Child Protection Risk Assessment and African American Children: Cultural Ramifications for Families and Communities

Sheryl Brissett-Chapman

Child welfare practitioners are increasingly employing formal and structured risk assessment processes to predict child vulnerability or to improve case decision making. In general, research has neither proved conclusively which set of risk factors are most critical for evaluating risk within a family and community, nor has it resolved the controversy regarding the importance of professional training and experience in risk assessment procedures and processes. There is, however, a beginning recognition of the importance of collaborative strategies that bring community representatives to the assessment table along with the traditional professionals. The author argues for urgency in the pursuit of a dialogue that examines varied definitions of harm and risk for children, and the implications of those definitions for cultural conflict, screening and intake, and resource allocation.

Sheryl Brissett-Chapman, Ed.D., ACSW, LICSW, is Executive Director, Baptist Home for Children and Families, Bethesda, MD.

Kenny stretched out, sprawling his long legs over the sofa in the living room of the boys' cottage in the residential facility for youths with behavioral and emotional disorders. By the age of 15, this handsome, dark-complected African American adolescent had lived in a number of settings. When Kenny was 10 years old, his parents, both struggling unsuccessfully with alcohol and drug addictions, had lived in an emergency homeless shelter for nine months with their four offspring. Shortly after, the result of a Child Protective Services report, the children were placed in several family foster homes, and separated from each other for the first time.

Kenny described one foster family that was so hostile that he had to break out of a locked room to steal food. In another foster home, Kenny became very attached to his foster parent, yet he still wondered why he was sent from that home to the group home. He acknowledged that he *had* threatened his teacher at school. He minimized the reality that in five family foster home placements, he was viewed as assaultive toward both peers and authority figures.

Bright, with exceptional interpersonal skills, artistic, athletic, ...and cautious, Kenny expressed immeasurable loss and grief as he spoke, "Dr. C, what am I gonna do? Where are we gonna go? Look at the predicament my folks have put us kids in!"

This article addresses the critical need for culturally competent assessments of the risk of child maltreatment in African American families and the implications for both policy and practice. The author, an African American practitioner specializing in child welfare and juvenile justice, puts forth a conceptual framework for integrating the challenges, synthesizing various cultural lenses, and urgently reconsidering the philosophical underpinnings of the evolving professional and systemic orientations to assessment of risk and subsequent case decision making regarding the placement of children.

The largest group of children in out-of-home care are African American. Most often they are poor, from poorly educated families, and are disadvantaged in the economic mainstream of the larger society. These children are placed in out-of-home care most frequently because of substantiated reports of child maltreatment, or as they grow older, because of legal or policy offenses they have committed against society. Too many African American children and youths in out-of-home care return to the very families and communities they initially counted on, with very little changed, and too often, exhibiting symptoms of a nature akin to posttraumatic stress due to feelings of abandonment and a lack of continuity of care.

It is not reasonable to discuss the spiraling and disproportionate national problem of African American children and youths being removed from their homes, and sometimes their communities, without first confronting the complex phenomenon generally referred to as child abuse and neglect, as well as other manifestations of family difficulties. What impediments are there to the likelihood of children receiving "good-enough" nurturing and caregiving from their families of origin? How might children be better supported and protected until they are able to care for themselves and any others who might be dependent on their future caregiving ability? Who are the gatekeepers for ensuring that each child's needs are adequately met? When, and how, should various members of the larger community respond to the voids and inadequacies that may or may not be readily apparent in the lives of thousands of African American children?

What is the role of government, as represented by the "official" child protective services system, in determining the vulnerability of children in the African American community, and how might this role effectively intersect with other "official" actors, such as the police, the courts, and professional "mandated" reporters (i.e., nurses, teachers, physicians, child care workers, and mental health providers)? How does the "community"—the natural and most invaluable resource for all family life—support the most challenged families in its midst? Ultimately, as these matters are sorted through, processes must be identified that allow for individuals, families, communities, and service systems to stay focused on the bottom line…the child's right to a childhood and a future.

Given these complex questions and the major need for additional research, we must incorporate into current risk assessment models a qualitative and interactive framework for understanding childhood vulnerability and risk in African American families. Simplistic linear models that focus on analyzing events and evaluating their significance have simply failed to serve African American communities and families due to widespread societal misinformation, ignorance, stereotyping, and a common inability to perceive individual, family, or community strengths and assets on the part of African Americans. Many child welfare specialists have advocated strongly for competent professionals, when addressing child maltreatment, to acknowledge cultural differences and the larger community context, and conduct pertinent systematic research [Garbarino et al. 1993; Cohen 1992; Pinderhughes 1991; Everett 1991; Harris 1990; Blick et al. 1990; and Holton 1990]. Culturally specific parameters are necessary for the effective practice of child protective risk assessment with African American families and their children.

Background

Legislative Responses

In 1974, the Child Abuse Prevention and Treatment Act [P.L. 93–247] established the National Center on Child Abuse and Neglect to ensure federal leadership in assisting states and communities with the prevention, identification, and treatment of child abuse and neglect through the allocation of funds appropriated by Congress. Eligible states received funding incentives to designate an agency for investigation; to establish a reporting system; to enact laws to protect children under age 18 years from mental injury, physical injury, and sexual abuse; and to provide guardians ad litum to represent children in the courts.

The Adoption Assistance and Child Welfare Act of 1980 [P.L. 96–272] focused on preventing the removal of children from their families, timely reunification of children with their families after they had been removed due to abuse or neglect, and adoption as a permanent plan for children who could not be reunited with their families within a reasonable time. In response to the exposure of "foster care drift"—children remaining in out-of-home care due to inadequate case planning and monitoring—this legislation encompassed the concept of making "reasonable efforts" to keep families together, providing permanency planning services, and placing children in the least restrictive settings. At the same time that this sweeping legislation was enacted, the child welfare field began to see the results of laws mandating reporting by professionals, and the identification of an increasing number of children of color in child protective reports. As far back as 1970, researchers noted that the threat of child separation appeared to be a particular problem for the families of underprivileged ethnic minority groups [Fanshel 1979; Price 1975; Neaves & Matheson 1970]. Indeed, some observers began to describe this decade as the "browning" of child welfare in America, due to the disproportionate number of substantiated reports emanating from the African American community and other communities of color.

The Family Preservation and Support Services Act, passed as part of the Omnibus Budget Reconciliation Act of 1993 [P.L. 103–66], complemented the earlier legislation by targeting resources for early intervention with families and providing additional supports for children in out-of-home care and in adoptive placements. The law provided funding for a comprehensive array of services, as well as for evaluation, resources, training, and technical assistance. It increased the effectiveness of state courts and spurred the development of statewide automated data systems [Brissett-Chapman 1995].

Child Abuse and Neglect Reports: Challenges to Practice

Although the trend in national social policy regarding vulner-able children and their families has been increasingly progres-sive, the rapid growth in suspected child abuse and neglect cases has, in effect, greatly inhibited the practical opportunity for actual child welfare practices to advance in similar fashion. Since 1980, alleged child abuse and neglect reports have more than doubled in this country [Child Welfare League of America 1986; National Center on Child Abuse and Neglect 1993]. In 1991, state child protective agencies investigated an estimated 1.8 million reports involving 2.7 million children [National Center on Child Abuse and Neglect 1993], compared to 929,000 reports in 1982 [Russell & Trainor 1984]. The recent legislative reforms in child welfare services, passed as part of the Omnibus Budget Reconciliation Act of 1993, may be viewed as a result of widespread national perceptions that the well-being of more and more American children is threatened by abuse, neglect, and family instability.

Ironically, this increased public recognition of the problem of child maltreatment and the subsequent expansion of caseloads compete directly with the requirements of financially strapped child welfare systems, which, in a downsizing economy, place emphasis on cost-containment, efficient and consolidated programming, and more theoretically, on outcome measurement. There appears to be too little interest and related capacity in the child welfare field for elucidating the complex-ity associated with effectively managing cultural distinctions presented by children and families. Practitioners typically seek concrete, narrow, and compartmentalized strategies to address the dynamic and often unfamiliar circumstances posed by fami-lies who generally neither solicit nor desire governmental in-tervention into "family affairs." All too often, the most visible consequences of child abuse and neglect are the severe psycho-logical, physical, and emotional impairment of children or the destabilizing family crises that result when authorities remove children from their families to ensure safety and protection [Brissett-Chapman 1995].

Characteristics of Reported Victims

In 1992, the National Center on Child Abuse and Neglect (NCCAN) collected data on child maltreatment from state child protective agencies to produce a critically needed national profile of child abuse and neglect as of 1991 [National Center on Child Abuse and Neglect 1993]. Much discussion ensued regarding the doubling of child abuse and neglect reports between 1980 and 1991. Some argued that the number of cases had actually increased, while others believed that practitioners were more willing and able to recognize the problems, particularly in cases of physical and sexual abuse. Some suggested that the social stressors and difficulties that many families face actually intensify the risk of child abuse and neglect (thus, the number of cases continues to increase), while others proposed that poor and ethnic minority children and their families are disproportionately reported, labeled, and routinely remanded into the child welfare system by practitioners who are socially and culturally distant from the actual family context.

Overall, the 1992 study conducted by NCCAN suggested that 52% of the total reports were made by professionals (12.4% by social service workers; 11.5% by law enforcement and justice system personnel; 15.6% by educators); 10.9% by anonymous persons; and 28% by family and friends [National Center on Child Abuse and Neglect 1993]. NCCAN's 1988 study suggested that although reports had increased, many professionals who recognized child maltreatment were *not* reporting it. Nearly half of all reported cases were *not* substantiated after investigation [National Center on Child Abuse and Neglect 1988].

Of the substantiated reports from the 45 states noted in NCCAN's profile [National Center on Child Abuse and Neglect 1993], the majority (44%) were cases of neglect; the remainder were distributed as follows: physical abuse, 24%; sexual abuse, 15%; other forms of maltreatment, 17%.*

---

* These categories are not exclusive. A victim may be assigned to more than one category.

The median age of victims was seven years; 7.6% (the largest age category) were children under one year of age. Fifty-three percent of the victims were female and 47% were male. Based on the reports in 42 states on ethnic and racial backgrounds, 55% of the children were Caucasian, 26% were African American, and 9% were Latino, a figure that is probably underestimated.

Culturally sophisticated processes for risk assessment are essential for child victims who come under the supervision of the child welfare system. Typically, reported child victims are young, are increasingly of color, and remain at high risk for child placement despite recent efforts at family preservation.

Risk Assessment: Role and Definition

In a technical brief prepared by the National Resource Center on Child Abuse and Neglect [1994], the fundamental practice of child protective service (CPS) was summarized as "making decisions that have a fundamental bearing on the present and future well-being of children. All aspects of CPS practice involve the balancing of the recognized right of parents to raise their children and the right of society to ensure that children are not intentionally or inadvertently harmed" [p. 1]. The practice of risk assessment in child welfare today is problematic since it is extremely difficult to achieve consensus on the focus of risk assessment. Should risk assessment instruments be viewed as structured decision-making processes or predictive clinical tools? In the context of shrinking resources and rising caseloads, should risk assessment approaches be geared appropriately toward improving agency or systems accountability or efficiency (i.e., consistent staff decisions, targeting resources from low- to high-risk cases, obtaining information about family functioning and effective, tailored intervention)?

Risk assessment also implies, for many, the ability to predict a given outcome. Will a high-risk family have a subsequent substantiated report of maltreatment? Will a low-risk family become involved in an initial occurrence of abuse and neglect?

What is the percentage rate of error, that is, false positives (those who are expected to abuse and neglect and do *not* do so) and false negatives (those who are *not* likely to maltreat a child and do so) [Cicchinelli 1991]?

Compounding the problem of defining risk assessment is the problem of defining "abuse and neglect." Although federal legislation sets forth specific core definitions of child abuse and neglect, each state interprets the definitions differently. To add to the complexity, each professional discipline has promulgated its own definitions without substantive consideration of state and federal parameters. As a result, there is no universal operational definition of child abuse and neglect, and the multiple and overlapping definitions challenge the very ability of professional helping systems to adequately and universally address the assessment of risks, the allocation of resources, the accurate assessment of the need for a child's removal from the family, or the opportunity to engage the involvement of other actors (i.e., neighbors, family, community institutions, allied disciplines) in ensuring that children are safe and adequately cared for.

Berkowitz, during a symposium on Risk Assessments in Child Protective Services [Cicchinelli 1991] discussed a number of particular risk-assessment issues. From an agency and systems perspective, Berkowitz pointed to the agency's need for (a) a relevant philosophy and supportive policies, (b) timely training and technical assistance, (c) user input for model development, (d) appropriate portrayals of the risk-assessment approach to external groups such as the courts, and (e) examination of the impact of the services' availability, staff time, and caseload size. Berkowitz also posed several general questions regarding risk-assessment models concerning (a) the development of different models for different decisions, (b) the inclusion or exclusion of specific factors, (c) the interaction of risk factors, (d) the incorporation of positive factors, (e) the level of reliability that should be required, and how it should be determined, and (f) enhanced sensitivity to cultural and ethnic differences [Cicchinelli 1991: 7]. Berkowitz and other participants at the forum emphasized the need for substantive research that is descriptive and exploratory. "Research should be process oriented, not only experimental or outcome-oriented" [Cicchinelli 1991: 33].

In the field of child protective services, *risk* is generally defined as the likelihood of harm to a child occurring or recurring once an allegation of abuse or neglect has been made [English 1989]. Risk assessment, therefore, poses questions regarding future caregiver or parental behavior and the effects of the child's environment, rather than simply the restatement of a documented history of child maltreatment. Child protective casework has always involved a reflective evaluation of the case situation in order to assess the risk of an incident of abuse or neglect. Caseworkers, however, have usually relied on intuition, experience, and interview engagement skills to ascertain future risk [Tatara 1989]. The use of a structured, formal risk assessment instrument is still a novel approach in the child welfare field, but one that is catching on quickly. This development, particularly as it interfaces broad policy positions and street-level service delivery, requires close examination of both its strengths and limitations [Pecora 1991].

DePanfilis [1988], however, suggested that the field is seriously underdeveloped in identifying clear guidelines in determining child safety. The continuum of purposes and objectives of the various extant risk-assessment systems, discrepancies in operational concepts of risk, and variations in systems instruments, timing, training, and implementation indicate the lack of an overall coherent framework for theory and practice. Although some progress has been made in this area [English 1994], it appears that there is no current way that any of these instruments or processes may be able to do much more than provide broad guidelines for actual case decision making. Indeed, risk assessment as a construct remains sufficiently confused within the field of child welfare that currently it fails to serve as insurance that child protective services investigations will result in the appropriate selection of family preservation or child placement as service responses.

The Cultural Lens

The importance of understanding the interface between socio-cultural issues and assessment of any type is coming to the fore, urging especially that African American families not be viewed from a single orientation of deficit or pathology [Boyd-Franklin 1989; Pinderhughes 1982]. Gibbs [1989] described important foci that must be evaluated if the African American adolescent is to be understood. The foci included attitudes toward self; speech and language; interpersonal relations; sexuality; anxiety and patterns of defense; coping and adaptive behaviors; family structure and roles; socioeconomic status and living arrangements; degree of integration-acculturation; social support system; communication patterns; help-seeking behaviors; school environment; educational program; peer relationships; and community assessment.

Indeed, the African American adolescent, with his or her highly visible and vulnerable status in today's society, serves as a barometer for understanding the interface between childhood and adulthood in the African American community. A systematic scanning of the struggles and victories of African American adolescents in any neighborhood or community and family institution yields a representative reading of the strengths and vulnerabilities of the respective African American community. Clearly, the community's ability to support family life translates directly to the level of "toxic" exposure to the sometimes arbitrary interventions of child protective service systems. An effective approach to understanding risks that may subject dependent young African American children to an unmodulated environment, one in which they are neither protected and nurtured nor appropriately stimulated and socialized, requires a synthesizing approach. Unlike the analytic, linear approaches referenced earlier, this synthesizing approach brings together multifaceted information from significant and potentially critical resources in order to provide timely and appropriate caregiving responses.

Jackson and Westmoreland [1992], for example, in their summary of problems facing African American children in out-of-home care, discussed the need also to understand the family of origin as the primary agent of socialization. "The length of time the child has had with biological parents at placement is important because the older the child is [at the time of placement], the more he or she has learned about the values and customs of the [biological] family's origin" [p. 45]. These authors describe the implications of strong kinship bonds and the impact of their absence on African American children, the effects of racism and oppression, the role of the family in providing racial socialization, the critical centrality and importance of communities as sources of positive identity and role models, and the impact of skin color and socioeconomic problems that affect the self-concept of the child.

More emphatically, Jackson and Westmoreland [1992] describe the disheartening results of poor educational experiences and parental inability to combat problem situations. Too often for the African American adolescent, the ultimate and most painful outcome is to be viewed as delinquent, and sometimes as "sick." Undoubtedly, the narrow focus of most risk-assessment systems on child and family characteristics and the history of child maltreatment has not served the African American child well. Practical, analytical, simple—matrix risk-assessment approaches often fail to capture substantive and interactive factors that may dramatically affect child and family well-being (see Sedlak [1992] for further discussion).

A Culturally Specific Frame for Risk Assessment

According to Starr et al. [1993], only a little more than half of the professionals in their study reported that structured risk assessment instruments were successful in improving casework decisions, facilitating documentation, and predicting the probability of abuse or neglect. Factors correlated with effectiveness were commitment of agency management, staff perceptions of the validity of the instrument, attitude and motivation for using a risk-assessment system, and provision of training.

The results of analyzing the accuracy of assessing risk by using predictors versus reliance on worker judgment, however, indicate that currently identified predictors of risk are not sufficiently accurate to determine whether a report should be investigated. These instruments should not be used as a substitute for worker judgment [Wells & Anderson 1992]. Davidson [1992] highlights this discussion further by suggesting many related legal problems, including generalizing risk-assessment tools across diverse child protection services, the lack of specific legislative authority, and deficient regulations. Still others [Gamble 1992] summarized the overall challenges of risk-assessment tools as confusion between causes and correlates in treatment planning, biases, lack of a theoretical base, vulnerability to mechanistic approaches to service planning, imposition of an "objectivity" framework onto the family, and a static versus developmentally focused orientation to practice.

In discussion with this author, Rose Herring, a 1996 doctoral candidate at the Howard University School of Social Work, reported preliminary findings of her study of 155 African American families served by Children's National Medical Center in Washington, D.C. It was noted that the Medical Center's Division of Child Protection risk-assessment instrument potentially served as an effective guide for inexperienced and inadequately trained practitioners but had no significant impact on the accuracy and predictability in judgment of seasoned professionals. The Division's Risk Assessment Matrix (RAM) included 10 of the most empirically agreed-upon risk factors associated with child abuse and neglect: previous reports; parental history of having been abused as child; age of parent/child; family composition; domestic violence; extended parent-child separation; parent/caregiver substance abuse; child mentally, physically, or emotionally impaired; caregiver or parent mentally, physically, or emotionally impaired; and low economic status.

Herring pointed out that risk factors should have more relevancy to the "values, lifestyles, and interactional patterns of the communities" that are being served. Thus, she incorporated 15 additional cultural and region-specific factors in the RAM instrument: medical evidence; school adjustment; parent with limited education; parent with limited support system; parent/child role reversal; inadequate extended family; child presenting sexualized behavior; peer relationship problem; family isolation; unsatisfactory marital relationship; mother emotionally/physically absent; child's exposure to harmful situation; inadequate living situations/overcrowding; developmental delays; and stepparent/paramour in home. Herring suggested that additional research should focus on the psychometric validity of the RAM instrument on risk-assessment processes and the impact of a high-powered quality assurance model coupled with staff development activities.

Perceptions and Attitudes of Child Welfare Professionals

Greater emphasis in professional training of child welfare practitioners should be placed on the complex dynamics of culture and on social acculturation. Most practitioners struggle with the need or desire for simple direct action and often shortcut the necessity of understanding historical and community contextual factors that influence family adaptation. Cross-cultural assessments, whether driven by race, ethnicity, gender, class, religion, or other social determinants, require a heightened element of time, valuation of the legitimacy of the perspectives of involuntary clients, and personal awareness of the professional's own values and cultural screens.

Process research should be ongoing in agencies and focused upon the characteristics of effective cross-cultural engagement and joint decision making between professionals and African American families at high risk. Practitioners should be trained to understand the significance of the worldview of African Americans and the implications for diagnosing and for planning interventions [English 1991]. Turner [1991], for example, describes the Africentric perspective, with its emphasis on the interconnectedness of all things, collective identity, consanguinal family structure, and consequential morality. Gould [1991] discusses the prominence of extended kinship bonds, communal identity, and self-help in the African American community as the basis for developing unique and effective child welfare interventions.

Engagement of the African American Community

Professionals throughout the child welfare system should question the validity of linear and individual client-based models of service planning. Collaborative strategies should be prioritized, bringing community representatives to the table as equal partners. Teams should engage in undominated dialogue that examines varied definitions of harm and risk for children and the implications for cultural conflicts, screening and intake, and resource allocation—public, private, and community-based.

Indigenous resources of the African American community, such as churches and social or educational institutions, should be cultivated as mediating structures that provide particular sensitivity to the types of factors that lead to child abuse in the African American community, that is, parents abused as children who continue the cycle of violence, social class, stress, social isolation, racism, joblessness, and diminished funding for social services (see Hampton [1991] for a discussion of an ecological framework for examining cultural factors).

Professionals should cultivate partnerships with extended families and kinship networks since surrogate caregivers may provide a support system for parents at risk and prove to be holders of the most accurate, predictive assessment information. If such persons are not engaged, cultural belief systems that are reinforced by the family's network may hinder or complicate positive case outcomes [Helfer & Snow 1985].

Conclusion

As outmoded and antiquated bureaucratic child caring systems fail to respond effectively to a growing number of African Ameri-

can children who come to the attention of child protective services, one can observe a frightening effect. As financial resources
continue to dwindle in contrast to demands and needs, we are
standing witness to the deprofessionalization of the governmental
response. As systems go into receivership and court supervision,
and as politicians lobby for their political survival, African
American children increasingly become fodder for untested and
nonsystematic interventions by many professionals into the lives
of their families and their communities. A cultural strength for all
people of color historically has been their investment in themselves
through the survival of their children and the insurance that their
offspring can adapt and lead the next generation. This article has
sought to drive home the urgency of developing comprehensive,
community-based, and culturally synthesizing approaches to evaluating potential and realized risks for the healthy development
of African American children. Only then can the elders, sparked
by their caregiving and generative roles within the community,
pass on the hopefulness. Then and only then will African American children cease to expand the "caseloads" in the child welfare and juvenile delinquency arenas. ♦

References

Blick, L., Giller, E., & Lloyd, D. W. (Eds.). (1990). *Enhancing child sexual abuse services to minority cultures. Proceedings of a think tank.* Huntsville, AL: National Children's Advocacy Center.

Boyd-Franklin, N. (1989). *Black families in therapy: A multisystems approach.* New York: Guilford Press.

Brissett-Chapman, S. (1995). Child abuse and neglect: Direct service. In R. L. Edwards (Ed.), *19th Encyclopedia of Social Work* (pp. 353–366). Washington, DC: National Association of Social Workers.

Child Welfare League of America. (1986). *Too young to run: The status of child abuse in America.* Washington, DC: Author.

Cicchinelli, L. (1991). *Symposium on "risk" assessment in child protective services* (Proceedings). Washington, DC: National Center on Child Abuse and Neglect.

Cohen, N. A. (1992). *Child welfare: A multicultural focus.* Boston: Allyn and Bacon.

Davidson, H. (1992). CPS risk assessment and the law: Unsettled issues. In *Fifth National Roundtable on CPS Risk Assessment* (pp. 153–166). Washington, DC: American Public Welfare Association.

DePanfilis, D. (1988). *Final report determining safety in child protective services and child placement decisions.* Charlotte, NC: ACTION for Child Protection.

English, D. (1994). *Case decision making in CPS: A discussion of issue and brief review of research. Proceedings paper.* Presented at National Center on Child Abuse and Neglect State Liaison Officers' Meeting. Washington, DC: Clearinghouse on Child Abuse and Neglect Information.

English, D. (1989). Washington State child protective intake study. An overview. In P. Schene & R. Bond (Eds.), *Research issues in risk assessment for child protection.* Denver, CO: American Association for Protecting Children.

English, R. A. (1991). Diversity of world views among African-American Families. In J. E. Everett, S. S. Chipungu, & B. R. Leashore (Eds.), *Child welfare: An Africentric perspective* (pp. 19–35). New Brunswick, NJ: Rutgers University Press.

Everett, J. E. (1991). Introduction: Children in crisis. In J. E. Everett, S. S. Chipungu, & B. R. Leashore (Eds.), *Child welfare: An Africentric Perspective* (pp. 1–14). New Brunswick, NJ: Rutgers University Press.

Fanshel, D. (1979). Pre-schoolers entering foster care in New York City: The need to stress plans for permanency. *Child Welfare, 58,* 67-87.

Gamble, T. (1992). Practice challenges to effective risk implementation. In *Fifth national roundtable on CPS risk assessment* (pp. 221–236). Washington, DC: American Public Welfare Association.

Garbarino, J., Kostelny, K., & Grady, J. (1993). Children in dangerous environments: Child maltreatment in the context of community violence. Advances in applied developmental psychology. In D. Cicchette & S. L. Toth (Eds.), *Child abuse, child development, and social policy* (vol. 8) (pp. 167–189). Norwood, NJ: Ablex Publishing.

Gibbs, J. T. (1989). Black American adolescents. In J. T. Gibbs, L. N. Huang, & Associates, (Eds.), *Children of color: Psychological intervention with minority youth.* San Francisco: Jossey Bass.

Gould, K. H. (1991). Limiting damage is not enough: A minority perspective on child welfare issues. In J. E. Everett, S. S. Chipungu, & B. R. Leashore (Eds.), *Child welfare: An Africentric perspective* (pp. 58–78). New Brunswick, NJ: Rutgers University Press.

Hampton, R. L. (1991). *Child abuse in the African-American community.* New Brunswick, NJ: Rutgers University Press.

Harris, N. (1990). Dealing with diverse cultures in child welfare. In *Protecting Children,* 7(3), 6–7.

Helfer, R. E., & Snow, L. F. (1985). Social and cultural issues. In V. L. Vivian (Ed.), *Child abuse and neglect: A community response* (pp. 113–121). Chicago: American Medical Association.

Herring, R. (1996). Personal communication.

Holton, J. K. (1990). *Black families and child abuse prevention: An African-American perspective and approach.* Chicago: National Committee for Prevention of Child Abuse.

Jackson, H. L., & Westmoreland, G. (1992) Therapeutic issues for black children in foster care. In L. N. Vargas & J. D. Koss-Chioino (Eds.), *Working with culture: Psychotherapeutic interventions with ethnic minority children and adolescents* (pp. 43–62). San Francisco: Jossey Bass.

National Center on Child Abuse and Neglect. (1988). *Study findings: Study of national incidence and prevalence of child abuse and neglect.* Washington, DC: U.S. Government Printing Office.

National Center on Child Abuse and Neglect. (1993). *National child abuse and data system: Working paper 2—1991 summary data component.* Washington, DC: U.S. Government Printing Office.

National Resource Center on Child Abuse and Neglect. (1994). *Risk assessment technical brief.* Englewood, CO: American Humane Association.

Neaves, D. C., & Matheson, D. K. (1970, November/December). Directions in research questions about policies and practices in parent-child separation. *Canadian Welfare,* 46(6).

Pecora, P. J. (1991). *Investigating allegations of child maltreatment: The strengths and limitations of current risk assessment systems. Technical report.* Seattle, WA: Washington University School of Social Work.

Pinderhughes, E. (1991). The delivery of child welfare services to African-American clients. *American Journal of Orthopsychiatry, 61*(4), 599–605.

Pinderhughes, E. (1982). Family functioning of Afro-Americans. *Social Work, 27,* 91–95.

Price, J. A. (1975). An applied analysis of North American Indians drinking patterns. *Human Organization, 34*(1).

Russell, A. B., & Trainor, C. M. (1984). *Trends in child abuse and neglect: A national perspective.* Denver, CO: American Humane Association.

Sedlak, A. J. (1992). *Demographic research and child abuse.* Proceedings paper. Washington, DC: American Psychological Association, Centennial Convention.

Starr, R. H., DePanfilis, D., & Morris, M. (1993). *Current issues in risk assessment.* Proceedings paper. Baltimore, MD: University of Maryland/Baltimore County.

Tatara, T. (1989). *CPS risks assessment survey of status on CPS risk assessment findings.* Washington, DC: American Public Welfare Association.

Turner, R. J. (1991) *Affirming consciousness: The Africentric perspective.* In J. E. Everett, S. S. Chipungu, & B. R. Leashore (Eds.), *Child welfare: An africentric perspective* (pp. 36–57). New Brunswick, NJ: Rutgers University Press.

Wells, S. J., & Anderson, T. (1992). *Workers' estimation of risk as a predictor of case substantiation. Publication information.* Washington, DC: American Public Welfare Association.

4

An Out-of-Home Care System in Crisis: Implications for African American Children in the Child Welfare System

Annie Woodley Brown and Barbara Bailey-Etta

An out-of-home care system that is itself in crisis lacks adequate resources to provide the services needed by families and children in distress. Increasingly, these families are composed of people of color, particularly African Americans. Using current child welfare statistics and a review of the literature, this article examines the nature of the crisis in child welfare, and how poverty and an array of social problems, as well as problems specific to the child welfare system, increase the overrepresentation of African American children and families in the out-of-home care system. Implications for child welfare practice and advocacy are also discussed.

Annie Woodley Brown, D.S.W., is Assistant Professor, Howard University School of Social Work, Washington, DC. Barbara Bailey-Etta, D.S.W., LICSW, is Assistant Professor and Director, Office of Field Instruction, Catholic University of America, National Catholic School of Social Service, Washington, DC.

Arican American families and children are adversely affected by an out-of-home care system in crisis. Their overrepresentation in a child welfare system that is overburdened and underfunded increases their risk for negative outcomes even when there is intervention. The number of children in out-of-home care is closely linked to the conditions under which families function and the societal supports available to assist them. African American families are disproportionately affected by negative social, political, and economic forces that undoubtedly contribute to their overrepresentation in the out-home care system. An array of problems—including racism, poverty, inadequate housing, substance abuse, HIV/AIDS, teenage pregnancy, incarceration, lack of appropriate social support systems, and violence—all combine to account for the growing number of African American children needing out-of-home care.

Families provide the basic socialization for children in preparation for their participation in the larger society. Far too many African American families, affected by some of society's most insidious ills, find themselves without the material and sometimes the psychological resources to provide basic care and nurturance for their children. The child welfare system, which has evolved to meet the needs of children and families in distress when children are endangered, is itself in crisis. Despite efforts over the last decade to retool policy and practice to prevent unnecessary placement of children in care [Gray & Nybell 1990], the number of children in out-of-home care has risen. The child welfare system, overwhelmed by the sheer number of children coming into care and placed in financial uncertainty by the politics of the reluctant welfare state, faces a formidable challenge at a time when sound policies and innovative programs are most needed.

Using an ecological perspective, this article examines the following questions related to the crisis in child welfare: (1) What are the historical antecedents to the present crisis? (2) What issues specific to the child welfare system itself contribute to the present crisis? (3) What is the relationship between other social problems and the crisis in child welfare? (4) What factors have contributed to the overrepresentation of African American children in the child welfare system? and (5) What are the implications for social work practice with African American children and families in the child welfare system? The ecological perspective provides a theoretical framework from which to view the present crisis in out-of-home care because it offers a holistic view of persons and their environments. The perspective forces us to broaden our unit of attention to include considerations of the environment: "people, organizations, service arrangements, ideas, systems, [and] time, as examples" [Mishne 1982].

Nature of the Present Crisis in Out-of-Home Care

The passage of the Adoption Assistance and Child Welfare Act of 1980 [P.L. 96–272] provided federal support for permanency planning as a guiding principle in child welfare. It established a national policy affecting permanency initiatives for children in out-of-home care and those at risk of entry into the system. It provided legislation that emphasized family preservation and reunification of children in care with their biological families; it made funds available to help with adoption if reunification was not workable, and it dealt with legal guardianship and long-term out-of-home care [Groze et al. 1994]. Through mandates for programs and some additional funding through Title IV-E, a concerted effort was made to end foster care drift and move children into permanent living arrangements. The act stipulated that states must monitor cases effectively, which included reviewing cases every six months and taking additional steps to assure each child a permanent home [DiNitto 1991; Fein 1991a].

Despite the focus on permanency and a reduction in the number of children in care from a high of close to half a million in the 1970s [Fein 1991a; Gustavsson & Segal 1994] to well below 300,000 in the early 1980s [Pecora et al. 1992; Gustavsson & Segal 1994], the number of children in care has significantly increased since the mid-1980s [Albers et al. 1993; Dillon 1994; Everett 1995; U.S. General Accounting Office 1995] (see figure 1).

Many factors—both internal and external, demographic and structural—contribute to the wide scope of the crisis of a system with diminishing resources and increasing responsibilities. These factors are interrelated and inextricably bound together, fueling the present crisis and rendering solutions elusive.

System Issues

Fein [1991b] noted that even more disturbing than the number of children in out-of-home care is the realization that the child welfare system is no system at all. "The lack of federal leadership in promoting professional standards of practice and effective policy initiatives has permitted 50 separate state 'systems'" [p. 576]. Everett [1995: 377] refers to a "patchwork of federal and state initiatives designed to support the principle of permanence." "Typically, the agencies lack the resources to deal with the more recalcitrant situations—those in which substance abuse, homelessness, domestic violence, and poverty exacerbate the abuse and neglect of a dysfunctional family system" [Fein & Staff 1993: 26].

Within the system, lack of adequate agency staff and resources, sporadic staff training, and unclear and sometimes contradictory policy mandates contribute to the crisis in the following ways: (1) lack of services to prevent initial placements; (2) a decline in the number of children discharged from out-of-home care; (3) increased reentry into out-of-home care following periods of family reunification that fail due to lack of supportive services; and (4) a decline in the number of family foster homes available for child placement.

The U.S. General Accounting Office (GAO) reported in 1995 that, next to funding, the most serious problem that affects the delivery of child welfare services in most states is that of staff-

FIGURE 1

Children in Out-of-Home Care, 1982 to 1994 (in thousands)

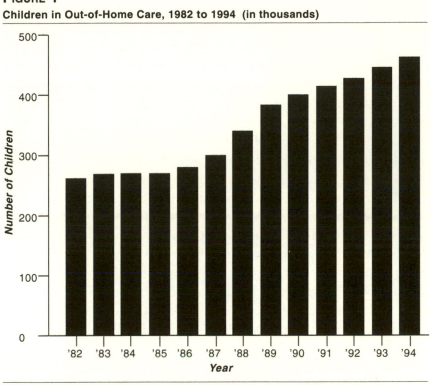

Source: Adoption and Foster Care Analysis and Reporting System (AFCARS), AFCARS State Workshop, September 1995, based on data by T. Tatara, *VCIS Research Notes*, No. 11, (August 1995).

ing. Ninety percent of the states reported difficulty recruiting and retaining caseworkers [U.S. General Accounting Office 1995]. The consequences of an inadequate number of staff members to provide and plan for supportive services to families and children undoubtedly include extended length of stays in the out-of-home care system and delays in family reunification. In fact, inadequate staffing compromises the very integrity of the out-of-home care system as a mandated service because staffing affects decision making at every level. The timeliness of decisions concerning reunification, adoption, or termination of parental rights is particularly vital, because failure to act keeps children in the system or in a particular status within the system much longer than is necessary. These problems become ever more critical as the out-of-home care components of child welfare systems in many states are placed in receivership. In the short term, such a measure further aggravates the crisis within the affected organizations, as manifested by staff apprehension, low morale, lack of adequate communication, and staff resignations.

The funds to accomplish much of the work with children and families in the out-of-home care system mandated by P.L. 96–272 have not been provided at the state or federal level [Fein 1991b; Pecora et al. 1992]. Shifting funding to a block grant basis via welfare reform can only increase the need for child welfare services for families and children. As pointed out in 1996, "child protection services would be converted to a block grant and subject to funding cuts at the same time that a large number of poor children and families would become ineligible for cash assistance or SSI because of other changes in the welfare bill" [Center on Budget and Policy Priorities 1996: 9].

"The supply of family foster homes has not kept pace with the growth of the foster care population" [Everett 1995: 385], adding to the crisis. In fact, from 1985 to 1990, the number of children in out-of-home care increased by 47%, but the number of family foster homes declined by 27% [Spar 1993]. Some major urban areas experienced as much as a 60% annual turnover in foster families [Everett 1995], a trend that is particularly evident in the African American community. Adequate staffing would help agencies to recruit, train, and retain families willing to provide care for children.

Although Tatara [1993] reported a two-thirds rate of reunification, many of the children reunified with their families of origin have returned to out-of-home care. Reentry estimates vary. Maluccio et al. [1994] reviewed studies indicating reentry rates from 10% to 33%. Undoubtedly, reentry is a factor in the number of children in care at any given time.

Societal and Family Factors

"Poverty, drug abuse, inadequate housing, and homelessness are factors cited in many reported cases of foster care placement" [National Center for Children in Poverty 1990: 61]. Child protection is the primary reason most children are referred for family foster care [Kadushin & Martin 1988; Tatara 1993]. Though family violence is found at all socioeconomic levels, the number of officially reported cases of child abuse is highest among the poor, and "the incidence of child abuse and neglect, as well as the severity of the maltreatment reported, is much greater for children from low-income families than for others" [National Center for Children in Poverty 1990: 59; Hampton 1991; Tatara 1991; Pelton 1994]. This could reflect a bias in reporting, since the poor more often use public facilities, but this correlation between poverty and child maltreatment could also reflect the reality that poverty exposes families to multiple stressors and, in interaction with individual coping capacities, compromises some parents' ability to provide effective parenting [National Center for Children in Poverty 1990]. The U.S. General Accounting Office [1995] report indicated that the number of children in family foster care eligible for federal matching funds by virtue of their biological family's eligibility for AFDC has increased by a larger percentage than has the number of children in care in general. Children from families who were on AFDC as reported by Albers et al. [1993] were less likely to be reunified with family members or placed in a permanent adoptive home compared with those children whose families were not on AFDC. In addition, those children whose families were on AFDC were likely to have longer stays in out-of-home care than those children whose families were not on AFDC.

When children from families who are poor are reported to the child welfare system, they and their families often have human service needs that go beyond the capacity of child welfare agencies alone to meet. The families are often connected to other major service delivery systems [Goerge et al. 1994] or need to be connected to such services if the children are to experience a successful outcome.

In considering the social and family factors contributing to African American children and families' involvement in the out-of-home care system, attention must be given particularly to the economic impact of the deindustrialization of the American economy and the subsequent loss of jobs experienced in African American communities across the country. Billingsley [1992] contends that racial and ethnic discrimination and a history of economic marginality have rendered African American families more vulnerable to the large-scale technological and economic changes in the social environment. As a result, African American families are altered by these changes, "earlier, more extensively and in a more negative way than families of other groups" [Billingsley: 130]. Consequently, these economic transitions have precipitated a sharp decline in the stable African American working-class population and have provided fewer opportunities for youth employment and economic incentives for family formation.

Urban areas have been left to absorb large numbers of truly disadvantaged persons. Communities have become destabilized by the overwhelming number of impoverished single female-headed households and by alternative economic activity that is more and more related to criminal and delinquent behavior. Families and children, with few of the social supports provided by stable neighborhoods and communities, are exposed to and experience increasing levels of violence, incarceration, and the ravages of substance abuse and HIV/AIDS. These problems all combine to increase the number of children needing out-of-home care and families needing services if there is to be any hope that any of these children will be reunified with their families.

Being born to young parents is associated with poverty for African American children and is a risk factor for entry of the child into out-of-home care, as is previous status of a parent as a child in care. Once a child is in out-of-home care, reunification of the child with the biological parents is often delayed because of the parents' inability to follow through with treatment plans for substance abuse or mental illness. Children from many of these families are entering care more troubled than in the past and with greater emotional, behavioral, and medical needs [Fanshel 1992; U.S. General Accounting Office 1995]. The child welfare system has been used by society as a substitute for unavailable multiservice systems designed to serve poor families [Albers et al. 1993].

African American Children and Families and the Out-of-Home Care System

Historical Perspective

Family foster care has it roots in ancient history [Kadushin & Martin 1988; Pecora et al. 1992; Everett 1995]. Less well documented in mainstream child welfare literature, however, is the fact that for African Americans, family foster care is undoubtedly rooted in their African cultural heritage, where societies were organized around extended families, clans, and tribes [Sudarkasa 1988]. Family foster care has historically been an integral part of the African American community. Even during slavery, informal substitute care was provided by other slaves to children left behind when parents were sold to other plantations. Moreover, after emancipation, "the extended family came to the rescue of thousands of related and nonrelated black children...who had no means of support" [Logan et al. 1990: 9]. Initially, African American children and families were excluded from the formal child welfare system as it evolved. Social welfare services, including child welfare services, were provided by the mutual aid, self-help efforts of churches, women's clubs, benevolent societies, fraternal organizations, and extended families [Ross 1978; Giddings 1984; Wesley 1984; Leashore et al. 1991]. Even with inclusion in the formal child welfare system, the provision of out-of-home care for children through informal adoptions and family foster care by relatives and nonrelatives has persisted [Hill 1977; Billingsley 1992].

Contemporary Perspective

In more recent times, racism and segregation have often denied African American families and children access to many of the services of the formal child welfare system [Close 1983], or provided the basis for differential treatment within that system [Stehno 1982; Albers et al. 1993]. Gould [1991] contends that once minority children enter the system, the system fails to evaluate their plight accurately, which has resulted in the provision of insufficient, inadequate, and oftentimes inappropriate and damaging child welfare services. Moreover, it has been found that these children enter the system in increased numbers, remain in the system longer than Caucasian children, do not receive as many in-home support services as Caucasian children, and have a disproportionate number of undesirable experiences [Gould 1991; Mech 1985; Billingsley & Giovannoni 1972]. African American children are more likely to be placed in transracial foster homes and adoptive homes than are Caucasian children, and more likely to enter care as young children [Fein 1991a]. Despite the development of policies to circumvent drift in out-of-home care, large numbers of African American children remain in the quagmire of bureaucratic systems that oftentimes do not understand them and/or lack the appropriate resources or alternatives to assist them and their families.

From exclusion very early on in the formal child welfare system, the number of African American children in out-of-home care in 1990 was larger than the number of children from any other group. Tatara [1993] reported that at the end of fiscal year 1990, 39.3% (159,600) of children in out-of-home care were Caucasian, 40.4% (164,000) were African American. Latino children constituted 11.8% (47,000) of the children in out-of-home care. Though states have some difficulty in reporting data for children in out-of-home care because of missing data, differences in kind of information collected, and inability to determine race and ethnicity, AFCARS [1995] data show trends of distribution in the different racial and ethnic groups in out-of-home care (see figure 2).

FIGURE 2

Children in Out-of-Home Care by Race, 1995 (N = 330,838)

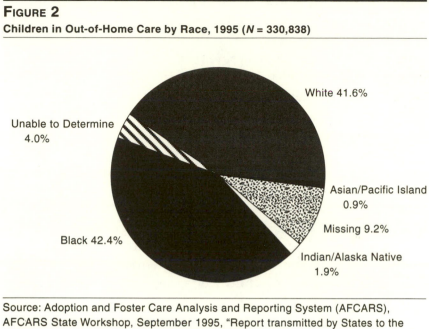

White 41.6%

Unable to Determine
4.0%

Asian/Pacific Island
0.9%

Missing 9.2%

Black 42.4%

Indian/Alaska Native
1.9%

Source: Adoption and Foster Care Analysis and Reporting System (AFCARS),
AFCARS State Workshop, September 1995, "Report transmitted by States to the
Administration for Children and Families (ACF)".

To place these numbers in context, it is important to note that in 1994, Caucasian children constituted 75% of the child population in the U.S., African American children constituted 15%, and Latino children constituted 10% of the total child population of the U.S. [Groze et al. 1994]. It is when we see the percentage of African American children as a part of the total child population of the U.S. compared to their percentage as a part of the out-of-home care population that the full impact of their overrepresentation in the child welfare system is realized.

The large percentage of African American children in out-of-home care has resulted in an interesting phenomenon—the increased number of African American children in kinship care in the formal out-of-home care system. This trend may reflect both the actual expansion of the number of African American children needing out-of-home care and the incorporation of pre-existing informal arrangements into the formal child welfare family foster care system. Kinship arrangements account for some of the recent growth in the population in out-of-home care [Testa 1992; Goerge et al. 1994]. "The proportion of foster children placed with relatives grew from 18 percent to 31 percent between 1986 and 1990 in 25 states, including California and New York" [U.S. General Accounting Office 1995: 11]. In some urban metropolitan areas such as New York City, reportedly half the children in out-of-home care in the 1990s were in kinship care [Dubowitz 1994]. A dramatic example of the increase in the use of kinship care in the child welfare system is provided by a comparative look at New York City over time. In 1986, the number of known kinship arrangements was 1,000; by 1992, it had increased to 24,000 [Child Welfare League of America 1995].

Ironically, a historical feature of the African American community (the provision of informal family foster care) has come to be seen by the formal child welfare system as a viable alternative, in many instances, to placement outside of the family. The perceived virtue of these arrangements and the desire of kin not to be treated like "foster parents" by the system, should not be allowed to obscure the fact that many of the families providing kinship care are often poor, and that they often have some of the same needs for supportive services as the biological parents. Kinship care arrangements should not be pursued by child welfare agencies as a cost-effective way to avoid providing supportive services to children and families in need. African American children in kinship care tend to receive fewer services than do children in nonrelative family foster care [Dubowitz 1994], and fewer services than their Caucasian counterparts in kinship care [National Black Child Development Institute 1989].

Implications for Child Welfare Practice, Education, and Research: A New Agenda

Child welfare workers must ally themselves with families to forge a proactive strategy to reduce the number of children entering the out-of-home care system. Such an alliance could be based on a strategy of empowerment for both child welfare workers and families [Hegar & Hunzeker 1988]. Solomon [1976] noted that empowerment-based practice would focus on the strengths of families, and that clients and workers could collaborate to solve problems. A proactive strategy for child welfare workers lies in the development of a family-centered, community-based practice. It is important to use the strengths of the community to help parents reaffirm their parental role. Networking with the extended family and community to assist with child rearing and a return to a consistent use of religious and fraternal organizations are strategies that need to be formalized in helping build a kind of social immunity or integrated social support system for children and families. Certainly, the use of kinship care is considered a return to the recognition of the use of extended families and friends who are considered "kin" to provide family foster care. This new interest in kinship care on the part of the formal child welfare system, however, provides an opportunity for important comparative research on the effectiveness of various types of placements, and for comparing the safety of relative family foster homes with the safety of nonrelative family foster home placements.

Agencies, and educational institutions that educate agency staff members and future human service workers, ought to recognize and support the need for collaboration among agencies, and for new initiatives to coordinate paths across the many different systems serving children—child welfare, health, mental health, and education—to reduce duplication of services and maximize the benefits of interventions. Additionally, empowered human service professionals and energized agency consumers have reasons for a strong joint advocacy role. They must make clear to Congress and the executive and judicial branches of government the nature of the crises facing the child welfare services delivery system.

Efforts must be pursued to establish partnerships between schools of social work and child welfare agencies to provide in-service training in cultural sensitivity and competency and the effective use of advocacy and lobbying to obtain appropriate services for African American children and families. The challenge for educators, practitioners, and researchers is "to view each child and family within a framework which encompasses the entire political, social, economic, cultural and spiritual experiences that shape the identity and behavior of the families and children with whom they work" [Dillon 1994: 138].

The ongoing shift in the provision of child welfare services to purchase-of-service contracting with voluntary agencies will likely be speeded up by social legislation that will affect funding and increase demands for unit cost analyses of services. Although child welfare services are big business, contracting and procurement for child welfare (to protect children and strengthen families, to prevent placement, or to achieve reunification once the child is removed) defy the kind of unit cost analysis characteristic of business. These changes have implications for social work practice, education, and research, because monitoring, training, and evaluation will be required to ensure that those in need of child welfare services receive the services they need. Despite widespread use of purchase-of-service agencies, little monitoring or evaluation of contracting has been conducted to determine its effects on services [Bailey-Etta, in press; Hart 1988].

Conclusion

The crisis in out-of-home care is not occurring in a vacuum. Forming the backdrop of the crisis is the continued deterioration of social conditions for many American families, and in particular African American families, who are disproportionately represented among the poor. The intense, complex, intractable nature of the problems faced by families in homes, neighborhoods, and communities poses an unprecedented need for special services from an already overburdened system.

The history of social welfare in the United States is one of reluctance to provide institutionalized social welfare services.

Concern for the welfare of children provided the impetus for much of the social welfare reform of the early 20th century and the consequent development of social work as a profession. We may now have come full circle. It may well be that concern for the welfare of children and families at a time of reduced opportunities for employment and declining protection against poverty will galvanize child welfare workers and other human service professionals to action—to use the social reform tactics of an earlier time in this country to confront the pressing problems of the present.

The majority of the children in the child welfare out-of-home care system during the time many of the previous reforms took place were Caucasian. In the current crisis, the majority of children in out-of-home care are African American. The history of racism and exclusion in this country poses a special challenge to policymakers concerning funding, programming, and best practices. The goals of permanence and continuity for all children in the child welfare system remain paramount, but these goals must be attuned to the realities of life and the devastating impact of social problems on families, especially African American families [Gray & Nybell 1990]. African Americans and other people of color are overrepresented as clients and underrepresented in the arenas where the decisions are made that will determine the direction of the child welfare system in the 21st century. ◆

References

AFCARS (Adoption and Foster Care Analysis and Reporting System). (1995). *AFCARS data*. Report transmitted by states to the Administration for Children and Families (ACF), from AFCARS State Workshop, September 1995.

Albers, E. C., Reilly, T., & Rittner, B. (1993). Children in foster care: Possible factors affecting permanency planning. *Child and Adolescent Social Work Journal, 10,* 329–333.

Allen, M. L. (1991). Crafting a federal legislative framework for child welfare reform. *American Journal of Orthopsychiatry, 61,* 610–623.

Bailey-Etta, B. (in press). Contracting as a strategy for organizational survival. In M. Gibelman & H. W. Demone Jr. (Eds.), *Cases in the privatization of human service: Perspectives and experiences in contracting.* New York: Springer Press.

Billingsley, A. (1992). *Climbing Jacob's ladder: The enduring legacy of African American families.* New York: Simon & Schuster.

Billingsley, A., & Giovannoni, J. M. (1972). *Children of the storm.* New York: Harcourt, Brace & Jovanovich, Inc.

Center on Budget and Policy Priorities. (1996). *The conference agreement on the welfare bill* (rev.). Washington, DC: Author.

Child Welfare League of America. (1995). *Foster family care fact sheet.* Washington, DC: Author.

Close, M. M. (1983). Child welfare and people of color: Denial of equal access. *Social Work Research and Abstracts, 19,* 13–20.

Dillon, D. (1994). Understanding and assessment of intragroup dynamics in family foster care: African American families. *Child Welfare, 73,* 129–139.

DiNitto, D. (1991). *Social welfare: Politics and public policy.* Englewood Cliffs, NJ: Prentice Hall.

Dubowitz, H. (1994). Kinship care: Suggestions for future research. *Child Welfare, 73,* 553–563.

Everett, J. E. (1995). Child foster care. In R. L. Edwards & J. G. Hopps (Eds.), *Encyclopedia of Social Work (vol. 1)* (pp. 375–389). Washington, DC: National Association of Social Workers.

Fanshel, D. (1992). Foster care as a two-tiered system. *Children and Youth Services Review, 14,* 49–60.

Fein, E. (1991a). Issues in foster family care: Where do we stand? *American Journal of Orthopsychiatry, 61,* 578–583.

Fein, E. (1991b). The elusive search for certainty in child welfare: Introduction. *American Journal of Orthopsychiatry, 61,* 576–577.

Fein, E., & Staff, I. (1993). Last best chance: Findings from a reunification services program. *Child Welfare, 72,* 25–40.

Giddings, P. (1984). *When and where I enter: The impact of Black women on race and sex in America.* New York: Bantam Books.

Gould, K. H. (1991). Limiting damage is not enough: A minority perspective on child welfare. In J. E. Everett, S. S. Chipungu, & B. R. Leashore (Eds.), *Child welfare: An Africentric perspective* (pp. 58–78). New Brunswick, NJ: Rutgers University Press.

Goerge, R., Wulczyn, F., & Fanshel, D. (1994). A foster care research agenda for the '90s. *Child Welfare, 73,* 525–549.

Gray, S. S., & Nybell, L. M. (1990). Issues in African American family preservation. *Child Welfare, 69,* 513–523.

Groze, V., Haines-Simeon, M., & Barth, R. P. (1994). Barriers in permanency planning for medically fragile children: Drug affected children and HIV infected children. *Child and Adolescent Social Work Journal, 11,* 63–85.

Gustavsson, N. S., & Segal, E. A. (1994). *Critical issues in child welfare.* Thousand Oaks, CA: Sage Publications.

Hampton, R. L. (1991). Child abuse in the African American community. In J. E. Everett, S. S. Chipungu, & B. R. Leashore (Eds.), *Child welfare: An Africentric perspective* (pp. 220–246). New Brunswick, NJ: Rutgers University Press.

Hart, A. F. (1988). Contracting for child welfare services in Massachusetts: Emerging issues for policy and practice. *Social Work, 33,* 511–515.

Hegar, R. L., & Hunzeker, J. M. (1988). Moving toward empowerment-based practice in public child welfare. *Social Work, 33,* 499–502.

Hill, R. (1977). *Informal adoption among Black families.* Washington, DC: National Urban League.

Kadushin, A., & Martin, J. A. (1988). *Child welfare services* (4th ed.). New York: Macmillan Publishing Company.

Leashore, B., McMurray, H., & Bailey, B. (1991). Reuniting and preserving African American families. In J. E. Everett, S. S. Chipungu, & B. R. Leashore (Eds.), *Child welfare: An Africentric perspective* (pp. 247–265). New Brunswick, NJ: Rutgers University Press.

Logan, S. M., Freeman, E. M., & McRoy, R. G. (1990). *Social work: A culturally specific perspective.* New York: Longman.

Maluccio, A., & Kluger, M. (1990). *No more partings: An examination of long-term foster family care.* Washington, DC: Child Welfare League of America.

Maluccio, A., Fein, E., & Davis, I. P. (1994). Family reunification: Research findings, issues, and directions. *Child Welfare, 73,* 489–504.

Mech, E. V. (1985). Public social services to minority children and their families. In R. O. Washington & J. Boros-Hull (Eds.), *Children in need of roots* (pp. 133–186). Davis, CA: International Dialogue Press.

Mishne, J. M. (1982). The missing system in social work's application of systems theory. *Social Casework, 63,* 547–553.

National Black Child Development Institute. (1989). *Who will care when parents can't? A study of Black children in foster care.* Washington, DC: Author.

National Center for Children in Poverty. (1990). *Five million children: A statistical profile of our poorest young citizens.* New York: Columbia University.

Pecora, P. J., Whittaker, J. K., Maluccio, A. N., Barth, R. P., & Plotnick, R. D. (1992). *The child welfare challenge.* New York: Aldine De Gruyter.

Pelton, L. H. (1994). Is poverty a key contributor to child maltreatment? In E. Gambrill & T. J. Stein (Eds.), *Controversial issues in child welfare* (pp. 16–21). Boston: Allyn and Bacon.

Ross, E. L. (1978). *Black heritage in social welfare: 1860-1930.* Metuchen, NJ: The Scarecrow Press, Inc.

Solomon, B. B. (1976). *Black empowerment: Social work in oppressed communities.* New York: Columbia University Press.

Spar, K. (1993). *Kinship foster care: An emerging issue.* Washington, DC: Congressional Research Service. Education and Public Welfare Division.

Stehno, S. M. (1982). Differential treatment of minority children in service systems. *Social Work, 27,* 39–45.

Sudarkasa, N. (1988). Interpreting the African heritage in Afro-American family organization. In H. P. McAdoo (Ed.), *Black families* (pp. 27–43). Newbury Park, CA: Sage Publications.

Tatara, T. (1991). Overview of child abuse and neglect. In J. E. Everett, S. S. Chipungu, & B. R. Leashore (Eds.), *Child welfare: An Africentric perspective* (pp. 187–219). New Brunswick, NJ: Rutgers University Press.

Tatara, T. (1993). *Characteristics of children in substitute and adoptive care: A statistical summary of the VCIS national child welfare data base.* Washington, DC: American Public Welfare Association.

Tatara, T. (1995). U.S. child substitute care flow data for FY 1993 and trends in the state child substitute care populations. *VCIS: Research Notes.* Washington, DC: American Public Welfare Association.

Testa, M. F. (1992). Conditions of risk for substitute care. *Children and Youth Services Review, 14,* 27–36.

United States General Accounting Office. (1995). *Complex needs strain capacity to provide services.* GAO/HEHS-95-208. Washington, DC: Author.

Wesley, C. H. (1984). *The history of the National Association of Colored Women's Clubs: A legacy of service.* Washington, DC: The Association.

5
Achieving Same-Race Adoptive Placements for African American Children: Culturally Sensitive Practice Approaches

Ruth G. McRoy, Zena Oglesby, and Helen Grape

A disproportionately large number of African American children are entering the public child welfare system, and many are in need of planning for adoptive placement. Although agencies specializing in adoption of minority children have been extremely successful in achieving same-race adoptive placements for African American children, funding and support for some of these initiatives have been withheld due to federal and state legislation designed to limit the consideration of race as a major factor in the selection of adoptive families. This article analyzes these issues, and describes successful placement practices used by a private agency in California and a public agency in Texas. Suggestions for culturally competent practice are elaborated.

Ruth G. McRoy, Ph.D., LMSW-ACP, is Ruby Lee Piester Centennial Professor in Services to Children and Families, University of Texas at Austin, Austin, TX. Zena Oglesby, M.S.W., is Executive Director, Institute for Black Parenting, Inglewood, CA. Helen Grape, LMSW-ACP, is Program Director, Region III, Children's Protective Services, Texas Department of Protective and Regulatory Services, Dallas, TX.

Recent statistics on out-of-home care reveal that a growing number of children are entering care and a disproportionately high number of these children are African American. The number of children in out-of-home care has increased from about 273,000 in the mid-1980s to almost 500,000 in 1992 [Children's Defense Fund 1994]. The proportion of all children of color in the out-of-home care system is three times their proportion in the nation's population [McKenzie 1993]. For example, in states such as New Jersey, Maryland, Louisiana, and Delaware, over 50% of the children in care are African American. Although accurate statistics on children in care needing adoptive placements are unavailable, experts estimate that between 30,000 and 50,000 U.S. children are legally free for adoption [North American Council on Adoptable Children 1995]. About 40% of these children are African American; in major urban areas like New York City and Detroit, about 80% of the children needing adoptive placement are African American [McKenzie 1993; Jones 1993].

Reasons for Out-of-Home Placements

Several factors account for the growing number of placements in out-of home care and the increased need for adoptive families, including parental drug use, poverty, and increased reporting of abuse and neglect. Although the majority of the children in care are at least of school age, the out-of-home care population is beginning to include a larger number of infants, primarily due to parental substance abuse. According to the Children's Defense Fund [1992], more than 4.5 million women of childbearing age use illegal drugs and only 14% of those who need treatment receive it.

African American children represent only 15% of the total U.S. child population, and almost 44% of all African American children live in poverty [Children's Defense Fund 1996]. A rise in reports of suspected and actual child abuse and/or neglect is a frequent concomitant of poverty. In fact, poverty is the greatest predictor of the removal of children of any age from their biological parents and placement in out-of-home care [Pelton 1989; Lindsey 1991]. As African American children are dispro-portionately poor, they are more likely to be removed from their homes and placed in out-of-home care.

Other factors such as lack of understanding on the part of protective service workers of cultural differences and variations in child rearing have sometimes led to African American chil-dren being separated from their families and placed in out-of-home care [Stehno 1982; Leashore et al. 1991]. In one state, one in 20 African American infants born in one year were placed in out-of-home care, compared with one in 100 Caucasian infants in the state [Morton 1993]. After entering the child welfare sys-tem, African American children are also more likely to remain in care longer than Caucasian children and receive fewer ser-vices, and their families may have fewer contacts with workers [Close 1983]. According to Stehno [1990], practitioners in New York were found to be less likely to arrange visits between Afri-can American families and their children than they were for their Caucasian counterparts.

Once many of these African American children become le-gally free for adoption, traditional public and private agencies often find it difficult to recruit suitable adoptive families for them. The media have recently drawn attention to Caucasian families who are seeking to adopt African American infants and young children transracially. This article examines the numer-ous issues confronting service providers involved in adoption decision making for African American children in out-of-home care. Federal and state policies designed to facilitate transracial adoptive placements are discussed and strategies used by Afri-can American placement programs for achieving inracial (same-race) placements are described.

Adoptive Placements for African American Children

Adoptive placement workers, supervisors, and administrators today are finding that adoptive placements for African Ameri-can children are influenced by many factors, including the availability of Caucasian prospective adoptive families and the limited supply of healthy Caucasian infants, the availability of culturally competent placement workers and culturally sensitive adoption agency policies and procedures, systemic obstacles to adoption by African American families, and changing state and federal adoption policies. Each factor is discussed below.

Availability of Caucasian Prospective Adoptive Families

Although current nationwide data on adoption in the United States is unavailable [Schulman 1993], estimates suggest that the number of Caucasian infants and young children available for adoption has decreased, while the number of Caucasian prospective adoptive parents has increased. Simon and Alstein [1987] report that approximately two million Caucasian couples are seeking to adopt. Most, however, are seeking infants. As only about 25,000 infants under two years of age were placed for adoption in 1986, the likelihood of receiving an infant for placement is slim for many of these couples. Given the small number of Caucasian infants available for adoption, and the growing number of African American children needing placement, some adoption agencies are encouraging Caucasian prospective adoptive parents to consider adopting transracially.

Availability of Culturally Competent Placement Workers and Specialized Minority Programs

Although the demographic profile of children in care is becoming a profile of children of color, the majority of adoption agency workers are Caucasian females. Adoption agencies are offering only minimal training to enable staff members to become culturally competent to meet the needs of children and families [Rosenthal & Groze 1990]. Moreover, private and public agencies have been reluctant to either establish or use specialized minority adoption programs [McKenzie 1993], although a study by the North American Council on Adoptable Children (NACAC) has found that these specialized programs are more likely to make successful adoptive placements of African American children than are traditional programs. NACAC reported that minority placement agencies place 94% of their African American children inracially, compared to traditional agencies that place only 51% of their children inracially [North American Council on Adoptable Children 1993b; Simon et al. 1994]. These minority specialization programs have successfully demonstrated that African American families can be recruited and retained, and can be viable resources for African American children.

Systemic Obstacles to Adoption by African American Families

Many adoption agencies find that they have a large number of approved waiting Caucasian families but a limited supply of approved waiting African American adoptive families. Some believe the myth that African American families are either not available to adopt or are not interested in adopting [Sullivan 1994]. According to Hill [1993], however, a National Urban League African American Pulse Survey revealed that three million (or one-third) of African American household heads were interested in formally adopting. Other studies have reported that when family composition, income, and age are controlled, African American families adopt at four times the rate of Caucasian families [Mason & Williams 1985] . Many African American families, however, have considered adopting but have been screened out of the process. For example, according to a National Urban League study of 800 African American families who applied to adopt, only two were approved for adoption. This disproportionately high number of African American families who are screened out of the process, combined with the large number of families who are actually interested in adoption, suggests that African American families can be found for waiting children if obstacles are removed.

Several researchers and adoption advocacy groups have studied the low approval rates for African American prospective adoptive families. Rodriguez and Meyer [1990] conducted a comparative study of minority adoptive parent applicants and adoptive parents from five large cities who were associated with eight private and five public traditional agencies and three private agencies that specialized in minority adoptions. They found that agency policies, lack of sufficient minority and trained staff members and some minority community attitudes were obstacles to successful recruitment of families for older minority children. They also found that successful agency practices included increased coordination and communication between agencies, personalized presentations of children, a culturally sensitized staff, use of adoption subsidies, use of single parents as adoptive resources, advocating foster care-adoptive placements, and educating minority communities about adoption. Similarly, the North American Council on Adoptable Children [1991] also reported that obstacles to adoption by African American families included such factors as agency fees and inflexible standards, as well as institutional/systemic racism and lack of minority staff members.

Regardless, some agencies have yet to confront obstacles to African American families adopting and continue to place African American children transracially [McRoy 1995]. In some cases, these placements began as transracial family foster care placements; after months and sometimes years in family foster care while awaiting legal termination of parental rights or placement planning, the foster parents and children become attached and removal of the children for adoptive placement becomes very traumatic for all parties involved. Sometimes, Caucasian family foster care providers have fought to adopt an African American child in their care despite the adoption agency's desire to place the child with an African American family [McRoy 1994; 1995]. Caucasian foster families have recently waged highly publicized legal battles over their right to adopt a particular African American infant or young child. Concerns that an agency's race-matching policies may delay or deny the placement of an African American child with an available transracial adoptive family have led in some cases to changes in both state and federal law pertaining to the use of race in adoption decision making [McRoy 1995].

Changing State and Federal Adoption Policy

States as well as the federal government have recently begun to change existing laws that tend to restrict transracial placements. In Texas, Florida, Wisconsin, and Pennsylvania, state statutes prohibit discrimination on the basis of race in adoption. In fact, a change in state law in Texas prohibits the state Department of Protective and Regulatory Services from making a foster care placement decision on the presumption that a same-race placement is in the best interests of the child. An independent psychological evaluation of the child must be completed to justify any consideration of race or ethnicity in placement planning. Moreover, the law stipulates that any employee who attempts to remove a child from transracial family foster care for the purpose of same-race adoptive placement, or who denies or delays a placement in order to seek a same-race family, is subject to immediate dismissal [Texas Family Code 1995]. The failure of many traditional agencies to find African American adoptive families is being considered acceptable practice and an emphasis is being placed on moving children quickly from out-of-home care into adoption with available Caucasian families.

On a national level, U.S. Senator Howard Metzenbaum of Ohio introduced S. 1224, the Multiethnic Placement Act (MEPA) in an attempt to "do something to help children who were being denied the opportunity to be part of a stable and caring family, when a same race family was not available" [Metzenbaum 1993]. The legislation, P.L. 103–382, signed into law by President Clinton in 1994, prohibits any foster care or adoption agency or entity that receives federal financial assistance from denying a placement solely on the basis of race, but allows for consideration of the cultural, ethnic, or racial background of the child and the capacity of the foster parents to meet the needs of a child of this background [McRoy & Hall 1995]. The act also requires that agencies "engage in diligent recruitment efforts of potential foster and adoptive parents who reflect the racial and ethnic diversity of the children needing placement" [U.S. Department of Health and Human Services 1995: 5].

Specialized Minority Adoption Programs

The aforementioned state and federal policy changes have resulted from the assumption that African American families are not readily available to adopt, and to locate minority families interested in adoption necessitates delays in the placement process [McRoy 1995]. Specialized minority adoption programs, such as the Institute for Black Parenting, Project Hustle, and One Church, One Child, have successfully challenged this assumption and have demonstrated that African American families can readily be found for African American children.

The Institute for Black Parenting

The Institute for Black Parenting (IBP) was originally founded in 1976 as the social service and research component of the Association of Black Social Workers of Greater Los Angeles. In 1988, the state of California provided funding to enable IBP to become the first licensed minority adoption agency in southern California. This full-service nonprofit African American adoption and foster placement agency now serves Los Angeles, Orange, San Bernadino, and Riverside counties in California. In 1995, IBP was selected to be the lead agency in Los Angeles County to provide family preservation services. The agency has made 330 adoptive placements since 1989, has served 880 children in care since 1990, and has received over 4,000 inquiries from African American prospective adoptive parents from all over the United States. Adoptions by African Americans increased by 39% in California from 1989 to 1991 [Los Angeles Times 1992].

The increase in African American families adopting was largely due to the development of a culturally sensitive approach to recruitment and retention. IBP uses many of the same types of recruitment options that other agencies use, including radio and television public service announcements, brochures and flyers, and church-based activities such as adoption Sundays and flyers in church bulletins. IBP has found that although recruitment, strongly emphasized by many traditional adoption programs seeking to place inracially, is important, retention is paramount. To retain families, IBP designed a program that offers services that can be viewed as a reversal of traditional state agency practices. For example, instead of having office hours from nine to five, agency staff members work flexible hours during the day and until nine or later at night. Instead of investigating a family, the agency educates the family. All staff members are trained in cultural competency. If conflicts develop between a worker and a prospective adoptive family, the family is allowed to change social workers, unlike the practices of many traditional programs.

After investigating the reasons that many agencies lose families between the initial orientation meeting and the actual application process, IBP began a new "Rapid Response" program, in which a staff member visits the family within 72 hours of the initial orientation meeting. Rapid Response is part of a federally funded program aimed at retaining the maximum number of qualified adoptive applicants by making the application process as easy as possible for them. The program accomplishes this by demystifying the bureaucratic process, clarifying applicants' initial questions, and addressing applicants' concerns. Rapid Response workers are also available to visit prospective applicants in their homes before they attend their first orientation meeting. Home visits frequently take place during evenings and weekends. Following the orientation meeting, applicants participate in 25 hours of training, 10 hours of which focus on adoption. The remaining 15 hours of parent training are conducted using the "Effective Black Parenting" curriculum, developed after more than a decade of extensive research and field testing [Scraggs 1993]. Rapid Response workers go to the home as well and answer questions that the family may have been reluctant to ask during a group orientation. Some families want to know such things as "Will I be disqualified because my brother has been in jail or if one of my children didn't finish high school?" Because many families are aware that they will have an opportunity in private, after the orientation meeting, to ask the hard personal questions, attendance at the orientation meetings has risen by 43%. The Rapid Response program has been found to increase applications by 33%.

During the study process, "status letters" are sent to the family at regular intervals to give them an update on exactly what is happening in their application. If the agency is waiting for a fingerprint check or for medical reports, the information is conveyed to the family. Families who have been approved are given up-to-date information in their status letters on the number of places their homestudy has been sent and the number of children for whom they are being considered. Also, for families who have been approved and are awaiting a placement, the agency offers "while-you-are-waiting" meetings in which families are brought to the agency quarterly, and given refreshments and an opportunity to mingle with others who are waiting. They view photolisting books and talk about possible children they might receive. These specialized practices have proven successful in recruiting and retaining African American adoptive families in the Los Angeles area.

On the day the Multiethnic Placement Act became law, the Institute for Black Parenting (IBP), which had received funding from the state of California since 1987, was notified that an expansion it was planning was no longer fundable due to the state's interpretation of the new law. These events have left social workers and administrators confused as to what, if any, efforts could be made to achieve same-race placements for minority children. Although the agency still receives federal funding for specific projects, IBP is hopeful that state funding will be continued despite the agency's emphasis on finding African American families in a state that is attempting to terminate any specialized "minority programs."

Project Hustle

In Texas in 1993, Project Hustle, a public agency/private contractor collaboration project, was developed within Children's Protective Services as an accelerated minority recruitment/ placement program designed to place children within 12 months following the date of termination of their biological parents' rights. The project was implemented in the Ft. Worth/Dallas counties, where 66% of the children waiting for adoption were African American and 8.6% were Latino.

To ensure open communication, at the beginning of the project all participating agencies and groups were mandated to attend a workshop on cultural competency sponsored by the Dallas Minority Adoption Council. Private agencies were assured that the families they recruited and developed would receive the same consideration as the families recruited and developed by the CPS agency staff.

One hundred and forty children were identified for the project; their cases were allocated among four specialized recruitment teams coordinated by a project director and two program managers. Teams consisted of placement staff members, representatives of private placement agencies, ministers, and foster and adoptive families. Each team was assigned a caseload of 35 to 39 children. Weekly daytime and monthly evening meetings were scheduled to assess the status of the children in the project.

Recruitment strategies included the use of videotapes about adoption as well as the media to publicize the need for minority adoptive families for specific children. "Adoption expos" were held in minority communities to provide an opportunity for interaction between children in need of families and families considering adoption. The staff responded to all inquiries about adoption within a maximum of 72 hours, and special orientations were scheduled on children immediately after the adoption expos. Members of adoptive parent groups established mentoring programs that included assisting with completion of adoption applications and tracking the status of applications in the system. Families interested in the children were either immediately scheduled for a training class for foster and adoptive families, or assigned to special contracted private agencies for homestudies. Those assigned to special agencies were still required to complete the group adoption preparation training at a later date.

Eight months later, at the end of the Hustle project, 84% of the children had either an adoptive family identified or selected, or had completed placements. Placement options had been identified for almost 8% of the children; only 9% of the children had no viable options (although several had foster parents who were willing to commit to permanent foster care).

Because of the success of the project, Project Hustle II was started in Dallas in 1994 and 142 primarily minority children were identified and assigned to it. Sixty-one percent of these children were placed. The project clearly proved that minority families will and do adopt. Success does not lie in traditional public welfare outreach strategies, however. Intensive efforts were made through work with parent groups and especially the minority adoption councils. The success of recruiting and retaining minority families can be attributed directly to mentoring programs, quick and responsive agency feedback, and locating meetings and orientations in targeted areas.

Other programs, such as One Church, One Child, founded by Father George H. Clements in 1980 in Chicago, have been particularly successful in recruiting and retaining families. Father Clements not only adopted several African American teenagers but encouraged African American churches around the nation to identify members who might consider adopting. The success of the program led Florida to pass legislation to establish the One Church, One Child program. Like Project Hustle and IBP, One Church, One Child offers individualized home studies and schedules training around work hours. One Church, One Child programs have been responsible for thousands of African American adoption placements nationwide [O'Neil-Williams 1996].

Unfortunately, over time, the number of specialized minority adoption agencies has declined. In the mid-1980s, an estimated 17 specialized agencies existed; today, only about 10 can be identified [Oglesby 1995]. The threatened loss of funding from federal or state governments for specialized minority adoption programs would further reverse progress made in successful recruitment and retention programs. These programs advocate for same-race placements but are willing to consider transracial adoption as an option for children for whom same-race placements cannot be found with genuine effort within a reasonable time frame.

Adapting Traditional Agencies for Culturally Sensitive Practice

Traditional adoption agencies have been successful in working with Caucasian families seeking to adopt infants and young children. The current population of children needing adoption, however, has changed from primarily Caucasian to primarily minority, from infants and young children to a large number of older children. Ann Sullivan [1994], Program Director of Adoption Services of the Child Welfare League of America, noted that adoption programs that follow sound, culturally competent adoption practices such as having both staff members and board members who reflect the children to be served, offer flexible hours, accessible office locations, and reasonable or no fees, can place not only African American infants but also older children with African American families.

Program Strategies

An analysis of adoption programs and services for minorities reveals that most do not charge fees and generally focus on finding families for older children [Jones 1992]. Their program strategies can be used as a guide to adapt traditional programs for cultural competency and overcome obstacles to adoption by African American families. The Multiethnic Placement Act mandates that all agencies develop a comprehensive recruitment plan that includes both targeted and general campaigns. To improve the success of recruitment efforts, traditional agencies might consider the following three types of programs:

1. Establish a recruitment unit designed to recruit and process minority families (Project Hustle began as a specialized recruitment unit). This recruitment unit may be created within an existing agency and often entails reducing the workers' caseloads so that they can respond to the target population

swiftly. All workers in the unit should be culturally competent, bicultural/bilingual if necessary, and responsible for making both matches and placements.

2. Establish an out-stationed office made up of agency employees placed in the target community. The unit may have a name that does not identify it as part of the larger agency (e.g., Tayari Adoptions in San Diego). This approach seems to engender ownership by the community and builds trust. All adoption recruitment and processing are handled through this office, which may be established in a church or other existing facility within the target community.

3. Obtain state funding for a private nonprofit agency to facilitate minority adoptive placements (e.g., The Institute for Black Parenting). This type of arrangement can develop strong public-private partnerships and facilitate the finding of families for public agency children outside of the geographical territory. It can also expedite family processing and child placements.

Policies and Procedures

Most importantly, policies and procedures must be sensitive to the needs and cultural context of African American families. The following procedures can improve service delivery:

1. Encourage interagency coordination, cooperation, and communication between agencies with children and agencies with waiting families to facilitate matches. Form collaborations with other agencies to develop joint recruitment programs. Work closely with the state agency and private agencies to review policies and procedures that might impede placements. Link the state agency with African American religious and community organizations that might know families who are interested in adopting. Work closely or contract with minority specialized agencies to help find families for African American children.

2. Make use of research knowledge about what types of families are most likely to adopt children with special needs. For

example, although most agencies prefer to place children with two-parent families, minority single parents have been found to be very likely to consider adopting children with disabilities and older children [Rodriguez & Meyer 1990]. Agencies should encourage prospective single-parent adopters by adapting policies and practices to reflect the characteristics of these applicants.

3. Educate workers as well as families about the availability of adoption subsidies and medical assistance for special-needs adoptions. These subsidies may make it possible to facilitate adoptions by foster parents, as well as other potential adoptive persons.

4. Provide adequate funding to specialized minority adoption programs. Although the majority of children that many agencies seek to place belong to racial minority groups, some agencies still resist establishing and/or fully funding minority recruitment and placement programs.

5. Modify agency procedures to screen in, rather than screen out, prospective adopters. Many large bureaucratic programs (and even some small programs) are not user-friendly. Respond quickly to all inquiries and adjust office hours, group meeting times, and procedures for child-specific recruitment to the needs of the target population—African American families. Some agencies respond to initial phone inquiries of potential adopters by mailing a large packet of information containing a 10- to 15-page application form, physical exam forms, reference forms, and other miscellaneous materials. If the forms are not returned, the agencies mistakenly assume that the family has decided not to proceed. Send a one- to two-page application and follow the Rapid Response or Project Hustle procedures discussed earlier in this article. (Since adoption application forms often are designed for couples, new or adapted forms should be provided for single persons interested in adoption.) Offer to conduct home visits and classes in the evenings and on weekends in addition to weekday sessions. Routinely evalu-

ate the agency's adoption program to remove impediments
that discourage families interested in adopting.

6. Establish a sliding fee scale, or preferably, eliminate fees.
    Specialized minority agencies typically do not charge fees
    because African American families question why they should
    have to pay to "open their homes and hearts to children in
    need" [Jones 1992]. Moreover, it is important for agency
    workers to be sensitized to some African American fami-
    lies' concern about adoption agency fees due to the nega-
    tive historical association with the buying and selling of
    African American children [Rodriguez & Meyer 1990].

7. Set up minority adoption task forces or adoption councils
    to provide advice on ways to improve the cultural sensitiv-
    ity and competency of the agency's policies and procedures.

8. Recruit African American workers for the adoption program.
    Specialized programs have reported that the presence of
    minority staff members tends to give credibility to the pro-
    gram, build trust, and put African American families at ease.
    Train all workers in cultural competency to enable them to
    be sensitive and flexible in their approaches to prospective
    adoptive applicants and to conduct culturally sensitive and
    competent assessments of families. Send workers to national
    and regional training opportunities on minority adoptions.

Conclusion

Just as some agencies have successfully designed culturally competent adoption services to meet the needs of African American
adoptive families, other traditional child welfare programs, such
as protective services and out-of-home care, should be evaluated and modified to better meet the needs of African American biological families and perhaps prevent unnecessary out-
of-home placements. Federal and state child welfare policies
must be aimed at solving the problems of the disproportionately high number of African American children being removed
from their biological families, the delays in termination of

parental rights, the inequities in length of stay in out-of-home care, and the obstacles to African American adoptions [Williams 1991; Morton 1993; McRoy, 1990, McRoy & Hall 1995; McRoy 1995]. It is these factors, not policies promoting same-race placements, that are responsible for the growing number of older minority children remaining in out-of-home care.

A close examination of the children in care and the families seeking to adopt reveals that the majority of transracial adopters are seeking infants and young children and the actual number of such adoptions is small. According to the National Health Interview Survey, adoptions of African American children by Caucasian parents account for only about 1% of all adoptions [Stolley 1993]. It is estimated that transracial adoptions account for only about 1,000 to 2,000 placements of African American children each year [Brooks 1991]. For example, of the 2,443 adoptions completed in 1992 in New York City, only 100 are estimated to have been transracial placements [Jones 1993]. The Multiethnic Placement Act (MEPA) will probably enable a small number of Caucasian foster parents to adopt minority foster children who have been in their homes since infancy. It will have no significant impact on the growing number of children in out-of-home care [The Economist 1994].

When many of the obstacles to adoption by African American families are eliminated, however, African American families can be successfully recruited and retained in large numbers. If the existing specialized minority programs were expanded and used for placement planning by traditional adoption agencies, and if many more programs were established and funded, it is likely that African American children could be as easily and readily placed with African American families as Caucasian children are currently placed with Caucasian families. Unfortunately, however, workers are now being challenged to find ways to justify the placement of African American children with African American families and to justify the use of specialized minority programs, due to the restrictive laws limiting consideration of race.

Ironically, although MEPA and the Texas legislation suggest that race should not be a primary factor or a factor at all in adoption decision making, race matching has been standard practice in the placement of Caucasian children. Historically, very few Caucasian children have been placed across racial lines. The rationale for these same-race placements of Caucasian children has been based on the large supply of Caucasian families and the limited supply of Caucasian children. It will be interesting to observe whether in the future the new legislation will be interpreted to facilitate transracial placements of Caucasian children as well as of minority children. ♦

References

Brooks, D. (1991). Black/white transracial adoption: An update. *OURS, 24*(4), 10–21.

Children's Defense Fund. (1996). *The state of America's children yearbook*. Washington, DC: Author.

Children's Defense Fund. (1994). *The state of America's children yearbook*. Washington, DC: Author.

Children's Defense Fund. (1992). *The state of America's children*. Washington, DC: Author.

Close, M. (1983). Child welfare and people of color: Denial of equal access. *Social Work, 28*, 13–20.

Hill, R. (1993) *Research on the African-American family*. Westport, CT: Auburn House.

Jones, C. (1993, October 24). Role of race in adoptions: Old debate is being reborn. *The New York Times*, p. 1.

Jones, M. (1992, November-December). Adoption agencies: Can they service African Americans? *Crisis, 8*, 26–28.

Leashore, B., McMurray, H., & Bailey, B. (1991). Reuniting and preserving African American families. In J. E. Everett, S. S. Chipungu, & B. R. Leashore (Eds.), *Child welfare: An Africentric perspective* (pp. 247–265). New Brunswick, NJ: Rutgers University Press.

Lindsey, D. (1991). Factors affecting the foster care placement decision: An analysis of national survey data. *American Journal of Orthopsychiatry, 61*, 272–281.

Los Angeles Times. (1992, June 10). More black families adopting babies. *Los Angeles Times*, p. A2 .

Mason, J., & Williams, C. (1985). The adoption of minority children: Issues in developing law and policy. In *Adoption of children with special needs: Issues in law and policy* (pp. 81–93, Washington, DC: American Bar Association.

McKenzie, J. (1993, Spring). Adoption of children with special needs. In I. Schulman (Ed.), *The Future of Children, 3*(1), 62–76. Los Altos, CA: David and Lucile Packard Foundation.

McRoy, R. (1990). An organizational dilemma: The case of transracial adoption. *Journal of Applied Behavioral Science, 25*, 145–160.

McRoy, R. (1994). Attachment and racial identity issues: Implications for child placement decision making. *Journal of Multicultural Social Work, 3*(3), 59–74.

McRoy, R. (1995, June 5). Lower barriers to black adoptive families. *Insight on the News Magazine*, pp. 18–21.

McRoy, R., & Hall, C. (1995). Transracial adoptions: In whose best interest? In M. Root (Ed.), *Multiracial people in the new millennium* (pp. 63–78). Newbury Park, CA: Sage.

Metzenbaum, H. (1993, July 15). Floor statement of Howard M. Metzenbaum introducing the Multiethnic Placement Act of 1993 (S. 1224).

Moore, E. (1984, April). Black children facing adoption barriers. *NASW News*, p. 9.

Morton, T. (1993, Spring). Ideas in action: The issue is race. *Child Welfare Institute Newsletter*, 1–2.

National Association of Black Social Workers. (1994, April). *Position statement on transracial adoptions*. Detroit, MI: Author.

North American Council on Adoptable Children. (1991). *Barriers to same race placement*. St. Paul, MN: Author.

North American Council on Adoptable Children. (1993a). *Transracial adoption position statement*. St. Paul, MN: Author.

North American Council on Adoptable Children. (1993b, Dec.). *NACAC policy statement on race and adoption*. St. Paul, MN: Author.

North American Council on Adoptable Children. (1995, Summer). "Multiethnic placement act policy guidelines issued" *Adoptalk*, pp. 2–3.

O'Neil-Williams, P. (1996, Nov. 6). Personal communication.

Pelton, L. (1989). *For reasons of poverty*. New York: Praeger.

Rodriguez, P., & Meyer, A. (1990). Minority adoptions and agency practices. *Social Work, 35,* 528–531.

Rosenthal, J., & Groze, V. (1990). Race, social class and special needs adoption. *Social Work, 35,* 532–539.

Schulman, I. (1993, Spring). Adoption: Overview and major recommendations. In I. Schulman (Ed.), *The Future of Children, 3*(1), 4–16. Los Altos, CA: David and Lucile Packard Foundation.

Scraggs, I. (1993, June). Adoption unit growth. *Taking care of our own*. Los Angeles: Institute for Black Parenting.

Simon, R., & Alstein, H. (1987). *Transracial adoptees and their families*. New York: Praeger.

Simon, R., Alstein, H., & Melli, M. (1994). *The case for transracial adoption*. Washington, DC: American University Press.

Stehno, S. (1982). Differential treatment of minority children in service systems. *Social Work, 27,* 39–45.

Stehno, S. (1990). The elusive continuum of child welfare services: Implications for minority children and youths. *Child Welfare, 69,* 551–562.

Stolley, K. (1993, Spring). Statistics on adoption in the United States. In R. Behrman (Ed.), *The Future of Children, 3*(1), 26–43. Los Altos, CA: David and Lucile Packard Foundation.

Sullivan, A. (1994, Spring). On transracial adoption. *Children's Voice, 3*(3), 4–6.

Texas Family Code. (1995). Sect. 162.308. *Race or ethnicity*.

The Economist. (1994). Black or white, p. 33.

U.S. Department of Health and Human Services. (1995). *Policy guidance on the use of race, color or national origin as considerations in adoption and foster care placements*. Washington, DC: Author.

Williams, C. (1991). Expanding the options in the quest for permanence. In J. E. Everett, S. S. Chipungu, & B. R. Leashore (Eds.), *Child welfare: An Africentric perspective* (pp. 266–289). New Brunswick, NJ: Rutgers University Press.

6

African American Families and HIV/AIDS: Caring for Surviving Children

Alma J. Carten and Ilene Fennoy

This article presents the preliminary findings of a national project undertaken to examine the medical/ health, social service, and legal needs of African American children who have experienced or will experience the death of one or both parents as a result of HIV/AIDS. The project seeks to guide the development of culturally competent policies and practices across delivery systems responsible for managing the care of these children and their families. Services have expanded for the children but much remains to be accomplished to achieve culturally competent, integrated care systems for surviving children and their caregivers.

Alma J. Carten, D.S.W., ACSW, is Associate Professor, New York University, New York City, NY. Ilene Fennoy, M.D., M.P.H., is Director, Ambulatory Medicine, Brooklyn Hospital, Brooklyn, NY.

Surveillance reports from the Centers for Disease Control [1994] indicate that of the 32,000 women who died of AIDS-related causes reported through December 1994, 23,000 were between the ages of 25 and 44 years of age, the period in which women are most likely to have dependent children. Eighteen thousand of these women were African American and Latino. Studies of infected women in New York City suggest that the women have on average two children each. Based on 1994 cases alone, an estimated 42,000 children are currently at risk of losing their mothers to AIDS [Norwood 1989]. If current trends continue, an estimated 125,000 children will become motherless by the year 2000 [Levine & Stein 1994]. The largest percentage of these children will be African American and Latino, concentrated in the urban cities of New York, Newark, Miami, San Juan, Los Angeles, and Washington, D.C. (table 1). Of the estimated 42,000 children at risk of losing their mothers, approximately 5,000 will be HIV positive; the remaining 37,000 will not be infected with the disease [Centers for Disease Control 1994]. Most will be children whose lives are already compromised by poverty, the drug culture, and the minority experience in the United States. Policymakers and health and human service providers face the daunting task of determining what the needs of this group of children are, and the best ways of meeting their needs in the absence of their parents.

Caring for Surviving Children

Women acquire HIV through intravenous (IV) drug injection (48%), sex with an injecting drug users (19%) and sex with an HIV infected person represents (13%) of cases [Centers for Disease Control 1994]. A large proportion of African American children whose mothers were IV drug users will likely be absorbed into extended families and cared for in formal kinship foster care arrangements with public child welfare agencies. Caldwell et al. [1992] examined 1,600 cases of children whose mothers were diagnosed with AIDS. The sample was drawn from seven

TABLE 1

AIDS Cases in Children Less than 13 Years Old (Cumulative Totals through December 1994) (*N* = 6,209)

City	AIDS Cases	Percent of Total
District of Columbia	177	2.85
Los Angeles	163	2.63
Miami	354	5.70
Newark	248	3.99
New York	1,463	23.56
San Juan, PR	205	3.30
Remaining USA & Territories	3,599	57.96

cities having the highest incidence of reported AIDS cases. Findings revealed that 40% of the children whose mothers were IV drug users were in out-of-home care, as compared to 14% of children whose mothers did not use drugs.

Gamble [1993] and Rotherman-Borus and Draimin [1994] found that in a significantly large percentage of cases involving African American children, relatives (usually grandparents and aunts) assumed care of the children. Moreover, child welfare trend data over the last decade indicate that the crack cocaine epidemic of the early 1980s resulted in dramatic increases in substance abuse-related child protective service reports and in the number of African American children entering out-of-home care [U.S. General Accounting Office 1990; National Committee for the Prevention of Child Abuse 1989]. Following this growth in the use of out-of-home care, a significant growth took place in the number of children placed in the homes of relatives under formal foster care arrangements under state jurisdiction [National Commission on Family Foster Care 1991; Thornton 1991].

These data suggest that public child welfare agencies already have a central role in managing the care of African American children exposed to substance abuse and those surviving the AIDS-related death of a parent. These agencies will likely assume an expanding role as the number of children surviving the death of a parent due to AIDS continues to rise.

Children suffering the premature loss of a parent as a result of AIDS present new needs that differ significantly from those of children traditionally served by the child welfare system. They will also need to draw upon services provided by many health and human service systems. At this writing, however, little systematic inquiry has been made concerning the range of new legal, health, and social service needs of these children and their caregivers.

Purpose

The Children Left Behind is the name of an exploratory project conducted under the auspice of the Black Leadership Commission on AIDS, a New York City-based agency that advocates for appropriate AIDS and related public policy development for the African American community at the local and national levels. The agency developed the project to encourage cohesive policy formulation for African American children surviving the death of a parent from AIDS. It identifies critical issues to guide culturally competent public policy formulation for children living with HIV/AIDS and surviving the AIDS-related death of a parent; and encourages an interdisciplinary, coordinated approach to meeting the multiple needs of these children and their caregivers. The project is being carried out in three stages: (1) gathering information from the highest case concentration cities about the appropriateness, availability, access, and utilization of medical/health, legal, and social support services, and emerging models of service delivery; (2) convening an interdisciplinary mix of health and human service professionals in a two-day summit to review findings; and (3) creating an action plan and set of principles to guide culturally competent public policy development. This article discusses the preliminary findings of the fact-gathering stage. The discussion identifies areas that can directly improve clinical care and service delivery for African American children in out-of-home care, as well as areas for further research.

Data Collection

Four sources of data collection were used: (1) a review of the social work and child welfare literature, using the descriptions of child welfare services, cultural competence, African American, HIV/AIDS, and orphans; (2) a telephone survey of 12 voluntary agencies and one program in a public hospital, all providing services to AIDS-affected children and families in New York City, Newark, Miami, Los Angeles, and Washington, D.C., to obtain general information about the agencies and kinds of services provided, the service needs of African American families, and the impact of service reductions and health care reforms; (3) clinical interviews conducted by primary care physicians and social workers with caregivers of HIV-positive children receiving medical care at a large urban voluntary hospital to identify factors that influenced access to medical services; and (4) two focus groups with surrogate caregivers from a voluntary child welfare agency providing specialized foster care services to HIV/AIDS-affected children. The focus groups were structured to elicit information on the health and mental health status of the children; access, availability, and service utilization; and respondents' perception of the quality, availability, and usefulness of services.

Limitations

The information-gathering process was subject to the following limitations: (1) the literature review was not exhaustive; (2) the number of surrogate caregivers participating in clinical interviews and focus groups was small and drawn exclusively from one medical facility and one agency, which limits generalizability; and (3) the agency survey revealed that most agencies do not keep discrete data on African American families, but collect information under the ethnic category of "black," which includes African American families and others of African descent such as Caribbeans, Haitians, and Africans.

Despite these limitations, several relevant findings were

made that are useful for planning services for children under state jurisdiction, and also have implications for continued research.

Literature Review

Since the mid- to late-1980s, the child welfare and social work literature on women, HIV/AIDS, and children has increased substantially. Early reporting focused on managing the care of infants and adolescents infected with the disease, but gave scant attention to planning for the long-term care of children surviving the death of a parent due to HIV/AIDS. The pioneering work of Levine [1993] and Levine and Stein [1994] was the first to focus on the plight of children who would lose one parent, usually the mother, to the disease before reaching the age of majority. These social scientists identified a comprehensive array of services they anticipated that children, facing the inevitable death of a parent, would need to support them during the experience and in the aftermath of the parent's death.

Subsequent reporting has not kept pace with the need for new information to yield adequate policy and service development for children and their caregivers. Since African American children are overrepresented in the population of children affected, there is much to learn about how this group of children and their caregivers are faring, and the extent to which existing service systems are accommodating new needs.

Characteristics of Respondents

The Agencies

Thirteen agencies participated in the survey. One Los Angeles agency reported serving a predominately Latino population. The other 12 agencies reported that African American clients, or clients of African descent, constituted the largest racial groups served. One Los Angeles agency served as an umbrella organization for 17 satellite programs. The remaining 12 agencies were small or medium in size and organized around a specific service such as residential care and transitional housing, intensive case management, nursing and home health care, and specialized foster care services. All agencies had in place a referral system to link families to needed services such as respite care, bereavement counseling, and legal assistance. A small number of specialized agencies were identified in the private sector as having a single mission—finding permanent adoptive homes for surviving children. In most locations, however, this remained a responsibility of the public child care agency.

The Families

The clinical sample consisted of 15 African American children and their caregivers. All of the children tested HIV positive. Seven were male and 8 were female; they ranged in age from infancy to adolescence (mean = 6.57 years). Only three of the children were in the care of a biological parent; eight were with a grandparent or other relative. Eleven of 15 caregivers were between the ages of 21 and 44 years, and four were 45 to 65 years old. Two-thirds of the children exhibited mild or no symptoms of HIV infection.

Of the 17 foster parents participating in the focus groups, 16 were African American. The children in their care ranged in age from infancy to adolescence. All respondents were caring for more than one child; the other children in the home included foster sibling groups and their own children. Unlike the children in the clinical interview group, the HIV status of the children whose caregivers participated in the focus group varied. The older children were not HIV positive. Some of the younger children were HIV positive but because of their age could still seroconvert; others were HIV positive. Respondents were relative (either grandparents or aunts) and nonrelative caregivers. All of the nonrelative foster parents had been previously certified as foster parents before assuming responsibility for children whose parents were diagnosed with HIV/AIDS. Five foster parents were employed in either full-time or part-time work. Eleven of the 17 were single heads of households.

The situations of the biological parents of the children varied. Some were deceased; others were living with the diagnosis of HIV or AIDS, stabilized in drug treatment, or actively abusing drugs, and two were reported to be homeless.

Findings

Agency Survey

The survey of agencies indicates that the demand for services far exceeds the supply. Agencies have endeavored to respond to emerging needs and rising demands for service by expanding services, using new funding provided under the Ryan White Act [P.L. 104–34], existing Medicaid funding, and allocations under the Social Security Act for child welfare services. They have also endeavored to counter the effects of reductions in federal and state funding by obtaining support from foundations and individual contributors. The development of services appeared to be largely reactive, however, resulting in a patchwork system of services to meet new needs as they arose. Services were also observed to be unevenly developed across the cities surveyed. For example, some local districts have yet to fully develop an adequate system for providing specialized family foster care services. Moreover, a revised social welfare policy authorizing the same procedures for relative caregivers as for nonrelatives for foster care board payment rates and access to services [Miller v. Youakim 1979] has not been fully implemented in some of the cities surveyed.

New York City, on the other hand, has fully implemented a program of kinship care throughout the system. Of the approximately 50,000 children on the out-of-home care caseload, 27,000 are placed in the homes of relatives, with more than half placed with grandparents [New York City Child Welfare Administration 1993]. New York City also has a well-established network of preventive services agencies and foster care agencies in the voluntary sector. Included among these are a small number of community-based, minority-governed agencies, established with the intent of developing innovative models of culturally competent services in high-need, underserved neighborhoods. The public child care agency has collaborated with all of these agencies to expand programs as the demand for new and different kinds of services has increased in the wake of the crack cocaine epidemic.

New York City is also moving toward the use of a managed care model for out-of-home care and other health and human services. There is considerable concern, however, that the change from a per diem to a capitated payment system can potentially compromise the quality of care for children with marked mental health needs. These children are often in need of long-term, high-cost specialized services. Moreover, small neighborhood-based agencies (models of service delivery that have been increasingly supported in policy and practice over the last several years because of improved consumer accessibility and utilization) will have less capability to survive in a managed care environment.

Respondents' views about managed care proposals varied. Most of the agency respondents were concerned about the potentially negative effects that a cost-driven model could have on delivery systems serving children and families suffering the effects of the AIDS epidemic. These concerns warrant closer examination as managed care as a model for delivering child welfare services continues to evolve.

Respondents indicated that African American children were likely to be in the care of grandparents or other relatives. In particular, grandparents taking on the role of caregiver were said to be in need of additional support. For example, those caring for children in informal arrangements were not receiving additional Social Security benefits and were in need of financial assistance. Grandparents also needed help with transportation for medical visits for themselves and the children. They were often overwhelmed by stress and anxiety as they dealt with both their own serious illnesses (e.g., diabetes and heart disease) and those of a chronically ill child.

According to the agencies responding, their African Americans clients generally expressed frustration about getting assistance with respite care and psychosocial support for themselves. The agencies further reported that African American clients were suspicious of medications because of the nation's history of using African Americans in medical experiments. In the focus groups, the caregivers unanimously expressed the need for more information about the effects of medication on children. They felt that medical providers did not give clear information about the progress of HIV in children, and they were confused as to the age at which children could be considered no longer at risk of becoming HIV positive.

Respondent's Themes

Three themes emerged from the analysis of the clinical interviews and focus groups with surrogate caregivers: (1) uncertainties about guardianship and custody, which affected health care decision making for children; (2) constraints on achieving early permanency planning for children in situations where the biological parent retained parental rights and actively abused drugs while living with the diagnosis of HIV / AIDS; and (3) difficulties encountered by surrogate caregivers endeavoring to cope with the demands of managing the heightened health care needs of the children. These themes are elaborated below in the discussion that incorporates excerpts from the focus groups.

On matters of guardianship and custody, respondents indicated a lack of clarity about the status of the children. For example, of the 15 patient families interviewed, only three had biological parents represented. One caregiver claiming custody said that financial benefits for the child were in the AFDC budget of the biological mother because she was the legal guardian. Eight of the 15 children were in the care of a relative, but only one acknowledged being advised to become a kinship foster parent or legal guardian. Nine of the families indicated that the question regarding advice on kinship foster care and / or their welfare budget was not applicable to them. Thus, it appears that some families remain unclear about guardianship and associated benefits, and therefore are unclear on rights of medical decision making.

In addition to the lack of clarity about guardianship and medical decision making, respondents' experiences further suggested that permanency planning decision making was constrained in those cases where biological parents were unsuccessfully coping with addictions and the prospect of death. A nonrelative caregiver who wanted to adopt a young child she had cared for since birth said:

> There needs to be separate rules for HIV/AIDS pediatrics. If you don't see your child in six months, and the mother returns and starts visits, the rules require an additional six months of visits before termination of parental rights. I feel that mothers should not have access to abandoned babies after six months. Babies need more stability and family.

Respondents were also faced with coping with the heightened health care needs of the children. Whether they are HIV positive or not, children require frequent medical visits. For children who are HIV positive, these visits have to be made on a scheduled basis to monitor the effects of in utero drug exposure or HIV infection on development and changes in immune function. Visits are also needed on an emergency basis when complications arise. The 15 families with an HIV-positive child illustrated this in their interview, with seven families making three or more visits each month to health care professionals, even though the disease process in these children primarily reflected absent to mild symptoms. This was also the case with the focus group respondents. Most made frequent visits (often for more than one child because most were caring for sibling groups) to primary care physicians, specialists, and social workers.

> When I got them they were always very sickly, constantly going to the doctor. Now they have occasional ear infections. Once a month I take the boys to get an IV drip. I had to take the five-year-old to see a psychiatrist

because of his behavior in school. He wasn't listening and hated the teacher. The pediatric clinic doctor and social worker suggested that he see a psychiatrist.

Furthermore, the children were dealing with the serious illness and the prospect of death of one or both parents and, possibly, the death of a sibling as well. We have learned from families coping with childhood cancer that this kind of situation calls for the provision of mental health care services, particularly for the children who are not ill. Statements made by one focus group participant illustrated the mental health care needs of a noninfected adolescent trying to cope with the situation of a biological parent and significant feelings of separation, abandonment, and loss.

> The older girl's mother wanted her to go to some of the meetings and counseling at her rehab program. By being 14, the girl is ashamed. The mother gave her some books and when we got out of the car she ran home, turned everything face down, and wrapped her coat around everything so nobody could see what it was. She doesn't want to go with her mother to the meetings. The girl is aware of the mother's problems and asked me (they call me mommy) "If something happens to my mother, would you keep us?" I said "Sure." "Would you adopt us?" I said "Sure. You are my children now." The boy doesn't think about it.

Pressures were also imposed by agency demands, beyond those for seeing to it that the children received appropriate medical follow-up services related to their AIDS status. For example, there were agency requirements for on-site medical visits for children, visiting requirements with biological parents, and meetings with social workers for an established number of appointments each month. Additional requirements included training to remain current on specific agency policies, as well as specialized training for caregivers of HIV/AIDS-affected children, and state-mandated training to maintain foster parent certification. Participants expressed frustration when biological parents failed to keep prearranged visits and believed that many agency-required appointments were duplicative and unnecessary. They agreed that foster parent support groups and training related to their foster parent certification status were essential.

While caring for chronically ill children is a full-time job in itself, a number of the respondents were also managing employment responsibilities.

> The baby was waking up at 1:00 A.M., 2:00 A.M., 3:00 A.M., 4:00 A.M. I could not get up in the morning. I was going to work late, taking a taxi to get there as soon as possible. He really did not start sleeping at night until eight months old. Now he is sleeping through the night and it's much easier.

The experiences of the focus group participants suggested that the many activities they had to undertake to respond to the complexity of the medical and mental health needs of the children have not been matched by a corresponding increase in agency-provided support services. Only four families in the clinical interview group reported receiving services as needed. Homemaker services were identified as needed by another four respondents. Moreover, caregivers' responses indicated that bureaucratic protocols and service reductions imposed systemic obstacles to obtaining services such as respite care and baby-sitting that were essential for supporting them in their caregiving responsibilities.

> I work from 9:00 A.M. to 2:00 P.M. My niece married over the summer and I requested a foster parent to baby-sit so I could go to the wedding. You have to give them (the agency) two weeks notice. I didn't hear from the agency so I took them with me to Florida. I didn't get help in paying their way.

And one foster parent, coping with the combined effects of bureaucratic protocols and reductions in services, reported:

They cut the board payment and baby-sitting. We pay
the baby-sitter out of the board payments now. I am
getting $1,128 and the baby-sitter gets $900. So now I
have to give her a decrease, I don't know if she will stay.
The city says I can get her as a provider mother. So now
she has to take the class. I have to go to the training office.
The social worker said that if I can get the baby-sitter to
take the class they will certify her as a provider mother.

Despite these problematic experiences, relative and nonrelative caregivers alike showed tremendous strengths and were
deeply committed to the children. The experiences that made
their childcaring responsibilities more difficult, as expressed in
the themes discussed above, were consistent for all respondent
groups, and have implications for policy and practice.

Policy and Practice Implications

The state will become the legal guardian for a large proportion
of surviving African American children. These children can
potentially experience the adverse affects of many layers of
decision making that will emerge, since the administrative
responsibility for their care and custody will be delegated to
local social service districts. Many local jurisdictions share this
responsibility with private child welfare agencies. These agencies in turn place children with surrogate caregivers. Although
foster parents have no legal status with regard to decision making, it is they who are confronted with the problems of day-to-
day decision making for the children.

It is imperative that where legal authority rests for making
decisions on the child's behalf is made clear, since for this group
of children many medical decisions and choices must be made.
For example, if the child is HIV positive, choices will have to be
made regarding the many investigational studies of drugs
offering hope of slowing the progression of the disease and/or
treating specific complications. And children who are HIV negative still have complicated medical needs, due to the inability

to differentiate their status from that of their infected siblings for the first 12 to 15 months of their lives. Furthermore, they may have been exposed to medications in utero in an effort to diminish maternal-fetal transmission, which may have adverse effects on their development. As such, they may be involved in investigational studies to determine the effects of the medications on the developing organism over many years, and choices will again have to be made regarding the scope of investigational and therapeutic medical services in which they will participate.

To the extent that health policy for children requires that a competent adult with parental rights sanction all but emergency care for the child, lack of clarity concerning guardianship/custody has the potential to deny children access to timely and appropriate care. Given the increased medical needs of the children, and the potential for investigational therapies to be of importance to their overall well-being, child welfare policies for children placed in foster family boarding homes must be reexamined and modified, as appropriate, to create structures for guardianship and clarity in decision making that best meet the needs of these children.

The agency survey revealed that California is working on such an approach, at least for children cared for in Pediatric AIDS group homes. At this writing, the state has introduced legislation that would give these facilities authority to provide medical treatment to children who are wards of the state, and thus avoiding the red tape of applying for permission to the public child care agency before providing any form of medical treatment.

Permanency Planning

The Adoption Assistance and Child Welfare Act of 1980 (P.L. 96–272), favors family preservation and early reunification of children with biological parents. For most children, this must remain a primary goal of child welfare services. Placement instability and prolonged stays in out-of-home care, however, may result for children whose parents are dealing with the problem of drug abuse while confronting their own mortality from a disease that is often erratic and overwhelming in its debilitating symptomatology. Parental ambivalence places children at risk of experiencing multiple and different placements and caregivers, and constrains planning for their long-term care. For example, focus groups respondents acknowledged that they had bonded with their children and were willing to adopt, yet current policies posed considerable obstacles to their interests even though it was an absolute certainty that the children in their care would not be reunited with their biological parents.

New York State offers two helpful examples for encouraging early permanency planning for this group of children. Its "standby" guardianship law gives terminally ill parents the option of naming a guardian while retaining custody of their children until the time of the parents' physical or mental incapacity or death. New York City's Early Permanency Planning Program is designed to find family foster homes for children before the death of their parents, placing children with families that will eventually adopt them. Both concepts represent beginning efforts at the state and local levels to solve the dilemma of permanency planning for surviving children. The large number of surviving children nationwide, however, would benefit from policies developed at the national level that would establish standards and provide resources that encourage structured permanency planning with the initial out-of-home placement, rather than the present experience of forced ambiguity while waiting for the parent's death or disappearance.

Supporting Families in Caregiving Responsibilities

Without exception, focus group respondents identified additional demands experienced in the role of fostering chronically ill children. As noted earlier, their experiences indicated that the procedural demands of the child welfare system failed to give consideration to the enormous demands placed on their time in managing the heightened health care needs of children, or their need for support and respite services.

Although the foster parents in this survey faced considerable obstacles, they were also able to develop resources and support networks that helped them to cope with the demands of child care and with service reductions. Some relied upon adult daughters for respite and baby-sitting. Almost all reported that considerable emotional support came from their church and religion. They also acknowledged the understanding and skills they themselves had developed concerning the health and mental health needs of their children, obtaining essential services, and evaluating critically the usefulness of services and interventions. In addition to being effective advocates in garnering needed services for the children, they were able to clearly articulate the kind of services that would help them in their childcaring responsibilities.

Implications for Further Research

Although recent research has expanded our knowledge of kinship caregivers and their strengths and needs [Wilson & Chipungu 1996], findings from this survey suggest the need for further inquiry into the situation of African American grandparents caring for surviving children. Two further areas of research present themselves as a result of this study. First, policy research should examine the effects of massive down-sizing, service retrenchment, and a new managed care environment on the ability of health and human services to provide an appropriate level of care to children who are in need of intensive and long-term services. Second, because these families are surrounded by an environment of death and dying, clinical research could tell us more than we now know about how children and their caregivers are affected by, and coping with, these dramatic and cumulative losses.

Whether they are relatives or nonrelatives, the surrogate caregivers of children surviving the AIDS epidemic not only provide a viable resource to child welfare agencies but a critical service to society in general. Human service providers have a responsibility to learn more about what these caregivers' needs are and to develop relevant and appropriate services that support them in this demanding role. As the number of surviving children in the child welfare system increases—and funds and care systems shrink—providers must pay close attention to the reported experiences of caregivers and listen to their requests. This would help ensure the maintenance of appropriate levels of services based on realistic appraisal of the supportive services these children need. ◆

References

Caldwell, M. B., Fleming, P., & Oxtoby, M. (1992). Biologic, foster and adoptive parents: Caregivers of children exposed perinatally to Human Immunodeficiency Virus in the United States. *Pediatrics, 90*(4), 603–607.

Centers for Disease Control and Prevention. (1994a). *Surveillance Report, 6*(2).

Centers for Disease Control and Prevention. (1994b). Revised classification system for human immunodeficiency virus infection in children less than 13 years of age. *Pediatric AIDS and HIV Infection: Fetus to Adolescent 1995, 6*(2), 114–121.

Gamble, I. (1993). *In whose custody?* New York: New York City Human Resources Administration.

Levine, C., & Stein, G. (1994). *Orphans of the HIV epidemic: Unmet needs in six U.S. Cities.* New York: The Orphans Project

Levine, C. (Ed.). (1993). *A death in the family: Orphans of the HIV epidemic.* New York: United Hospital Fund of New York.

Miller v. Youakim, 440 U.S. 125 (1979).

National Commission on Family Foster Care. (1991). *A blueprint for fostering infants, children & youth in the 1990s.* Washington, DC: Child Welfare League of America.

National Committee for the Prevention of Child Abuse. (1989). *Substance abuse and child abuse fact sheet.* Chicago: Author.

New York City Child Welfare Administration. (1993). *Foster care overview, fiscal years 1992–1993.* New York: Author.

Norwood, C. (1989). *Aids orphans in New York City: Projected numbers and policy demands.* International Conference on AIDS, June 4–9, Volume 5, Abstract #M.E.P. 40.

Office of the Inspector General, U.S. Department of Health and Human Services. (1990). *Crack babies.* Washington, DC: U.S. Government Printing Office, 709-926:30010.

Rotherman-Borus, M., & Draimin, B. (1994). *Interventions for adolescents whose parents live with AIDS.* Washington, DC: National Institute for Mental Health, Grant # MH49958-03.

Thornton, J. (1991) Permanency planning for children in kinship foster homes. *Child Welfare, 70,* 593–601.

United States General Accounting Office. (1990). *Drug exposed infants: A generation at risk.* Washington, DC: Author.

Wilson, D. B., & Chipungu, S. S. (Eds.). (1996). Kinship Care Special Issue. *Child Welfare, 75.*

7

"Of Mind, Body, and Spirit": Therapeutic Foster Care— An Innovative Approach to Healing from an NTU Perspective

Shawan D. P. Gregory and Frederick B. Phillips

This article examines Progressive Life Center's (PLC) innovative Therapeutic Foster Care (TFC) program, and its incorporation of a unique clinical approach, NTU (pronounced in-to) psychotherapy, into its program model. PLC is an African American private nonprofit community-based organization that strives to improve the delivery of mental health services through culturally competent therapeutic techniques. PLC expanded its services to include TFC for seriously emotionally disturbed children, ages 2 to 18. All PLC services are delivered within the spiritual and cultural framework of NTU.

Shawan D. P. Gregory, M.S., is Director of Quality Assurance, and Frederick B. Phillips, Psy.D., is President, Progressive Life Center, Inc., Washington, DC.

The Progressive Life Center, Inc. (PLC) was founded in 1983 as an African American, private, nonprofit human services organization. Its mission is to improve the quality of African American life through the development and provision of quality mental health-related services to individuals, families, local governments, and community and private organizations. PLC provides a continuum of individual, child, youth, and family services, striving to improve the delivery of behavioral health care services through culturally competent, therapeutic techniques. Its staff of 90 professionals provides helping and healing services in Washington, D.C.; Prince George's County, Maryland; and Baltimore, Maryland.

PLC is recognized for its culturally specific services and programs, which are based upon the principles of NTU (pronounced in-to), an Africentric, spiritually based, therapeutic framework. Although developed primarily for African Americans, NTU is suitable and effective for persons of a wide range of cultural backgrounds. Among the services provide by PLC are behavioral health care, substance abuse treatment and prevention, home-based family counseling, adoption placement, parent training, adolescent rites of passage programs, program evaluation, and management consultation and training.

In 1989, PLC expanded its services to include therapeutic foster care for seriously emotionally disturbed children and youths ages two to 18 in the state of Maryland and the District of Columbia. Therapeutic foster care at PLC encompasses various clinical and educational services, including parent training, rites of passage, in-home family therapy, planned and unplanned respite care, preservice and ongoing training, a foster parent support group, 24-hour crisis intervention, a foster parent advisory board, and multifamily retreats. All PLC services are delivered within the spiritual and cultural framework of NTU.

The NTU Philosophy

NTU is PLC's underlying philosophy and therapeutic framework, and forms the basis for PLC's approach to therapeutic foster care. NTU psychotherapy is culturally congruent to the African American population that is the agency's primary client base. The word *NTU* comes from the Bantu peoples of Central Africa and describes the spiritual essence that underpins and suffuses all material phenomena. This unity, called variably among African subcultures as *Sunsum*, *Spirit*, and the *Vital Force*, is positive in its force and universal to all people. It unites individuals with one another and connects them to all else that exists.

NTU emphasizes the interrelatedness of intrinsic factors, (which are psychic and immaterial), and extrinsic factors (which are social and material). This interrelationship fuels the ability to both influence and respond to problems of daily living. NTU psychotherapy is both culturally and spiritually based and enables people to function authentically and harmoniously within their systems of living. NTU's core tenet, the ubiquity of spirituality, provides the foundation, purpose, and direction of PLC therapeutic intervention.

PLC's clinical approach is consistent with the NTU philosophy, which organizes its approach to healing around four basic principles that incorporate the African-centered philosophy of health, life, spirituality, and energy [Phillips 1990; Foster et al. 1993]. The four clinical principles are harmony, balance, interconnectedness, and authenticity.

Harmony is the concept of natural order, implying that relationships should be purposeful, orderly, and spiritually based. It is our life task to be in harmony with ourselves and with our environments. Good mental health, then, is defined by a harmony of individuals with the natural order; it follows that healing is a natural process.

Balance is inextricably related to harmony, and is sometimes used synonymously with harmony. Balance suggests a process such as the mediation of seemingly conflicting or opposing forces of nature. Balance is a centering of spirit and energy. It is often symbolized in African philosophy by the *Mandala*, a holograph that reflects the tendency to reestablish balance by forcing integration when any one aspect of the whole gets too far out of equilibrium.

The principle of *interconnectedness* describes the oneness of the universe. The essence of this oneness is the spiritual, healing energy that connects all material manifestations. The experience of interconnectedness encourages a sensitivity to the environment in a way that actualizes the interdependency of life. Through interconnectedness, we are conscious of the "We who are I." To put it differently, we grow in our awareness of the extended self. Within the NTU philosophy, the highest value lies in the interpersonal and spiritual relationship among human beings.

Relationship assumes the *authenticity* of the person. The relationships we build within the larger family and community of people define the quality of our own being. Knowledge of self is fundamental to living and authenticity. The priority within NTU is the development of cultural awareness as a necessary first step to self-knowledge.

NTU psychotherapy uses the Seven Principles of Kwanzaa developed by Karenga [1977] as guidelines for healthy living.

1. Umoja (Unity): To strive for and maintain unity in the family, community, and nation.
2. Kujichagulia (Self-Determination): To define ourselves, create for ourselves, and speak for ourselves.
3. Ujima (Collective Work and Responsibility): To build and maintain our community together and to make our brothers' and sisters' problems our problems and to solve them together.
4. Ujamaa (Cooperative Economics): To build and maintain economic enterprises and to profit from them together.

5. Nia (Purpose): To make as our collective vocation the building and developing of our community and to be in harmony with our spiritual purpose.
6. Kuumba (Creativity): To do always as much as we can, in the way that we can, in order to leave our community more beautiful than we inherited it.
7. Imani (Faith): To believe with all our hearts in our parents, our teachers, our leaders, and our people.

The concepts of NTU psychotherapy are universal, and are equally applicable to European Americans, Latino Americans, and other racial/ethnic groups, with appropriate modifications for cultural diversity. The response to NTU psychotherapy was so significant that PLC decided to incorporate its philosophy and psychotherapeutic model into its approach to treating children and families in the therapeutic foster care program.

The Therapeutic Foster Care Program

The therapeutic foster care program at Progressive Life Center is called NIA (Nurturing Individuals Always). *NIA* also means "purpose" in Kiswahili. The therapeutic foster care program was the result of the convergence of four factors.

The first factor was the mental health problems of the urban and suburban children and youths. Aggressive behaviors in this population were becoming increasingly severe with the growing negative social forces that affect urban, suburban, and African American communities. The second factor was the recognition that traditional out-of-home care was inadequate to meet the needs of seriously emotionally disturbed (SED) youths, who need sustained and comprehensive mental health treatment. The third factor was the growing disillusionment and dissatisfaction with available institutional care for SED youths. The fourth factor was PLC's faith that its Africentric NTU-based psychotherapy would benefit SED children and youths.

Our first therapeutic foster care program was started in Washington, D.C., in 1990. In 1993, the American Psychological

Association's Division of Child Psychology recognized PLC's therapeutic foster care program as a national model program in service delivery for child and family mental health. Currently, four therapeutic foster care programs are located in Washington, D.C., and Maryland.

Child and Youth Characteristics

The children or adolescents targeted for the therapeutic foster care program must meet two principal eligibility criteria: (1) they must have a serious emotional disturbance that is identified via a DSM-IV diagnosis; and (2) they must have an I.Q. of at least 72 as measured by the Weschler Intelligence Scale for Children. Some children diagnosed with developmental disorders may be eligible for the program, providing the developmental disorder fits the criteria for placement, and the developmental disorder coexists with another diagnosable psychiatric disorder.

Children referred to our program have a history of neglect, abandonment, and physical and/or sexual abuse. They are overwhelmingly African American. In the majority of cases, they have parents who are unemployed, have medical or psychiatric disabilities, drug or alcohol addictions, and histories of physical or sexual abuse themselves. A significant number of children in care have parents who are deceased or whose whereabouts are unknown.

In the program's early development, children or adolescents who demonstrated aggressive, life-threatening behaviors were not eligible for placement; as the recruitment and program services have evolved, these children are now also admitted. Examples of aggressive, life-threatening behaviors that, at one point, were excluded from the program include threatening the lives of other, setting fires, use of a deadly weapon, sexually aggressive acts against other children, and participation in drug trafficking.

The common clinical pattern of these children is one of severe cultural deprivation, spiritual disconnection, lack of awareness of their own personal biography, disconnection from community and family, and an intense sense of not belonging. The most common traditional diagnosis is dysthymia and other major depressive disorders. The most frequent diagnosis for latency-age children is Attention Deficit Hyperactivity Disorder, while adolescents experience a frequent diagnosis of dysthymia or other major depressive disorders. Other diagnoses include oppositional defiant behavior, posttraumatic stress disorders, conduct disorder, and psychosis.

Over 50% of the children enter the program with a pharmaceutical regimen. Within 6 to 12 months after admission, their medication is either reduced or discontinued. Pharmaceutical regimens for children in care have been significantly diminished from 70% at admission to 42% during placement. The most common medicinal intervention with this population is Ritalin. Many children in out-of-home care have severe behavioral problems. Typically, these children may be physically and verbally assaultive. They may find following rules and respecting authority difficult, be distrustful, lack a sense of belonging, experience very low self-esteem and self-worth, lack a sense of identity, and have difficulty establishing and maintaining authentic relationships.

PLC maintains a fundamental belief that severely emotionally disturbed children and adolescents can be served in a home setting where there is a high level of structure, skilled supervision, and extensive clinical support services for the individual and family. Our approach to serving this population involves a network of support that includes mental health professionals, biological and foster families, community resources and mentors; educators and therapeutic recreation specialists, and medical personnel and clergy. Through intensive foster care services, we can move the client to a higher level of functioning and a less restrictive setting. The program goal is to return the clients to their biological families or a permanent living arrangement within 18 to 24 months of placement.

Foster Parent Recruitment

PLC's success in recruiting foster parents is attributed to its NTU approach. Foster parents are recruited within a 50-mile radius of our office sites. Recruitment methods include making presentations on waiting children before church congregations, and distributing brochures, posters, and other printed materials. The most effective recruitment method has been newspaper advertising that stresses PLC's Africentric approach. Radio spots, public television announcements, and talk shows are other vehicles for recruitment.

Persons interested in becoming treatment foster parents submit an application and attend an orientation meeting. After a substantive interview and application process, the prospective treatment foster parent must successfully complete the H.E.L.P. (How Empowerment Liberates Parents) training program. This training program spans five consecutive weeks and provides 32 hours of preplacement classroom and field placement training. The training includes an ACT (Actualizing, Coaching, and Teaming) internship for foster parents. The 10-hour internship is supervised by certified and experienced foster parents, who are teamed with prospective foster parents to provide hands-on training during the intern's field placement. The training includes lectures and workshops on education about emotionally disturbed children, the NTU principles, behavior management, crisis intervention, passive restraint, medication administration, communication skill building, effective discipline, parenting the child from a multicultural perspective, and the foster parent's role in facilitating reunification. The treatment foster parent must be able to meet all agency qualifications and requirements, and comply with agency policies and state regulations.

The Admission Process

The admission process for foster children consists of videotaping both the foster child and the foster parents, so that they each see the other's video before an actual meeting occurs. The admission process for the foster child consists of videotaping his or her interview and clinical assessment. The videotape is used to introduce the foster child to the prospective foster parents and is typically experienced as nonthreatening and noncommittal. This process allows the foster parents to determine whether they can meet the needs of the child and whether they are interested in parenting the child. The videotape process has been effective in eliminating premature introductions and reducing the number of failed placements. Foster parents are videotaped in their homes, affording the child the opportunity to become familiar with the home structure, environment, and family members before meeting them. This process has the added benefit of empowering the child in need of a placement, allowing him or her to choose the foster parents, and includes the foster child in the process of matching.

This initial introduction procedure for the children and treatment parents diminishes anxiety and fears of rejection. Permission is granted by the local authorities for videotaping the children and using the videos in matching children with foster families. Consents are also required for the foster parents. After reviewing the child's clinical record and his or her videotape, foster parents can decide whether they are interested in working with a particular child. If the parents decide to work with the child, the foster parent's video is sent to the child and his or her team to review. If all parties agree with the match, the match is approved and a formal introduction is scheduled. Foster parents rarely are rejected by the children. The children are not informed about foster parents who choose not to parent them, but are notified only of the family(ies) who are interested in them. This process ensures a successful placement beginning and diminishes the risk of failed placements. In our first year of child placements, 10 children were placed, with no failed placements. In our second year, 30 children were in placement, with three failed placements. The average number of child placements agencywide is 30 per year. The average number of failed placements agencywide is three. Failed placements represent unplanned discharges from the program.

PLC provides transition homes for those children who are returning from out-of-state placements with other agencies. The transition homes are temporary placements for children requiring a therapeutic environment during their gradual introduction to their treatment parents and their move into a PLC therapeutic foster home. Transitional parents are certified under the same training as treatment parents and are required to supervise the child or adolescent 24 hours a day. Most children coming from out-of-state placements do not have educational placements secured and require supervision during the day until their schooling begins.

Program Services

After the placement, PLC maintains services for the foster child, foster parent, and biological family.

Services for Children

Transition rites of passage. This period last four weeks, beginning with a Welcoming Ceremony, and provides a structured gradual transition for the child from the current residence into the new foster home. This transition is marked by cultural rituals and ceremonial activities. Children are prepared during this period for the Rites of Passage component of their treatment program. It is in this phase of the transition that the seven Principles of Kwanzaa are introduced. The four-week transition culminates with a Crossover Ceremony that signifies a successful transition, completion of goals, and the child's ability to bring his or her transition to a close.

Rites of passage. All foster children are required to participate in our rites of passage program. The program's duration is four to nine months, it prepares latency-age children for adolescence, and adolescents for adulthood. All groups are gender-specific, and are culturally and spiritually focused. The children/adolescents review the Seven Principles of Kwanzaa, and begin practicing them every day by accepting additional family and community responsibility and other structured activities. The children are given African names and are educated about their culture.

Therapy. All clients engage in weekly in-home family and in-office individual therapy; play and group therapy are provided as needed. Therapeutic intervention ranges from three to six hours per week per child. Psychiatric consultation and psychological evaluation are provided for each client.

Retreats. Retreats take place at a sequestered environment out-of-town and are scheduled on an ongoing basis for the children during the year. A team of clinicians supervises the children in the absence of their foster parents. The retreats include clinical, social, cultural, and recreational activities.

Education incentive programs. These programs are designed to encourage and motivate academic success. Monetary incentives and awards are given to children who strive for academic excellence, and who have few absences.

Tutoring. This help is available for those clients who need it, and can be provided in-home or on-site.

Support Services for Foster Parents

In-service training. Beyond the preplacement training, a minimum of 30 hours of ongoing training annually is required for treatment parents.

In-home family therapy. Each treatment family participates in weekly in-home family therapy.

Foster parents' support group. This group meets monthly to provide a nurturing environment for treatment parents to discuss specific incident problems and successes. Suggestions on parenting are offered. Group members engage each other in joining and networking.

Crisis intervention. Therapists are on-call around the clock to provide help in crises. All crises are followed up with an incident report. Treatment parents access the crisis hotline by dialing direct to the office or paging a therapist for assistance.

Multifamily retreats. These retreats are an integral component of the complete foster care program. The retreat is a communal experience structured to intensify the curative factors normally operative during the treatment process. Treatment families with their foster children, and in some cases biological families, attend these retreats annually.

Foster parent advisory board. This board consists of treatment parents who are responsible for advocating for other treatment parents and for the children in care. They act as liaisons for foster parents' grievances, plan and implement activities and special events, and represent the agency at conferences, meetings, orientations, and trainings. This board works closely with the project director.

Planned and unplanned respite. All treatment parents are required to take a respite at least one weekend per month. Treatment parents may take up to two weekends per month of "planned" respite. Treatment parents and the children in care use the same respite parents, establishing an extended family. Planned respite requires the coordination of transportation between treatment parents and respite parents. In a crisis, or "unplanned" respite, foster parents have access to respite as needed. The therapist is responsible for identifying a respite home, and transporting clients to that site when they are in crisis.

Services for the Biological Family or Other Caregivers

Parent training. Biological parents or caregivers who enter into a service agreement with PLC are given parent training, a natural support component that focuses on life skills, educating the parent about the special needs of the child, behavior management, and communication skills.

Family and group therapy. Biological parents or caregivers receive in-home family therapy and group therapy that sometimes includes the treatment foster parent as well. Parent-child interaction is observed, and parents are given the expert assistance they need to improve their relationships with their child and their parenting skills.

Twenty-four hour crisis intervention. Biological parents or caregivers have access to the agency hotline and can page a therapist for assistance in the event of an emergency during the child's transition period.

Respite. Planned and unplanned respite services are provided for the biological family or caregivers during the step-down phase of child's discharge. During the child's transition out of the program, caregivers have access to a respite home, providing support services for 30 to 90 days.

The Step-Down Program: Preparing for Reunification

As the foster child and the biological family or caregiver progresses toward reunification, PLC's Step-Down program prepares the young person for separation from the program with a transition back into the permanent home. The Step-Down phase provides diminished clinical and supportive services while assisting the youth and the identified family resource, whether a biological family or an adoptive family, with the adjustment back into the home or community over a period of 30 to 90 days. This array of services is provided during the child's or youth's treatment program and culminates in discharge from the program.

Program Outcomes

The principal objective of PLC's therapeutic foster care program is to identify children who would benefit from our services and place them in therapeutic foster homes that would facilitate their incorporation back into their communities and their biological family, or into a different permanent living situation. PLC is committed to ongoing evaluation of its programs. To evaluate our clinical intervention we use the Child and Adolescent Problem Checklist, which is administered to clients pretreatment and every six months thereafter. Treatment parents complete these assessments, which focus on emotional problems, academic achievement, and behavioral areas. Treatment parents also complete a six-month internal evaluation of clinical services in the form of a survey. In turn, treatment parents are evaluated semi-annually by clinicians through the use of an assessment tool with scale ratings to determine the foster parents' strengths, level of effectiveness in their work with the child in their care, and their compliance with agency requirements.

Evaluation efforts to date demonstrate that PLC's faith was justified: 74% of the youths improved significantly emotionally, 37% improved in school academically and 47% stabilized in their school situations, and 53% of the children showed significantly improved behavior. Eighty-three percent of the treatment parents indicated that they received direct clinical services frequently and consistently, while 90% indicated that the clinical intervention was effective and that they could see the child's progress in the healing process socially, emotionally, psychologically, and spiritually.

NTU'S Contribution to Treatment Foster Care

Spirituality is the core distinguishing principle in an African-centered philosophy of life and is the fundamental concept of healing in the NTU psychotherapy approach [Phillips 1990, 1996; Nobles 1986]. Healing involves a transformation of one's attitude and emotions, it is a personal experience. Bolling [1986] states, "A heightening of awareness of the correct values and ethical considerations is necessary first to wake the healing energies of the inner self." NTU therapy facilitates this process through the exposure of clients to the Seven Principles of Kwanzaa.

One of the rituals commonly used in NTU psychotherapy

within group processes for centering, empowering, and healing purposes is *libation*. Staff members, foster parents, and children alike engage in the practice of libation. Libation is conducted through the pouring of liquid into the earth for circular connectedness, and is accompanied by the calling forth of the names of family and historical ancestors. These ceremonies are often practiced during special events, such as foster parent graduations, Kwanzaa celebrations, retreats, and Welcoming and Crossover Ceremonies. The essence of the libation ritual is that we can all gain real strength from the recall of anchoring a family ancestor into our consciousness. Though the "strength" may come through the emotional or spiritual avenues, it is available on the physical and mental levels also. It has been our experience that immediately following a libation ritual, both foster parents and children feel emotionally better, physically stronger, mentally clearer, and overall empowered.

NTU has given the therapeutic foster care programs both purpose and direction for clinical intervention. In the African tradition, the NTU therapist/healer counters the despair of clients by giving them hope, which liberates the soul. The therapist seeks to purge the falsehoods from the abused self of the client's bodymind, flushing out the poisons from the body and soul. This process allows clients to rediscover their authentic self. It allows for the unfolding of the NTU healing spirit-energy. The healer assists the client system to synthesize all its scattered energies, thereby empowering the bodymind. The therapist's work, then, is one of seeing, hearing, and knowing the spirit-energy of the client system bodymind, and helping with the awareness, realignment, and integration process. The healer becomes a conduit for the healing process to take place. The healer encourages the client to "go with the flow" and remain centered in his or her own life-sustaining spirit-energy as he or she harmonizes in a healing relationship with the client system [Phillips 1996].

The goal of NTU psychotherapy is to restore harmony, balance, interconnectedness, and authenticity to the bodymind in order to facilitate the internal healing spirit-energy. Succinctly, the role of the NTU therapist in this process is that of a spiritual guide, assisting the organism to become aware of, and stimulate, its self-healing mechanism. The healer inspires and energizes the client system through the infusion of positive healing energy within the framework of authentic human love.

PLC's therapeutic foster care programs are short-term placements of up to two years. We do not maintain a large number of children in care for any lengthy period of time. Short-term placements with intensive care are preferred, and a constant "revolving door" movement of children through the system of care, avoiding the probability of children getting stuck in the system, is our purpose. This short-term intensive care allows our agency to serve more children more efficiently and effectively. It is a program that allows children to realize and actualize their goals, to "grow on, instead of hold-on." ♦

References

Bolling, J. (1986). Ori: The personality/character soul and the practical inner healer (unpublished paper presented at the third Orisha Conference, October 4, 1986).

Foster, P., Phillips, F., Belgrave, F. Z., Randolph, S. M., & Brarthwaite, N. (1993). An Afrocentric model for AIDS education, prevention, and psychological services within the African American community. *Journal of Black Psychology, 19*, 123–141

Karenga, M. (1977). *Kwanzaa: Origin, concepts, practice.* Los Angeles: Kawaida Publications.

Nobles, W. W. (1986). *African psychology: Towards its reclamation, reascension, and revitalization.* Oakland, CA: Black Family Institute.

Phillips, F. (1990). NTU psychotherapy: An Afrocentric approach. *Journal of Black Psychology, 17*, 215–222

Phillips, F. (1996). *Spirit-energy and NTU psychotherapy.* Hampton, VA: African American Mental Health, Cobb and Henry Publishers.

8

African American Female Adolescent Identity Development: A Three-Dimensional Perspective

Joyce West Stevens

African American female adolescents have unique identity issues that structure developmental tasks. Qualitative data from a longitudinal research project are used to explicate a three-dimensional model of the identity developmental process in early-age African American female adolescents. The limitations of a gender analysis model of voice and connection are noted. It is suggested that the African American female adolescent experiences a relational crisis in both racial and gender identity development. Moreover, African American female adolescents develop skillful, unique, expressionistic, and assertive styles of relating to negotiating perceived hostile environments. Practice implications for child welfare are outlined.

Joyce West Stevens, M.S.W., D.S.W., DCSW, is Assistant Professor, Boston University School of Social Work, Boston, MA. This article is a revised version of a paper presented at the Council on Social Work Education 42nd Annual Program Meeting. The research on which this article is based is funded by a grant from the Hubie Jones Fund for Urban Social Work Practice, Boston University.

F eminist theorists contend that gender is socially constructed and the female developmental trajectory should
be based on mutuality, care, and connection rather than
separation [Belenky et al. 1986]. Certainly, the idea that a positive sense of self develops vis à vis primary relationships that
foster interdependence, care, and connection advances knowledge and enriches our view of human development. Even within
this conceptual framework, however, African American female
adolescents have unique identity issues that structure their
developmental tasks. This article uses qualitative data from a
longitudinal pregnancy prevention research project to conceptualize a model of identity development in early teenage (11
through 14 years) African American females. Implications for
clinical practice in child welfare conclude the article.

Theoretical Considerations

Identity Formation in Adolescence

Psychodynamic theory posits a recapitulation conceptualization
of adolescence that suggests that the resurgence of early developmental conflicts results in intrapsychic restructuring. This
internal restructuring represents the quintessential process of
identity formation [Blos 1967; Erikson 1968, 1969]. Palombo
[1988] has argued persuasively that this conceptualization has
become such an accepted view of adolescent development that
it is rarely questioned. Nevertheless, Erikson [1968, 1969] framed
identity as anchored in social life:

> We deal with a process located in the core of the
> individual and yet also in the core of his communal
> structure, a process which establishes, in fact, the identity
> of these two identities.

Erikson forces us to recognize the significance of social
referents of behavior and affect, yet his identity construct is
problematic. For one thing, he sees identity as unitary, formed

in late adolescence with an outcome of either consolidation or foreclosure. More importantly, formulations of both race and gender in the identity construct are theoretically flawed. For instance, it is reasoned that female identity is realized through spousal attachment and that African American identity is decidedly compromised. African Americans living in a hostile racist environment, it is argued, form negative identities.

Such cultural biases make for serious problems when theorizing about African American female adolescents. Hence, traditional theorizations of adolescent development must be modified or new models must be developed. Interestingly, Phinney et al. [1990] have used the basic Erikson paradigm to interpret empirical research data concerning ethnic identity formation. All things considered, African American adolescents experience multitextured socialization experiences from which complex identities develop. Dill [1990] has argued that the African American experience in America is a dialectical one. She suggests that there is a "simultaneity of conflict and interdependence which characterizes black-white relations" [p. 70].

The Impact of Race on Identity Formation

In American society, race has been constructed in such a way that certain undesirable characteristics are attributed to minority racial groups based on a social hierarchy of unequal power and privilege. Structures are then created to control, constrain, or eliminate those who are racially marginalized within the power hierarchy. Consequently, the least powerful or privileged (African Americans) commonly carry out transactions in oppressive and hostile environments. Indeed, the social geography of race is such that members of both minority and majority races experience racial identity problems [Frankenberg 1993]. Presently, scholars use various conceptual frameworks (assimilation, accommodation, multiculturalism, ethnicity, dual perspective) to describe the adaptation and adjustment of racial/ethnic minority groups within a majority culture [Atkinson et al. 1994; Chau 1991; De Hoyos et al. 1986; Devore & Schlesinger 1996;

Norton 1978; Pinderhughes 1979]. Bifurcation—the sense of a double consciousness or the experience of living in two worlds—is one framework commonly used to explain adjustment [Chestang 1972; DuBois 1903]. The concept, however, suggests far more complexity than is commonly interpreted by scholars.

The internalization of oppression has been the most salient conceptualization of bifurcated adaptation when it is explicated as a model of duality / opposition. When interpreted in this vein, bifurcation suggests a deficit or victimized view of adaptation. Moreover, explanations of the African American experience vis à vis a lens of oppression and victimization eschew explications of affirmative implications of African American history and culture. Simply put, such explanations leave out the ethics of African American resistance; what African Americans affirm about being Black and what they affirm about being American [Cone 1972; Murray 1970]. At best, the concept of a double consciousness represents identity as complex.

Actually, racial self-devaluations may be experienced as normative if considered as integral features of the bicultural self-development process [Cross 1991; Boykin 1983, 1986].* As such, the development of identity in African Americans encompasses behavioral and psychological responses that mediate, negotiate, and repudiate oppressive conditions. The author maintains that negative and positive racial self-valuations may coexist while personal integrity is sustained. A strengths perspective would clarify bifurcation as providing self-experiences for the development of bicultural competence or cultural flexibility. As a matter of fact, biculturalism may be a valid concept to expli-

---

* The terms *Afro-American* and *Euro-American* used later in this text are not to be confused with the current scholarly debate generated by Mary Lefkowitz's argument [1996] regarding the knowledge claims of Africentrism. A model of ethnic/racial identity, initially developed by Cross [1971, 1991], has been widely adopted to explicate identity development. Moreover, this model has been useful in cross-cultural counseling. Regarding counseling minorities and culturally diverse populations, see especially the work of Carter [1995], Helms [1984, 1986], Sue & Sue [1990], and Vontress [1971, 1976]. Finally, the theorization of broad and comprehensive value orientations, as in the Afro-American and Euro-American conceptual models, is indebted to the early work of work of anthropologist Florence Kluckhohn [1961].

cate the experiences of African Americans' cultural flexibility, since cultural meaning systems define socialization experiences [Bruner 1990; De Anda 1984]. Inherent in the notion of biculturalism is the idea that a Euro-American and Afro-American cultural ethos* are both constituents of the identity formation of African Americans. Moreover, both domains represent coherent realms of cultural integrity [Boykin 1983].

Gender Identity Formation

Female adolescents experience a normative relational crisis at the emergence of adolescence, since awareness develops at this time that it is socially expected that one must separate and disconnect from family. Heretofore, self-development has taken place in relation to others, providing a sense of connection, care, nurturance, and mutuality. Societal demands for severance of parental ties and the devaluation of gender relational values bring self-esteem considerations to the forefront [Gilligan et al. 1988; Surrey 1991]. To be sure, the African American female teen experiences this normative crisis, but her developmental trajectory is confounded as she undergoes a similar crisis due to her cultural group membership. A paramount issue for African American female adolescents is a perceived social expectation of, or demand for, separation from family and from one's fictive kinship group.

The concepts of the fictive kinship group and the cultural reference group are used interchangeably. While they both share similar meanings, the idea of kinship suggests a closer attachment. Further, it represents a cogent conceptual translation of the African American folkloric expression of "play kin." Societal oppression of minority groups gives members a sense of shared experiences. Cultural dissonance is a core dilemma that comes to the forefront for the African American female at the onset of adolescence. Moreover, she perceives, in a new way, not only the societal devaluation of her gender, but more importantly, societal devaluation of her as a member of a racial

---

* See note on prior page.

minority, her reference group. On both accounts, this real and perceived devaluation is played out in the school setting, where cultural values are transmitted that are markedly different from feminist and Afro-American prosocial values.

The female adolescent does not want to separate from what is valued. Rather, she seeks to change the content of her relationships in such a way that developmental changes are validated and her racial/ethnic group affiliation is supported. The self is formed and re-formed within the context of the cultural group, which is the matrix for the creation of personal meaning and self-narrative. Indeed, biographical narratives of African American luminaries document the observation that Afro-American group identity carries enormous meaning and purpose [McClain 1986]. Hence, the experience of isolation/separation from the group can be problematic, painful, and may contribute to poor mental health. Moreover, disconnection from one's cultural reference group not only generates guilt and shame, and creates cultural dissonance, but also deprives the individual of the psychological supports needed to cope with the stress of a racist society.

Identity Complexity

The identity formation of the African American adolescent female is multidimensional and complex. A core developmental task is synthesizing coherent meaning systems from three experiences of socialization: (1) mainstream society (Euro-American worldview); (2) a devalued societal status (affected by the status convergence of gender and race); and (3) cultural reference group (Afro-American worldview). The salient generalized description of the African American cultural ethos is communalistic, holistic, emotionally expressive, personalistic, and oral; the Euro-American ethos is individualistic, acquisitive, competitive, materialistic, impersonal, and linear [Atkinson et al. 1993; Boykin 1983; Collins 1990; Cross 1991]. Likewise, Boykin [1983; 1986] has conceptualized a triadic model of socialization. The model, termed a Triple Quandary Paradigm, argues that the Euro-American and Afro-American cultural ethos are noncommensurable. The African American female adolescent's negotiation of the experiential domains of Afro-American, Euro-American, and racial minority status is confounded by the socialization experiences of gender.

Female prosocial values of connection, care, empathy, and mutuality converge with similar Afro-American values [Collins 1990]. Such prosocial values are seen as contrary to those of the established culture. Consequently, they are devalued in mainstream society. Certainly, these triadic socialization experiences involve psychological processes. Although the effort here is to place this analysis within the realm of social-cultural life, one notable psychological process of adolescent development must be mentioned. At the onset of adolescence, there is an inner urgency for coherence and synthesis, augmented by formal operational thought [Palombo 1988]. Identity complexity and social identity are presented as heuristic explications of the developmental tasks of the African American female adolescent. Saari [1991] refers to *identity complexity* as the conscious experience of self as versatile, creative, and differentiated, noting in particular that conflict may exist in coherence. Identity complexity, as so defined, may well be placed within a phenomenological paradigm, and not exclusively in a psychodynamic one, as Saari asserts [Atwood & Stolorow 1984]. Identity is not as much an achieved state of independence from parental ties as an evolving differentiation in relation to self, others, and the surrounding world, while sustaining a connection to significant others. It is the psychic connection to significant others that makes coherence within differentiation possible.

A coherent differentiated self reflects experiences of complexity, choice, fluidity, creativity, and articulation. Such experiences of self are organized by meanings created from social-cultural life. Social identity here is conceptualized as the cultural anchorage of the self. A social identity differs from the concept of social role in that social identity has to do with the meanings embedded in social roles, not just the role itself. A social identity develops by engaging in social and personal meaning-making actions that are legitimated by the praxis of daily life. For instance, it seems reasonable that social identities are commensurate with various social roles assumed by an individual [Stevens 1994].

In sum, the significant psychosocial developmental tasks of African American female adolescents are (1) the development of coherent meanings from triadic socialization experiences; (2) the development of bicultural competence while sustaining connection to family/fictive kin; and (3) the negotiation of strategies of resistance for self-liberation to counteract racial victimization and gender devaluation. The development of healthy social identities for the African American female adolescent must be anchored in those social experiences that provide worth and value as an African American female. At the same time, however, the African American female adolescent must develop bicultural competence. The felt demand, at adolescence, to move outside the confines of both one's blood and play kinship group may be experienced as self-threatening. The psychological stress of both racial victimization and gender devaluation is more keenly experienced in adolescence than in earlier developmental periods. Nevertheless, social victimization and devaluation may be consistently resisted and opposed in variant behavioral/psychological responses. When destructive behaviors are used to manage identity problems in oppressive environments, however, a survival existence is maintained, not a liberated one [Ward 1991].

Methodology

The Research Setting

A public middle school in a large northeastern city was selected for the research site. The school is located in an inner-city community where 43.3% of the children ages birth to 17 years live below the poverty level. Of the 254 students enrolled in the school, 78% are African American, 5% are Caucasian, 16% are Latino, and 1% are Native American. The school reports that close to 100% of the students are eligible for the free lunch program.

The Research Design

The Pregnancy Prevention Intervention Research (Growing Up: Learning to Make Choices) was initiated in January, 1994, with visits to the school for (1) participant observation of the school-community environment; (2) formal and informal meetings with administrative and staff members; and (3) evening meetings with parents. The present study is part of this Pregnancy Prevention Intervention Research, a longitudinal study, incorporating quantitative and qualitative measures. A 10-week intensive curriculum (Self-Image Life Skills and Role Model Mentoring curriculum) was tested among a group of at-risk early-age African American adolescent girls. The curriculum's expressed foci were psychosocial and ethnic identity developmental issues.

Qualitative raw data were collected by audiotaping the Self-Image Life Skills Curriculum group sessions and the planning/reporting meetings of college student mentors with research investigators. At their meetings the mentors, in addition to planning recreational-cultural field trips, shared observations about their interactions with study participants. Memo notebooks were maintained by the leaders of the group sessions and the college mentors throughout the data collection phase of the research. Notebooks were used for recording observation field notes, ideas, and impressions. The notebooks and audiotapes were the principle sources of data. The data collection took longer than planned due mainly to temporal obstacles, such as school closing or early school dismissals.

Data Analysis

For the analysis of the qualitative data, the tape-based data from the Self-Image Life Skills group sessions and the Role Model Mentor meetings were transcribed and reviewed, along with memo notes. Content analyses were used for the raw data, which were examined thematically. Common themes that emerged from the text-based data of the curriculum were identified and conceptualized [Miles & Huberman 1984]. Examples from the text-based data are presented here to document findings. The themes reflect the efforts of participants' to negotiate the triadic socialization experiences of (1) a Euro-American ethos; (2) a devalued societal status (affected by the status convergence of gender and race); and (3) an Afro-American ethos.

Findings

Only preliminary results from the qualitative data are reported at this time. The two themes set forth below, although seemingly unrelated, are integrally connected in that they speak to the manner in which the girls endeavored to assert themselves. The themes convey significantly how the girls begin to construct a sense of personal identity and self-efficacy. Moreover, the themes represent coping strategies in the management of disempowering interactions. The themes are representational, composite statements of the girls' concerns. The quoted statements were, at some point, articulated by the girls and are meant to capture the quintessential nature of the theme or composite. The theme itself is parenthetically noted; for example: (1) "You gotta be able to thump, argue, and curse!" (Self-Assertion in Relating to Others); and (2) "My mother is a crazy person!" (Self-Assertion and Understanding Parental Restrictions).

Thumping, Arguing, and Cursing

Most striking about the study girls was their boisterous, confrontational, and combative behavior. They engaged in "loud mouthing" or "facing off" when relating to one another. In other words, they engaged in high volume social interactions and stylistic performances. Their stylistic expressions of orality, expressive individualism, and signification are characteristic of an Afro-American stylistic cultural idiom [Boykin 1983; Gates

1988]. The findings suggest that high-volume activities affirm a sense of self and give the girls a way to manage their devalued race and gender status within a school setting. In short, the girls in the study were not silent girls, but were vociferous, demanding respect when they felt they were being disrespected by peers and adults.

The girls' behavior, at times, took on the timbre of friendly one-upmanship bantering, but it could become mean and ugly, escalating easily into fights. Generally, the girls seemed contentious and quick to show anger, for fear they would be put down by someone. A mentor's field notes comment on the girls' obstreperousness, as observed at the university campus orientation visit and the initial meeting with the mentors:

> The girls were extremely boisterous and loud. At the very first, they seemed intimidated by their surroundings, but once we got outside, I think that they felt a lot more comfortable because they knew they could go where they wanted. At the meeting with (University Administrator), Carla (mentor) was getting a piece of gum for herself and offered some to the rest of us. I wanted one, Sarah (mentor) also took one, and Carla offered gum to the girls. Yolanda (teenage girl) said, "Look, she's trying to say your breath stinks"—showing she obviously did not trust us. Carla most definitely did not mean a thing by offering the gum.

The mentor here attributes the girls' boisterousness and loudness to feelings of uneasiness in the university environment, but this kind of behavior generally characterized the girls' demeanor and manner of relating in other settings as well. This behavior was not only observed by those of us engaging in the research, but was well known to school personnel. The girls were frequently involved in fights during and after school, and their behavior would result in "talk" or "gossip" among school staff members, who saw fights only among the girls, not among the boys.

School suspensions were mainly due to fights, and most fights were about boys. Among the girls, interestingly, fantasied or genuine romantic liaisons with male peers were a basis for valuations of self-worth and self-definition. The experience of a devalued gender status may have been operative in relationships with male peers, especially where affective responses were of a romantic nature. According to the girls' self-reports, many male peers pursued multiple romantic relationships and rarely made a commitment to a single girl. Field notes from the author's observations contain an instance of fighting that was due to the romantic involvement of two girls with the same boy:

> Then Queenie and Palama get into a serious argument. They are in a crossfire of accusations about who [he] likes best. They have quieted the others. They are angry and full of rage. They are shouting, cursing, about something that has occurred yesterday, in school, about a boy. And then, in a wink of the eye—it all seemed to have happened so fast. Palama, cursing, calling names, jumps up out of her seat—so does Queenie—both girls facing each other—ready to fight. I try and separate them— talking to them to calm them down. Other girls join in to get them to sit and calm down—they do not hear us. But, it seems clear that the group is turned on and excited by the turn of events. They are smiling—laughing. While attempts are made to separate the girls, Queenie manages to kick Palama. They start hitting and kicking each other even though, once this occurs, they are forcibly restrained. There is an uproar—shouts and screams.

Although the study girls tended to develop assertive coping strategies, they seemed most vulnerable in their relations with male peers, especially those with whom they wanted romantic attachments. The girls seldom expected male peers to be accountable or responsible for behaving in the same ways they found unacceptable in female peers.

As stories were shared, the girls were asked to explain themselves and describe their actions and vernacular expressions. This was accomplished with little difficulty because the girls saw research team members not only as offering help but also as interested persons who could learn from them. We wanted to know how they made sense of the social world around them, and therefore the meanings they attached to their own actions. Interestingly, the girls did not see themselves as loud or boisterous. They described themselves as being able to "thump, argue, or curse." Their ability to engage in such actions was a source of pride. Even shy and reticent girls saw value in being able to act in this manner, because it warranted respect from peers. The term *thump* was unknown slang to the research team. Further, the context in which all three words were used was equally unknown, but the girls willingly shared knowledge, or, as they said, "We'll let you in on what's goin on."

"Thumping," the girls explained, "means you can take care of yourself, watch your back, and not have people mess with you, and you fight if you have to." Though the phrase is simple and clear, the gesturing and posturing in which it was expressed rendered a dramatic display of bravado. In the vernacular lexicon of African American teenagers, Folb [1980] translates *thump* to mean "fight." In the following transcription, group members explain what it means to argue and curse in an interaction with school staff members.

Field-Taped Transcription:

> GROUP MEMBER 3: Miss Block, Ellen. She thinks she's our mother. She's always trying to tell us what to do, even though she's a teacher. I would respect her, but she's mean. She's got two kids of her own, but she's mean. Like the last time, Ann and me went into the office and she goes, "May I help you?" And Ann says, "No you cannot because I'm looking for Miss Garland." And she just sits there and yells at us. If a person acts like that, how can they help you? What's the sense of you telling 'em your problems. I just kept on walking. I was mad at

her and I was yelling, but I kept on walking and told her Miss Jacob told me to come and sit. She said, "Where are you going?" And I said, "to sit right there." And she said; "No you're not." And I said, "Yes I am." And I sat down and she said; "Get up and get out." And I said, "Miss Jacob told me to come in here." And she was like— get up.

GROUP MEMBER 4: We don't curse people, we just argue.

GROUP MEMBER 3: Like when I was talking about Miss Block just now, when she was yelling at me, like no you're not sitting here and I was like yes I am. That's what we call arguing.

GROUP MEMBER 4: Cursing means you better get outa my face before I make you get out of it. You better leave me alone, cause I didn't do nothing to you and you better leave me alone...

GROUP MEMBER 3: Miss Block, now we didn't go up in each others face.

The transcript concretely demonstrates the characteristic manner in which these girls saw themselves interacting with adults within their school environment. They did not see themselves in conflict with authority figures as much as asserting strength ("yes I am"), independence, ("get outa my face"), and demanding respect. They saw Miss Block as not respecting them. She was seen as not courteous or warmly responsive. In other words, the girls did not automatically defer to age—an adult did not automatically warrant respect, she had to earn it. All in all, the girls were in direct conflict with school authority figures; deference to the hierarchical status of school personnel was simply not a consideration for the girls. Findings suggest that the study girls experienced difficulty in negotiating the school setting. In short, the study girls had not yet developed a flexible cultural style that would assure successful adjustment in a Euro-American school environment—they had not yet developed social competence in the school environment. Most girls had not incorporated a social student identity that would conform with school norms.

Furthermore, verbal interactions among peers have a central role in the daily life of African American teenagers: words are used as tools to exercise power and control and to manipulate and control one's social-psychological space [Folb 1980; Smitherman-Donaldson 1977]. Verbal interactions that are commonplace among peers have been transferred to interactions with adults. Implicit in the girls' thumping, arguing, and cursing are strategies to display a sense of power that will influence the behavior of not only peers, but of adults as well. Though one would think that there might be a clear demarcation of the kinds of verbal interactions with peers and with adults, this was not true of the study girls. Additionally, most girls were not just in conflict with school staff members, but with their parents as well.

My Mother Is a Crazy Person

The mothers of the girls in the study tried to set reasonable limits, and do things that they thought would benefit their daughters. Nonetheless, these women clearly found dealing with their daughters very difficult. Parents often resorted to extreme verbal abuse in efforts to demand compliance with discipline regimens. Mothers and daughters were engaged in verbal combat. Parents frequently initiated requests for supervision of their daughters from relatives or the courts in conditions of badly deteriorated parent-child relationships. Most girls were in a different psychological place than parents, and therefore saw parental efforts at discipline and supervision as irrational. Though this posture is not unusual for adolescents, these parents faced realistic fears about social risk in their communities. The following excerpts from group sessions are illustrative.

Field-Taped Transcription:

> GROUP MEMBER 3: Yeah. My Mama is like, "Those little boys be talkin nasty to you. They be asking you for sex." I be like lookin at her like she stupid, like she got two heads on her shoulders.

> GROUP MEMBER 4: When a boy call, or a boy come to my house and wanna see me or whatever and we just sittin and chillin. My mother come there sayin, "You better not be havin no babies with some chump!" I be like hold up, wait a minute. I'm like chill with the babies.

> GROUP MEMBER 5: They always bringin up babies.

> GROUP MEMBER 5: They scared we might get pregnant.

The anxiety of mothers appeared to be reality based, as the possibilities of early sexual activity and pregnancy were real-life concerns. Many of the mothers themselves had been adolescent mothers. Moreover, concern about premature sexual activity and parenthood was expressed about the girls but not the male siblings. The girls saw a gender bias in maternal concern about their social activities. Although the girls could articulate some understanding of their mothers' "irrational behavior," they had little understanding of the environmental risk of their communities or their own emotional and sexual vulnerabilities. Like most adolescents, they were quick to adopt bravado stances and saw themselves as invulnerable. Moreover, the girls saw themselves as engaging skillfully in arguments with their mothers.

Field-Taped Transcription:

> GROUP MEMBER 1: Alright, my mother is real strict, OK. Something happen to her when she was little and something happen to my older sister when she was small, so she's strict on me and my other sister, so she'll tell me to do something and I won't do it, and I know if I don't do it, somethin gonna happen. She's gonna be mad, so I

go on and do it anyway. Cause I...you know... I'm stubborn, I guess.

Later in the same session:

> GROUP MEMBER 1: But, it's not just that. It's just that she don't know how to talk to nobody, when you want to ask her something she just keep on talkin about it. She calls other people [meaning relatives here] and tries to tell them about you—"Don't let her stay at your house. If she runs away let her stay on the streets." And, I don't think she has a heart and I guess she's so cruel. She's got nerve problems and everything. She's crazy!

The girls in the study were rarely ever in a conflict-free relationship with their mothers. Mothers appeared to respond from a base of fear about what might happen to their daughters; parental anxiety at times was uncontrollable. As a consequence, parental discipline and supervision were ineffectual. Mothers, in particular, resorted to physical force and cursing in their discipline efforts. The girls, in turn, felt at times berated by their mothers, and "cursed and argued" back, creating a cycle of escalating conflict.

> "It was like before I turned 13 and I came home late. And she started yelling, calling me and my friends bitches. Told me to get rid of those bitches, not have them come around any more. And my mother started hitting me and stuff like that...my mother's big, OK? She's big, big hands, big knuckles. She busted my nose and I was bleeding all over the place. I feel trapped. I hate my mother. She's just crazy."

Despite such conflict, the study girls desired and felt an intimate relationship with their mothers. They wanted the new developmental changes they were undergoing to be recognized and understood. Above all, they wanted their mothers to trust that they could make decisions and become competent problem solvers. Apter [1990] has suggested that, in arguing with their mothers, adolescent girls become differentiated in their gender identity in that internalized controls and a sense of power are developed. To be sure, this appeared to be the case with the girls in this study.

Discussion

Preliminary findings suggest that the study girls tried to project identities valued by persons in their proximal environments. The study girls' socialization experiences were anchored in an African American cultural idiom. The complexities of identity development were derived from the management of concrete psychosocial developmental tasks: (1) the development of co-herent meanings from triadic socialization experiences; (2) the development of bicultural competence while sustaining connec-tion to family/fictive kin; and (3) the negotiation of strategies of resistance for self-liberation to counteract racial victimiza-tion and gender devaluation.

The study findings tended to confirm results of other stud-ies that suggest that parents and adolescents experience discrep-ant realities in family life [Jessop 1981]. The girls in the present study wanted their mothers to accept them on their own terms. They thought their mothers were overly anxious about their interest in boys. Likewise, the mothers seemed greatly concerned about their daughters' well-being, but they had extreme reac-tions to their daughters' rule-breaking and misconduct behav-iors. Parental discipline and supervision were consequently problematic. Carrying out protective functions in parenting African American children induces considerable psychological stress for African American mothers [Collins 1990].

Convention informs us that there are three primary social-ization tasks that African American parents perform: (1) keep-ing children safe (physically and emotionally) from the dan-gers of street life; (2) protecting children from overt forms of racism and oppression; and (3) helping children develop bicultural competence. From the daughters' reports, the mothers seemed anxious and fearful in the performance of these tasks. Perhaps this accounted for the imposition of severe and strict discipline regimens. It seems, from the daughters' reports, that their mothers unwittingly required the girls to relinquish their connection with their peers. The mothers mistakenly believed that peers were associated with street culture. The daughters perceived such requests as demands for disconnection from their fictive kinship group. As a result, such requests exacerbated the daughters' resistance to parental supervision.

Anderson [1994] has suggested that African American teenage girls increasingly engage in typically masculine behaviors such as abusive language and violent attacks to gain respect and assert a sense of self. These claims are questionable since, to some degree, physical aggression, rowdiness, and verbal assertiveness are common modes of expression among adolescents regardless of gender and race [Larson 1983]. African Americans, in particular, have historically used a vernacular lexicon to express aggression and power in social interactions, such as the ritual insult games of "playing the dozens" or "signifying." Such games, often carried out in a humorous or joking manner, are meant to discredit or embarrass another. *Playing the dozens*, in particular, has been defined as ritualized or spontaneous insults directed most often at another's mother (the dirty dozens), or at an opponent (the clean dozens). *Signifying* represents rhetorical understatements and may be seen as a metaphor for black language skills [Ellison 1964; Folb 1980; Gates 1988].

Not surprisingly, African American female adolescents, too, employ these ritual insult games for organizing the context of their social environments. The girls of the study commonly engaged in the clean dozens. They tended to see themselves in competition with female cohorts for the attention of male peers; female peers were therefore seen as opponents or competitors. Ordinarily, the girls engaged in the specific verbal game of "he said, she said." Girls were constantly reacting to character or behavioral allegations made about them. The game represents, as do all games of this nature, attempts to assert oneself, and to manipulate and control others [Folb 1980; Goodwin 1990].

Manipulation and control are not used here in a pejorative sense, but are meant to suggest ways of exercising some measure of control in one's environment. Yet, the verbal games engaged in by the study girls were centered on boys. The focus of social discourse among the girls was about real and imagined romantic affiliations with boys. Moreover, such verbal games are enacted within a social space of high volume discourse [Kochman 1981]. In short, African American girls are loud girls.

Granted that the study girls presented herein engaged in boisterous and loud behavior, yet, this obstreperous behavior can be viewed metaphorically. "Loudness," Fordham [1993] compellingly argues:

> is meant as one of the ways by which African American women seek to deny the society's efforts to assign them to a stigmatized status...therefore, "those loud Black girls" is used here as a metaphor proclaiming African American women's existence, their collective denial of, and resistance to, their socially proclaimed power-lessness, or "nothingness." (p. 25)

Way [1995] presents a counterargument to the interpretation of loud, brassy behavior in inner-city African American girls, suggesting that such descriptions are stereotyped and therefore represent a negative view of urban African American adolescent girls. Interestingly, Way does not view loudness as typified adolescent behavior. Yet, loudness need not be seen as negative, since adolescents may outgrow loudness while retaining assertiveness.

Given the limitations of such generalizations, a case can be made, nevertheless, for interpreting the girls' brassy assertive behavior as an emotive stylistic expression that is cultural [Boykin 1983]. More important are the meanings the study girls attached to their argumentative behavior. They clearly saw "arguing" as a demonstration of self-assertiveness and sense of power. The behavior may well indicate resiliency and serve as a protective element in negotiating hostile racist environments. Moreover, skill in argumentation can afford African American females opportunities for meeting psychosocial developmental relational needs of self-differentiation, as well as connection [Apter 1990; Gilligan et al. 1988]. Nonetheless, in concrete terms, arguing and other obstreperous behaviors cause trouble in the school setting.

Loud obstreperous behavior is not tolerated in a school setting. It is usually interpreted as antisocial or as behavior that should result in disciplinary action. The loud behavior of the study girls often resulted in the filing of misconduct reports by school staff members. When African American girls construct identities to defy racial/cultural devaluation, are they at the same time asserting a diverse female identity? Do they in fact voice claims of self-affirmation of their difference? These are questions that require future exploration and study.

Additionally, self-esteem concerns were salient in the management of sexuality and gender development among the study girls. Their romantic interest and involvement with male peers tended to diminish an ethic of caring in female peer relations. Self-reports of the study girls suggested that they were not yet sexually active. Nevertheless, the girls seemed constantly preoccupied with real and imagined romantic affiliations. Most reports, however, indicated that personal self-esteem was often compromised in such affiliations as girls saw themselves competing with each other for a boy's attention or interest. As a result, the girls engaged in physical fights and verbal insult games with their female peers.

It was difficult to discern the context the girls were using to make value judgments about norms of behavior for males and females. The literature is relatively taciturn about the development of sexual desire among female adolescents [Tolman 1994]. Decidedly, assertiveness is a useful skill in the management of hostile environments, yet the girls tended to assume more vulnerable passive postures when relating to males than to their female peers. It has been suggested elsewhere that early romantic attachments and single-partner dating may place African American female adolescents at risk for premature childbearing [Stevens 1994]. Moreover, early physical maturation can strongly influence female adolescents' decisions about dating and sexual activity [Gargilo et al. 1987].

The demands of social life require that adolescents assume complex differentiated identities without pathological fragmentation. To do so presupposes that the individual becomes an active and confrontational agent in negotiating the realities of living while sustaining self-coherence and authenticity. The notion that a firm identity develops and is set at a particular point in time for all time seems curiously out of date in a postmodern age. African American adolescent females, then, must create complex, multifaceted social identities.

African American females, at the onset of adolescence, experience a normative crisis of connection/disconnection with parents and their fictive kinship group. Nonetheless, psychosocial competencies must be developed to negotiate relationships within the dominant culture for cultural/bicultural competence [Freeman 1994]. The minority female must synthesize her triadic socialization and develop coherent systems of cultural and personal meaning. Experiences of complexity are heightened during adolescence as flexible and variable interchanges take place in the social domains of family, school and peer relations. It seems reasonable to suggest that African American adolescent girls may be at risk for antisocial and delinquent behaviors if management of racial identity issues is unsuccessful.

Practice Implications

The ethnic identity of culturally diverse children in placement is of paramount importance to the field of child welfare. Child welfare agencies routinely place children outside their immediate and extended kinship groupings. Acting-out adolescents are usually placed in residential group homes rather than in family foster care.

Most ethnic identity considerations in child welfare have a political context, as in the case of transracial adoptions. Ethnic/racial identity, however, must be addressed routinely, whether placement occurs within or outside the child's kinship group, especially in the case of adolescents.

African American adolescents in residential placement settings are often in the minority, and minority staff members are largely absent as well. The ethnic/racial minority adolescent in this kind of setting may face special problems in identity development. For instance, the predominate Caucasian environment of the group home may be perceived as hostile and oppressive. Aspects of ethnocultural transference and countertransference among adolescent residents and staff members can be consistently confronted in case conferences and clinical sessions, so that maximum therapeutic benefit can be achieved from the group home milieu [Comas-Diaz & Jacobsen 1987, 1991]. Moreover, agencies must make available training programs that will instruct practitioners about the influences of culture and race in clinical practice. In fact, empirical research findings have suggested that, in cross-race clinical dyads, practitioners with immature racial identity ego statuses are not likely to achieve positive therapeutic outcomes [Carter 1995; Helms 1984]. African American adolescent females require supportive environments to explore matters of ethnic/racial and gender identity issues.

Moreover, direct clinical practice, whether individual or group, can assist female adolescents in mediating their identity socialization experiences. Self-differentiation within the context of family is not the same as disconnection from familial bonds. Developmental markers, such as identity management, while sustaining connection with familial ties and one's reference group, serve as assessment indicators when evaluating coping strategies in adolescent adjustment in the social contexts of school, home, and peer relations. Preplacement, culturally sensitive, clinical intervention programs can be designed to enable the minority (African American) female adolescent to manage identity developmental tasks successfully.

The need to sustain kinship and reference group connections is critical in African American adolescent identity development. Sensitive attention must be given to cultural/ethnic identity considerations in the delivery of placement services for minority adolescents in the child welfare system. Increasingly, effective service delivery systems employ intervention strategies to prevent the removal of children from their kinship networks. If child welfare services are to benefit, however, from a focus on abuse prevention, additional research on informal social support networks will be necessary. The effectiveness of such support systems in sustaining and strengthening families, especially those families at risk for maltreatment, could greatly influence abuse-prevention programs [Thompson 1995]. ◆

References

Anderson, E. (1994). *Streetwise.* Chicago: University of Chicago Press.

Atkinson, D. R., Morten, G., & Sue, D. W. (1993). *Counseling American minorities: A cross cultural perspective* (4th ed.). Madison, WI: Brown & Benchmark.

Atwood, G., & Stolorow, R. D. (1984). *Structures of subjectivity: Explorations in psychoanalytic phenomenology.* Hillside, NJ: Analytic Press.

Apter, T. (1990). *Altered loves: Mothers and daughters during adolescence.* New York: Fawcett Columbine

Belenky, M. F., McVicker, C. B., Goldberger, N. R., & Tarule, J. M. (1986). *Women's ways of knowing: The development of self, voice, and mind.* New York: Basic Books.

Blos, P. (1967). The second individuation process of adolescence. *Psychoanalytic Study of the Child, 22,* 161–186.

Boykin, A. W. (1983). The academic performance of Afro-American children. In J. T. Spence (Ed.), *Achievement and achievement motives* (pp. 321–362). San Francisco: W. H. Freeman & Company.

Boykin, A. W. (1986). The triple quandary and the schooling of Afro-American children. In U. Neisser (Ed.), *The school achievement of minority children* (pp. 57–75). Hillsdale, NJ: L. Erlbaum Associates.

Bruner, J. (1990). *Acts of meaning*. Cambridge, MA: Harvard University Press.

Carter, R. T. (1995). *The influence of race and racial identity in psychotherapy*. New York: John Wiley & Sons, Inc.

Chestang, L. W. (1972). Character development in a hostile environment. *Occasional Paper no. 3* (series), 1–12. Chicago: University of Chicago Press.

Chau, K. L. (1991). Social work with ethnic minorities: Practice issues and potentials. *Journal of Multicultural Social Work, 1*, 23–29.

Collins, P. H. (1990). *Black feminist thought*. Boston: Unwin Hyman, Inc.

Comas-Diaz, L., & Jacobsen, F. M. (1987). Ethnocultural identification in psychotherapy. *Psychiatry, 50*, 232–241.

Comas-Diaz, L., & Jacobsen, F. M. (1991). Ethnocultural transference and counter-transference in the therapeutic dyad. *American Journal of Orthopsychiatry, 61*, 392–402.

Cone, J. H. (1972). *The spirituals and the blues*. Maryknoll, NY: Orbis Books.

Cross, W. (1971). The Negro to black conversion experiences. *Black World, 20*, 13–27.

Cross, W. E., Jr. (1991). *Shades of Black: Diversity in African-American identity*. Philadelphia: Temple University Press.

De Anda, D. (1984). Bicultural socialization: Factors affecting the minority experience. *Social Work, 29*, 101–107.

De Hoyos, G., De Hoyos, A., & Anderson, C. B. (1986). Sociocultural dislocation: Beyond the dual perspective. *Social Work, 31*, 61–67.

Devore, W., & Schlesinger, E. G. (1996). *Ethnic-sensitive social work practice* (3rd ed.). Boston: Allyn & Bacon.

Dill, B. T. (1990). The dialectics of Black womanhood. In M. R. Malson, E. Mudimbe-Boyi, J. F. O'Barr, & M. Wyer (Eds.), *Black women in America: Social science perspectives* (pp. 65–78). Chicago: University of Chicago Press.

DuBois, W. E. B. (1903). *The souls of black folk* (pp. 247–260). New York: Signet.

Ellison, R. (1964). *Blues people in shadow and act.* New York: Random House.

Erikson, E. (1968). *Identity youth and crises.* New York: W. W. Norton & Company, Inc.

Erikson, E. (1969). *Identity and the life cycle.* New York: International Universities Press, Inc.

Folb, E. A. (1980). *Runnin' down some lines: The language and culture of black teenagers.* Cambridge, MA: Harvard University Press.

Fordham, S. (1993). "Those loud Black girls": (Black) women, silence, and gender "passing" in the academy. *Anthropology and Education Quarterly, 24,* 3–32.

Frankenberg, R. (1993). *White women, race matters: The social construction of whiteness.* Minneapolis, MN: University of Minnesota Press.

Freeman, E. M. (1994). African-American women and the concept of cultural competence. *Journal of Multicultural Social Work, 3,* 61–76.

Gargilo, J., Attie, I., Brooks-Gunn, J., & Warren, M. P. (1987). Girls dating behavior as a function of social context and maturation. *Developmental Psychology, 23,* 730–737.

Gates, H. L., Jr. (1988). *The signifying monkey.* New York: Oxford Press.

Gilligan, C. (1982). *In a different voice.* Cambridge, MA: Harvard University Press.

Gilligan, C., Ward, J. V., & Taylor, J. M. (1988). *Mapping the moral domain: A contribution of women's thinking to psychological theory and education.* Cambridge, MA: Harvard University Press.

Goodwin, M. H. G. (1990). *He-said-she-said: Talk as social organization among Black children.* Bloomington, IN: Indiana University Press.

Helms, J. E. (1984). Towards a theoretical explanation of the effects of race on counseling: Black/White interactional model. *The Counseling Psychologist, 46,* 187–197.

Helms, J. E. (1986). Expanding racial identity theory to cover counseling process. *Journal of Counseling Psychology, 33,* 62–64.

Jessop, D. J. (1981). Family relationships as viewed by parents and adolescents: A specification. *Journal of Marriage and the Family, 43,* 95-106.

Kluckhohn, F. R., & Strodtbeck, F. L. (1961). *Variations in value orientations*. Evanston, IL: Row, Peterson.

Kochman, T. (1981). *Black and White styles in conflict*. Chicago: University of Chicago Press.

Larson, R. W. (1983). Adolescents' daily experience with family and friends: Contrasting opportunity systems. *Journal of Marriage and the Family, 45*, 739–750.

Lefkowitz, M. R. (1996). *Not out of Africa: How "Afrocentrism" became an excuse to teach myth as history*. New York: Basic Books.

McClain, L. (1986). The middle-class black's burden. In C. Page (Ed.), *A foot in each world* (pp. 12–14). Evanston, IL: Northwestern University Press.

Miles, M. B., & Huberman, A. M. (1984). *Qualitative data analysis*. Newbury Park, CA: Sage Publications.

Murray, A. (1970). *The omni-Americans*. New York: Outerbridge & Dienstfrey.

Norton, D. (1978). The dual perspective. In D. Norton (Ed.), *The dual perspective: Inclusion of ethnic minority content in social work curriculum*. New York: Council on Social Work Education.

Palombo, J. (1988). Adolescent development: A view from self psychology. *Child and Adolescent Social Work, 5*, 171–186.

Phinney, J., Lochner, B., & Murray, R. (1990). Ethnic identity development and psychological adjustment in adolescence. In A. R. Stiffman & L. E. Davis (Eds.), *Ethnic issues in adolescent mental health*. Newbury Park, CA: Sage Publications.

Pinderhughes, E. B. (1979). Teaching empathy in cross-cultural social work. *Social Work, 24*, 312–316.

Saari, C. (1991). *The creation of meaning in social work*. New York: The Guilford Press.

Smitherman-Donaldson, G. (1977). *Talkin and testifyin'*. Boston: Houghton Mifflin Company.

Stevens, J. W. (1994). Adolescent development and adolescent pregnancy among late age African-American female adolescents. *Child & Adolescent Social Work Journal, 11*, 433–454.

Sue, D. W., & Sue, D. (1990). *Counseling the culturally different: Theory and practice*. New York: John Wiley.

Surrey, J. (1991). The "self in relation": A theory of women's development. In J. V. Jordan, A. G. Kaplan, J. B. Miller, I. P. Stiver, & J. L. Surrey (Eds.), *Women's Growth in Connection*. New York: The Guilford Press.

Thompson, R. A. (1995). *Preventing child maltreatment through social support: A critical analysis*. Thousand Oaks, CA: Sage Publications.

Tolman, D. L. (1994). Doing desire: Adolescent girl's struggles for/with sexuality. *Gender & Society, 8*, 324–342.

Vontress, C. E. (1976). Racial and ethnic barriers in counseling. In P. B. Pedersen, W. J. Lanner, & J. G. Draguns (Eds.), *Counseling across cultures*. Honolulu, HI: The University of Hawaii Press.

Vontress, C. E. (1971). Racial differences: Impediments to rapport. *Journal of Counseling Psychology, 18,* 7–13.

Ward, J. V. (1991). A belief in self far greater than anyone's disbelief: Cultivating resistance among African-American female adolescents. In C. Gilligan, A. G. Rogers, & D. L. Tolman (Eds.), *Girls and psychotherapy-reframing resistance* (pp. 87–104). New York: Harrington Park Press.

Way, N. (1995). "Can't you see the courage, the strength that I have?" Listening to urban adolescent girls speak about their relationships. *Psychology of Women, 19,* 107–128.

9

A Rite of Passage Approach Designed to Preserve the Families of Substance-Abusing African American Women

Vanesta L. Poitier, Makini Niliwaambieni, and Cyprian Lamar Rowe

This article approaches the treatment of addicted African American women in ways drawn from traditional African culture. While the modern African American woman is clearly not the same as her continental African foremother, the reality of her life is still predicated on the basis of her culture and her material wealth or lack of it. The approach recommended here, a rite of passage, derives from the belief that the value orientations drawn from the African wisdom of the ages offers the best way to work with families to recover both sobriety and a powerful understanding and repossession of culture that will help to ensure not only sobriety but also ways of holding together and rebuilding the families of today and the future.

Vanesta L. Poitier, M.S.W., LICSW, is Director, and Makini Niliwaambieni, A.A.S., is Rites of Passage Coordinator, Partnership for Family Preservation Program, Washington, DC. Cyprian Lamar Rowe, Ph.D., is Assistant Dean for Student Services and Multicultural Affairs, School of Social Work, University of Maryland at Baltimore, Baltimore, MD.

Historically, drug treatment programs have been less than sensitive to women and to the cultural considerations that affect them, and women, as a whole, have seldom received adequate treatment. Although opportunities for women to receive treatment have recently begun to expand, in many cases, treatment for drug addiction alone is insufficient. For women to receive adequate care with sustainable results, it is critical that they and their children be involved in the recovery process. With the establishment in 1992 of the Women and Children's Branch of the Center for Substance Abuse Treatment (CSAT), a federal agency, it became apparent that the family is the most powerful resource for the survival of its own members [Amen 1992].

To be effective, the treatment approach must explore uncharted waters: family preservation as a primary factor in the treatment of substance-abusing women. The inclusion of family members and the understanding of the family's cultural context, when taken together, can be major deterrents to the protracted use of drugs. The withdrawal of destructive substances can reduce the negative forces that have the overall effect of disassembling the lives of women and their families.

The rite of passage is an innovative approach to treatment for African American women and their children whose existence has been marked by family dysfunction and substance abuse. It is designed to assist families recovering from addiction and addictive ways of living. It offers a balanced approach, rich in African culture and tradition, that empowers families to achieve the level of functioning necessary for sustenance of individuals and the families that individuals make together. The aim is to make families self-sustaining.

The rite of passage approach integrates four basic principles for a full human life, beyond mere existence: (1) Restraint, (2) Respect, (3) Responsibility, and (4) Reciprocity. If incorporated into an overall recovery program, these principles can inspire participants and their family members to make personal life changes and to grow mentally, spiritually, and physically healthy.

Since the family is the most powerful interpersonal resource for the survival of its members, effective treatment depends upon family preservation as a primary factor in the treatment process [Amen 1992]. This article expounds upon the thesis that an adequate prototype/model for the treatment of African American drug-abusing women and their families must proceed from a knowledge base of both cultural and gender-specific treatment modalities, and offers such a model.

Family and Culture

Drug use/abuse attacks, at its core, the families of African Americans. Not only does drug abuse lead to a suspension of attention to the life-preserving mandates implicit in every culture (those learned from history and the life-in-context of a living culture) but it also undercuts drastically a family's attention to the rudiments of communal life that can preserve it as a unit. A number of studies [Mondanaro 1989; Chasnoff 1988; Nobels 1985] report that the quality of family life and familial relationships are the victims of the plague of drug addiction.

According to Mondanaro [1989], the substance-abusing family is "characterized by chaos, unpredictability, and inconsistency." She also states that children from drug-dependent families tend to learn to accept and expect the unexpected. Thus, one can deduce that children exposed to drug abuse and other self-abusing behaviors will themselves mimic what they see, thereby continuing the cycle of destruction.

The obverse is also true: Positive role-modeling, mirroring [Comer & Poussaint 1976; Miller & Dollard 1941], empathic nurturing, parental interactions, and appropriate expectations [Bavolek & Comstock 1985] are essential elements in the nurturing and rearing of children and can lead to healthy, self-sufficient, and responsible adults.

Supporting this belief is one of the core tenets of African philosophy: the individual does not exist alone but rather cooperatively and collectively [Mbiti 1969]. Thus, whatever happens to the individual happens to the whole group, and whatever happens to the group has an impact on the individual [Mbiti 1969]. This core belief is stated in the adage: "I am because we are, therefore, I am."

To treat addiction in the African American community, and especially among African American women with children, we must understand the spiritual context of African life. Addiction is a pattern of behaviors that undermine the physical and psychosocial well-being of the primary addict. It also creates a correlative and respondent secondary addiction that seizes and corrupts the entire family unit, as well as a tertiary addiction that multiplies itself in all the interactions that the addict and her family members have with the world in which they live. We must, therefore, look at "family" in a much larger context.

Family in the African American context does not necessarily carry a solely nuclear meaning; it may refer to whoever resides in the "household" as well as those who share an extended relationship within a given community. Family may include a number of fictive relatives—persons who are or become very close to a person or blood family and, to all intents and purposes, are viewed as family and treated as such even in essential features of family life.

Relationships within the nuclear and extended families are guided by ethical principles recognized by Sudarkasa [1980] and others in their research into African kinship groups, discussed below. Here it is important, however, to make the point that in the African context, the meaning of family follows a design that, when overlooked, undermines the attempt to treat addicted women who come from this community.

Aphorisms such as "It takes a village to raise a child" and "If relatives help each other, what evil can hurt them" are not taken casually in the African context. They are indeed a constant reaffirmation of all belonging to all [Leslau & Leslau 1962]. Kuhn [1970] describes a natural family as an observed cluster of similar objects, sufficiently important and sufficiently discrete to command a generic name, that is, family. Comparatively,

Akbar [1976] likens the African family to a spider web in that one cannot touch the least element of the web without causing a vibration of the whole.

The separation and the mutual exclusion between the "drug addict" and the significant others in close proximity is indicative of the lack of understanding of the true meaning of key concepts like kinship and collectivity in African philosophy. Many drug treatment programs are based upon intervention strategies that continuously treat the addicted mother as a *monad*, a single, singular being whose disease and cure are located solely in the ability of the program to clean her up and refocus her energies on the elements of life that bring her least obtrusively to the attention of society, its mores, and its norms. This orientation to treatment is inadequate to the needs of any person dealt with outside of her or his culture. Its inadequacy and misplacement are dramatic when applied to persons whose cultural orientation and instrumentalities derive from the collective.

Unfortunately, the intervention strategies of many drug treatment programs continue to compartmentalize interventions into separate boxes marked "addict," "family," "society," and "underlying spiritual values." These atomized notions are clearly not empowering for women coming from a cultural context in which strength, loyalty, oneness, and union are basic values. These women are apt to resist the sorts of notions that come out of the perspectives in which the African family is characterized as "weak, disorganized, and vulnerable" [Moynihan 1965; Frazier 1932].

Family is that entity in which the individual personality is nurtured and developed. It is the place where responsibility to the group is learned through observation and practice; where self-esteem/self-worth is developed; and where respect, restraint and reciprocity are observed and learned. These qualities, in addition to reverence and humility before elders, are internalized through observation and practice. Family is the place where obedience is learned and group expectations of the individual are continually clarified as the individual's mission within the family and response to the family are made evident.

Family is also that place where children learn important life skills, such as compromise, negotiation, styles of showing belonging, and building intimacy. Family is that living organism in which are enshrined the vital teachings of the elders, whose wisdom and experience are the living endowment of the ages.

Familial relationships within the extended family must, therefore, be understood and made a part of the healing process called recovery. It cannot be emphasized enough that it is not the individual alone who must recover. It is that total world, in which the individual addicted mother has lived out the pathologies of addiction, that must be brought into the recovery process.

Culture is the way people are in the world. It brings together all things into what becomes for them "reality." Amen [1992] defined culture as a set of ideas used to influence and change behaviors in people into refined social qualities necessary to bring about a harmonious, stable, and prosperous society. Hence, it is only with a firm grasp on the living, moving, and motivating power of African culture that the addicted mother and her family can be moved to choose sobriety and ultimately familial, communal health.

It is to culture then that we should look for those healing elements that can be applied in the process of recovery for African American women and their families. These processes must be carried out in tandem and they must be animated and guided by a set of principles that are an age-old value articulation of African soul.

Relationships within the extended family are guided by ethical principles recognized by Sudarkasa [1980] and others in their research into African kin groups in indigenous African societies. These principles are consistently identified from group to group and found among the seven principles of Maat[1] [T'Shaka 1995]. They are "principles of wholeness" from ancient Kemet

(Egypt) to which many African historians trace the roots of more contemporary African indigenous groups. These principles are, as noted earlier, restraint, respect, responsibility, and reciprocity.

The traditional structure of African American families is obviously not what it was 40 years ago. Each decade within the past 40 years introduced some new challenge to the traditional family structure that persisted in some form through and since the Maafa[2] period [Richards 1989].

The 1980s and the 1990s have witnessed such a change in African American families that what were traditionally considered the family's wealth, that is, the children, are now too frequently given over to the force of public assistance, which values neither the notion of family nor its need to endure as a self-sufficient, self-perpetuating articulation of African American humanity. We are witnessing the intergenerational transmission of antifamily values. We are witnessing two or more generations of families addicted to illegal substances. And we are witnessing two or more generations of families who, as a result of these addictions, are unable to pass down cultural wisdom. We are witnessing families that are so dysfunctional that disrespect between parents and children, between children and children, between both and the many articulations of an invasive social structure, are the norm rather than the minuscule variant.

The depth of dysfunction challenges, at its most profound level, the ability of significant numbers of African American people to pass on "core culture" or even to experience family in the manner ideally described above. It is balanced, perhaps, only by the powerful embodiments of African American values in culturally functional institutions in the community.

The call of Sankofa, an Adinkra symbol and proverb from the Ashanti people of Ghana, West Africa, has been sounded loud and clear, and responded to by many among Africans from every walk of life in the diaspora. Sankofa is represented visually as "a bird who wisely uses its beak, back turned, and picks for the present what is best [seen] from ancient eyes, then steps forward, on ahead, to meet the future, undeterred." [Kayper-Mensah 1978]. Sankofa tells one that it is not taboo to go back and fetch what one forgot. It tells Africans in the diaspora to look to their traditions to correct challenges that face them today. This concept is applicable to the development of programs for women (and their families) who are recovering from substance-abuse.

Prototype for Family Preservation

Walker et al. [1991] state that "parental drug abuse has led to a dramatic increase in the national foster care caseload in recent years." They also note that an unprecedented number of African American children are entering care. The essential interconnection between these conditions is inescapable. Experts in the fields of child welfare and substance abuse are clear that services in each of the areas are "either unavailable, insufficiently brokered or uncoordinated" [Walker et al. 1991].

The literature suggests that if relevant services and programs are not implemented comprehensively, family preservation and reunification goals will not be achieved as intended. It has also been suggested that family preservation programs are basically ineffective intervention strategies for treating families characterized by extreme poverty, single parenthood, low educational attainment, and mental health problems [Dore 1993]. Furthermore, many of the reunification programs have been criticized for their inability to ensure the safety of children, leaving them vulnerable to abuse and neglect, and exposed to drugs and violence.

A number of authors have attempted to measure, in its totality, the influence of drug abuse on the quality of parent-child relationships. Some have offered prescriptions for change [Taylor 1991; Chasnoff 1988; Boykin et al. 1985; Edelman 1985]. Most often, they characterize these relationships as chaotic and lacking emotional warmth. The prescriptions applied, however, lack the characteristics of a reciprocal, interdependent, and evolving relationship between parent, child, and other family members, among whom are included all those relatives (blood or fictive) who constitute the extended family support network. The prescriptions also fail, on the whole, to discern what could have been missing culturally so that, despite the best intentions of workers, destructive familial behaviors remain.

The passage from destruction to self- and family reconstruction, regeneration, and resurrection, can be summed up in the phrase *familial recovery*. Familial recovery can best occur for African Americans when the recovery process is firmly and fully grounded in an African perspective, integrating fully and meaningfully the traditions from the African past, and also taking into full account the challenges that African people in America have experienced and continue to experience.

Program Design

A *rite* is a formal, cultural, often religious, procedure/ceremony. It is placed at critical cultural junctures to mark passage, on the one hand, from one symbolic state to another, and, on the other hand, to grant power and permission for the "new journey and responsibilities" required of the person/s undergoing the rite. Five major rites of passage have been identified and ritualized in the traditional African setting: rites of birth, puberty, marriage/parenthood, eldership, and passage [Warfield-Coppock 1994]. In the Akan tradition, for example, the "Outdooring" ceremony marks the first time a newborn is formally introduced to the village and given a name. From this point on he or she is formally part of the people.

For our program, the rite of passage is preparation of the individual, within a collective framework, for the coming phases of life. In this context, collective means that children and other family members are included. This rite of passage approach responds to the profound African belief that humans are fully themselves only as part of the "people" (that is to say, the village, the tribe, the nation) and to the profound realization that the essence of our existence as human beings is grounded in our connection to the Creator, the ancestors, the cosmos, one another within the construct of the family, and the community [Akoto 1994]. Some [1985] discusses the importance of the puberty rite among his people in Burkina Faso. Some had left his village at the age of four. Returning at the age of 20, he discovered that many of his family and friends would have little association with him because he had not participated in the ritual that would have prepared him for manhood. The council of elders, however, permitted him at the age of 20 to participate in this rite. The continental African section of Haley's landmark work *Roots* [1976], is replete with examples of such rites in which Kunta Kinte participated among his Mandingo people in the Gambia.

The family rite of passage approach encompasses and is designed for four phases: genesis, initiation, passage/transformation, and Sande Society—with four ethical principles found within the extended family structure as enumerated above: restraint, respect, responsibility, and reciprocity. The phases and principles are linked as follows: Genesis (Restraint), Initiation (Respect), Passage/Transformation (Responsibility), and Sande Society (Reciprocity). These phases and principles are interrelated and overlapped.

The overall objective of family preservation using the four principles can best be achieved in an environment that fosters and promotes communal living. The ideal environment consists of individual apartments equipped with kitchens, communal group and meeting rooms, a fully equipped child care center, recreational and exercise gym, a vocational training room, a medical/health area, and staff offices. The surroundings promote positive social interactions between families and decrease the opportunity for isolation and functioning outside of the collective.

Upon acceptance and admission to the program, each woman is required to complete a seven-day orientation process to acclimate her to her new surroundings, inform her of program expectations, and give her time to decide whether or not the program is for her.

Phase One: Genesis

The Genesis Phase is a four-month period during which the ethical principle of restraint is the primary focus. When a substance-abusing woman is able to declare, "I want to change my life. I cannot go on this way. I want to be a productive woman and mother!," she is ready to face the rigors of recovery. Each woman focuses on stabilizing herself in order to function, first, within her family; second, within the treatment center community; and, last, within the general community/society.

The participant is required to begin the process of dealing with those forces that led to her substance abuse. Only then can she learn to live without abusive substances, and, only then, can she learn what restraint means to a female individual within a family and within the larger communities of which she is a part.

According to Sudarkasa [1980], "restraint means that a person can't do...her own thing. That is, the rights of any person must always be balanced against the requirements of the group." This message is different from the one expressed by a do-your-own-thing society. Because of this tension, the principle requires discussion, examples, and a willingness on the part of the participant to embrace the metamorphic process.

Emphasis is placed on program requirements because group requirements and group standards must be adhered to by all members if they hope to meet their goals. This is true of all groups, be they familial, communal, or political. Parallels between all these various group contexts are consistently and persistently underscored in this approach.

In the case of family, adults must not only live up to standards and meet goals, they must also establish both standards and goals. They must, by example, resocialize their children by living the reality that these standards and goals aim to structure and preserve. These standards and goals are, at their most profound level, nonnegotiable since the perdurability of the family-and-group as family-and-group depends upon their observance.

If the participant's former emphasis has been, "It's my thing, I do what I want!," she may find that incorporating into her life principles of restraint and sacrifice for the good of the whole may be difficult. Hence, in the Genesis Phase there must be a focus on personal development within the context of group participation and group bonding. This is, after all, what happens in creatively functioning families.

During Genesis, in addition to attitudinal transformation, emphasis is also placed on detoxification, regular exercise, and nutrition. Individual psychotherapy, and training in parenting skills, daily living skills, problem-solving skills, and schedule-maintenance are all part of the Genesis Phase, during which women are paired with another participant until they are accepted into the Initiation Phase—the point at which they are reunited with their children. This process is approximately 120 days or four months in length.

Shared living in the Genesis Phase fosters group bonding, sharing, and "kinship building." Within the communal environment, each woman assumes a specific role. She also follows a strict daily schedule that eliminates "idle" time and increases productivity.

Rising each weekday morning at 6:00 A.M. (8:00 A.M. on weekends), the women participate in a guided group meditation from 6:30 A.M. to 7:00 A.M. After meditation, they return to their apartments, dress, prepare their own breakfasts, and clean up their living areas. Chores scheduled for community areas must be completed by 9:00 A.M., when group psychoeducational sessions begin. These extend to noon.

Afternoon sessions begin at 1:00 P.M. and last until 5:00 P.M., when individual therapy sessions and dinner preparation begin. Evening psychoeducational sessions begin at 7:00 P.M. and end at 8:00 P.M. Lights go out at 10:00 P.M. weekdays and at midnight on weekends.

During the first two months of Genesis, the women are not directly involved with parenting considerations. Preparation, however, is continually being made for that time when the children will arrive. Until then (the second half of the Initiation Phase), arrangements are made for biweekly, supervised visits with the children, depending upon each woman's progress during the phase.

Biweekly case management meetings are held between each participant and the treatment staff to assist the participant with matters of personal development. At this time, progress is underscored and remaining challenges recognized.

Group meetings with the women in this phase are held twice weekly to enable them to discuss their development as a collective. These meetings are guided by the treatment staff, and together with reports from both the psychoeducational groups and individual therapy sessions, help the staff and participants to assess each woman's readiness for the next phase.

Evaluation of readiness for movement to each subsequent phase is conducted by designated staff members and Phase IV women. Phase IV women constitute the Sande Society Council. The process of movement from phase to phase is in the tradition of the secret societies found among many groups in Africa. The secrecy is expected to be maintained by each woman. If the secrecy is violated, the penalty/consequence is determined by the Sande Council. (For example, a woman found to have revealed information to a noninitiate may have to defer to a Sande Society sister by doing her laundry or cleaning her room/house for a period of time.)

Concomitant with the movement of women through the Genesis Phase is the movement of children through their Genesis Phase. Children of Genesis Phase women meet weekly as a group to prepare for their transition into community living.

Transition meeting topics include discussion of the mothers' recovery, approximate dates for mother-child reunification, child-centered discussions wherein children are able to articulate their personal trauma resulting from their mother's substance-abusing behavior, and sharing of coping strategies and techniques. The children also undergo comprehensive developmental assessments to determine their educational, social, psychological, and medical needs.

Phase Two: Initiation

The Initiation Phase is guided by the ethical principle of respect: respect for self, respect for family, respect for staff members, respect for rules, and respect for community. This phase, like Genesis, also lasts four months, with the continuation of a strict daily schedule, daily-living skills building, individual psychotherapy, communal living, and collective responsibility for cleanliness. Central to this phase are the concepts of womanhood, sisterhood, and motherhood.

Sessions are designed to increase the participants' awareness of their personal developmental needs. Hence, continuing emphasis is placed on spiritual counseling, academic testing, and the building of parental skills. In this phase, a woman's primary role as mother is rigorously studied in an effort to foster the understanding that a woman's needs and desires must be secondary to her children's development and nurturance needs. The program strives to bring participants along the path of understanding that a child's development depends on the guidance, nurturance, and direction provided by a mother. The mother must provide clear, concise standards that are aimed at the commonweal, the welfare of the whole: the individual, the family, the extended family, and the community.

The women are helped to identify and implement new methods aimed at changing the trinity of the "me-myself-I" attitude dictated by addiction. Emphasis is placed on building problem-solving skills such as those required to work out daily living schedules for oneself and one's children. The collective living arrangements and community meetings all require honest, open interaction. This group interaction significantly advances the effort to change habitual attitudes. Attention is called to the effectiveness of communication engaged in between participants, and among participants and staff members. Special attention is directed to the women's interactions with, and responses, to their children.

What might be called the "diminution of frenzy" (the tendency to respond as if enraged), becomes a focus of parent-child interaction. Mothers are shown ways to diminish the intensity of negative reactions to their children, and to replace those negative reactions with purposeful responses. Since the negative habit is learned, the achievement of the positive habit of speaking to children must be preceded not only by unlearning the negative but also by a perceived amelioration of communication brought about by the positive. So important were the expressions of ideas through words among groups in Africa that many proverbs developed to remind everyone that words could be injurious and nonproductive as well as encouraging and empowering. Consider the following traditional African proverbs: "A harsh answer provokes strife, but one who speaks with gentleness is loved," and "Silence is better than useless chatter" [Leslau & Leslau 1985].

In preparation for reunification, women in the Initiation Phase are required to participate in mother-child bonding exercises in the second month. They are also scheduled to work in the child care facility with other women's children at various points during the day. The time spent in child care is a learning experience and develops the understanding that, although children can be very demanding, they can also bring great satisfaction. The benefit of this experience is that women grow in the awareness that they can learn or relearn the skills necessary for the positive rearing of children. Anticipation of a positive outcome and patience with the stumbles along the "growing way" can help them reach the level of maturity demanded in the rearing of children.

The halfway point of the Initiation Phase is marked by the reunification of the women with as many as four of their children on a full-time basis. The female children must be between the ages of infancy and 13 and males from infancy to 10.

Preparations are made with great care. They range from the physical disposition of the living arrangements to the psychoemotional, sometimes hidden, expressions of anxiety on the part of "recovering" mothers and children. Examples of these preparations would include moving into a new apartment and buying toys and food items appropriate to the ages of the children.

The mothers must also be prepared to deal with their fears concerning the uncertainty of acceptance versus rejection by their children. It involves a reassessment of their desire for reunification. In many cases, there is also the intense, sometimes frightening joy at the prospect of the children's coming.

Staff sessions with individuals and groups in the Initiation Phase focus on self-help sessions, assisting the women to achieve some critical skills, such as how to arrange schedules for themselves and their children, how to make appointments with doctors and teachers, how to set up parent-teacher conferences, and how to access and maintain medical, academic, and social records. There is a possibility that some of the women will feel overwhelmed by a sense of having to master many tasks "seemingly overnight." At such a juncture, the benefit of the group is incalculable.

Reunification of mothers and children. Self-esteem considerations must be a major focus of reunification. Children may have developed the feeling that their mothers neither wanted them before their coming nor cared for them after they were here. They may have perceived the psychoemotional and physical absence of their mothers as abandonment. It is not uncommon for children to view their mothers' return with some degree of skepticism. Reunion will require, among other elements, the following steps recommended both by the National PTA and the March of Dimes:

1. Learning to listen well;
2. Ability to get along by negotiation and compromise;
3. Establishment of fair and consistent discipline;
4. Making children responsible for doable tasks;
5. Keeping a sense of humor; and
6. Praising children appropriately.

These steps, followed consistently, can build self-esteem and pride in both parents and children. As the African proverbs remind us: "He who is taught by his mother is not taught by the world," "Children are the reward of life," "As you bring your child up, so will he grow," and "Without children, the world would come to an end" [Knappert 1989].

The children, depending upon results from previous testing, may continue their therapy and group sessions. They refer to each of the women in the program as "Mama" followed by a first name. This is intended to inculcate a sense of extended family. The older children, under the watchful eye of one of the mothers and a staff member, are given responsibilities for younger ones. The children attend school in the neighborhood and are escorted to school by their mothers. They also spend time among themselves, learning how to interact appropriately in a supervised, safe, and nurturing setting where redirection and relearning can take place when required.

Phase Three: Passage/Transformation

The third phase, Passage/Transformation, is guided by the ethical principle of responsibility. Much of what began in the Initiation Phase is continued, but with less direct supervision. During this third phase, the women must determine what assistance they need to meet their daily challenges. They must develop appropriate ways of asking for help. Seeking assistance is potentially one of the major downfalls of persons who feel that asking for help diminishes them in the eyes of themselves and/

or others. The fear of appearing foolish or of being refused can operate as major deterrents to seeking help.

Learning how to "pass over" into the core of psycho-emotional strength that enables one to assess one's strengths and needs is critical to independent living. It is during this phase, then, that the women are directly preparing for independent living with their children. The coming together of mothers and children to operate as functional families marks the real transformation.

Women are involved with their own academic development in this phase. Either in individual or small group tutoring, they prepare for the GED or college entrance examinations. Involvement in their children's educational development is accomplished through their participation in the PTA or other volunteer organizations at their children's schools. In addition to their work at school, the women may volunteer in a child care facility other than the one their child attends.

African history and culture field trips to places where the women's explicit knowledge of both can be enhanced are a major focus of this Passage/Transformation Phase. Much of the substance abuse that characterizes the lives of these women comes from a lack of self-knowledge and much of the self-directed violence by these women results from a sense of being without value. This is the result of ignorance of the culture and traditions of African Americans.

Historical-cultural sessions are conducted using videos and books that focus on the achievements of historical personalities such as Harriet Tubman, Ida B. Wells, and Marcus Garvey. These sessions serve as the starting point for discussions of issues pertinent to the self-esteem of the women and their children. In many cases, women are helped by appropriating history as a starting point for developing parallels to their continued enslavement by addiction. This may lead to the development of ideas about themselves that foster their esteem for themselves and their children, helping them to interweave their addiction in concepts of continued enslavement and modern-day racism.

Volunteer employment. Volunteer employment is the last part of the Passage/Transformation Phase. Volunteer employment enables the women to develop a good work ethic and appropriate skills. It is also an extraordinarily powerful way for women to prove, implicitly, to their children that they can be effective outside the home as well as inside the home. Responsibility and accountability, both to self and to groups, are developed in a setting/facility unrelated to the treatment center. That this can be a lesson to and for the children is indisputable. Mutual respect is one of its by-products, whose value cannot be overestimated.

Phase Four: The Sande Society

The Sande Society, as mentioned above, is the fourth and final phase of the program. The program relates this phase to the ethical principle of reciprocity. The title comes from the Bundu society in Sierra Leone, where it is one of the aspects of its people's highly developed ritual for initiating adolescent females into full societal participation [Boone 1986]. Entrance into the Sande Society is determined in the same manner as entrance into the first three phases, with one major difference: a private ceremony attended by each initiate-woman's mother and grandmother (if possible), female staff members, and the Sande Society Council members. This private ceremony is followed by a public ceremony attended by the women in phases one through three of the program, in addition to extended family and friends of each initiate.

During the private ritual, each woman receives an African name and Sande Society beads and is symbolically reminded of the challenges of life, while being received into the circle of womanhood. Each Sande Society member receives a new bead for each year in recovery and participation in the program. Sande Society members and women in the program's other phases participate in the public ceremony for each woman. The atmosphere is festive, and the ceremony includes a short speech by each new Sande initiate, an African dance performed by the women, and congratulatory speeches by family and friends who feel inspired to speak.

Becoming a member of the Sande Society is a great honor. As with every true honor, however, it carries a major responsibility. Each Sande Society member is expected to continue to work with the women in each of the other three phases of the program, as well as to provide their own and each other's children with support and love. As Sudarkasa [1980] states, "Reciprocity ties all together. Without the principle of reciprocity, the other principles would not stand."

The first four months of Sande Society membership are characterized by the participation of the Sande Society women in group activities held at the treatment facility, individual and group therapy, and parenting sessions. After this period, Sande Society members' independence increases and monitoring by the treatment center staff diminishes.

Officers are elected by members of the Society. These officers make up the Sande Society Council and preside over regular monthly "sharing sessions" during which members discuss their progress and challenges.

Sande Society members plan in several areas: social activities for themselves, their children, and their extended families; and quarterly empowerment dinners where successful women in varying phases of their recovery are featured speakers. These featured speakers are also invited to participate in the Sande Society: the circle is completed and shall remain unbroken.

Afterword

According to Richards [1989], "African culture is amazingly resilient." She is undoubtedly speaking of the core cultural content that underlies the many different specifics of African peoples. Despite the chaos of the present, therefore, that would tend to disperse African peoples and fragment their energies, African culture when attended to can be a powerful call of people back to their spiritual and creative core/centers.

Rediscovery and revitalization of that discipline is what must be sought to arrest the flight into patterns of intergenerational hopelessness and helplessness. A program design, holistic in nature, based on the traditions of African people, and inclusive of children, promises to shape order out of chaos and send people onward in the journey of healing for African American families, exposed to and affected by the debilitating effects of substance abuse. ♦

Notes

1 *Maat* is the cosmic, earthly, ethical, and social law that invisibly guides the heavens and the earth, conceived by the ancients of Kemet (Egypt).

2 *Maafa* is a Kiswahili word that means disaster. Proposed by Richards [1989] to describe the African enslavement period.

References

Akbar, N. (1976). Rhythmic patterns in African personality. In L. King et al. (Eds.), *African philosophy: Paradigm for research on black persons* (pp. 175–198). Los Angeles: Fanon Research and Development Center.

Akoto, K. A. (1994). *Nation building: Theory and practice in Afrikan centered education.* Washington, DC: PAWI.

Amen, R. U. N. (1992). *An Afrocentric guide to a spiritual union.* New York: Khamit Corporation.

Bavolek, S. J., & Comstock, C. M. (1985). *Nurturing program for parents and children— Program implementation manual.* Eau Claire, WI: Family Development Associates, Inc.

Boone, S. (1986). *Radiance from the waters.* New Haven: Yale University Press.

Boykin, A. W., & Toms, F. D. (1985). Black child socialization: A conceptual framework. In H. P. McAdoo & J. J. McAdoo (Eds.), *Black children: Social, educational, and parental environments* (pp. 33–51). Beverly Hills, CA: Sage Publication.

Chasnoff, I. J. (1988). *Drugs, alcohol, pregnancy and parenting.* Boston: Kluwer Academic Publishers.

Comer, J. P., & Poussaint, A. F. (1976). *Black child care*. New York: Simon and Schuster, Inc.

Dore, M. M. (1993). Family preservation and poor families: When "homebuilding" is not enough. *Families in Society: The Journal of Contemporary Human Services, 74*, 545–556.

Edelman, M. W. (1985). The sea is so wide and my boat is so small: Problems facing black children today. In H. P. McAdoo & J. J. McAdoo (Eds.), *Black children: Social, educational, and parental environments* (pp. 72–82). Beverly Hills, CA: Sage Publications, Inc.

Haley, A. (1976). *Roots: Saga of an American family*. Garden City, NY: Doubleday.

Kayper-Mensah, A. (1978). *Sankofa: Adinkra Poems*. Ghana Publishing Co.

Knappert, J. (1989). *The A-Z of African proverbs*. London, England: Karnak House.

Kuhn, T. (1970). *Criticism and the growth of knowledge*. MA: University Press.

Leslau, C., & Leslau, W. (1985). *African proverbs*. New York: Peter Pauper Press, Inc.

Mbiti, J. S. (1969). *African religions and philosophies*. New York: Praeger.

Miller, N. E., & Dollard, J. (1941). *Social learning and imitation*. Hartford, CT: Yale University Press.

Mondanaro, J. (1989). *Chemically dependent women: Assessment and treatment*. Lexington, MA: Lexington Books.

Nobels, W. (1985). *Africanity and the black family: The development of a theoretical model*. Oakland, CA: Black Family Institute Publication.

Richards, D. M. (1989). *Let the circle be unbroken: Implications of African spirituality in the diaspora*. Trenton, NJ: Red Sea Press.

Some, M. P. (1985). *Of water and spirit: Ritual, magic and initiation in the life of an African Shaman*. New York: G. P. Putnam's Sons.

Sudarkasa, N. (1980, November/December). African and Afro-American family structure: A comparison. *The Black Scholar*, 49–50.

T'Shaka, O. (1995). *Return to the African mother principle of male and female equality*. Oakland, CA: Pan African Publishers and Distributors.

Taylor, R. L. (1991). Child rearing in African American families. In J. E. Everett, S. S. Chipungu, & B. R. Leashore (Eds.), *Child welfare: An Africentric perspective* (pp. 119–155). New Brunswick, NJ: Rutgers University Press.

Walker, C., Zangrillo, P., & Smith, J. M. (1991). *Parental drug abuse and African American children in foster care*. Washington, DC: National Black Child Development Institute.

Warfield-Coppock, N. (1994). The rites of passage: Extending education into the African American community. In M. Shujaa (Ed.), *Too much schooling, too little education: A paradox of black life in white society*. Trenton, NJ: Africa World Press.

10

An Afrocentric Program for African American Males in the Juvenile Justice System

Aminifu R. Harvey and Antoinette A. Coleman

Though the juvenile justice system provides an array of interventions, culturally relevant programs are necessary to deal with the myriad social problems, including an escalating crime rate, facing high-risk African American adolescent males. This article presents an Afrocentric approach to service delivery for these youths and their families.

Aminifu R. Harvey, D.S.W., LICSW, is Assistant Professor, School of Social Work, University of Maryland at Baltimore, Baltimore, MD. Antoinette A. Coleman, Ph.D., LCSW, ACSW, is Associate Professor and Director of Field Education, Ethelyn R. Strong School of Social Work, Norfolk State University, Norfolk, VA.

With the increase in juvenile offenses among African American adolescent males, there is a growing impetus to use culturally innovative approaches to service delivery for these youths and their families. A number of authors have noted the importance of incorporating cultural strengths of African American families and communities into programs serving African American adolescents [Everett et al. 1991; Daly et al. 1995; Assante 1988; Akbar 1984]. Daly et al. [1995] contend that the reinforcement of one's group identity has a critical importance for African Americans, particularly adolescent males, in their efforts to attain positive ego strengths and self-esteem to cope effectively in society. Most services in the juvenile justice system have no culturally relevant interventions directed toward changing negative behaviors among these high-risk youths. The literature is also largely devoid of culturally relevant programs for curbing negative behaviors among African American adolescent males as they move into manhood [Hill 1992; Isaacs 1992]. Yet, a body of American literature exists that suggests that spirituality and collectivity are critical principles in the provision of services that promote the growth and development of African American youths [Oliver 1989; Perkins 1986; Pinkett 1993; Schiele 1994; Harvey 1994].

This article presents a range of social and psychological services for high-risk African American adolescent males and their families based on an Afrocentric approach that incorporates the principles of spirituality and collectivity. For the purpose of this article, *spirituality* is defined as living a life grounded in virtue and morality. The principle of *collectivity* refers to exhibiting behaviors that enhance one's group of origin.

The MAAT Center

The MAAT Center for Human and Organizational Enhancement, Inc., is a nonprofit African American-operated agency founded in 1986. *Maat* is an Egyptian word referring to living a virtuous and moral life [Karenga 1987]. The MAAT Center serves African American children, youths, and families, using an Afrocentric orientation to practice. This orientation views humanity collectively through shared *concern* for the well-being of others [Daly et al. 1995] and promotes an understanding of one's spiritual self [Pinkett 1993; Mbiti 1969] rather than an orientation that relies on individualism and material gain. Using this framework for practice, the MAAT Center provides a range of social and psychological community-based services to African American children and youths and their families who live in the District of Columbia. Referrals come from local juvenile court services and mental health agencies. Many of the children and youths referred have backgrounds of abuse and neglect, mental health and emotional problems, school and learning difficulties, and delinquent behaviors.

The MAAT Center developed and implemented a Rites of Passage program to serve adolescent African American males at risk for exhibiting delinquent behavior(s), and their families. The Rites of Passage program teaches African American adolescent males and their families from an Afrocentric orientation how to build character, self-esteem, and unity [Fraser 1994] among themselves as a family, community, and race of people— *African Americans.* The Rites of Passage program includes (1) in-home family therapy and individual adolescent counseling, (2) adolescent after-school groups, and (3) family enhancement and empowerment interventions.

The Rites of Passage Program

In-Home Family Therapy and Individual Adolescent Counseling

In this component of the Rites of Passage program, an agency therapist provides family and adolescent therapy within the home. In-home family therapy is fundamental to this Afrocentric

orientation because it is based on the African principle of natu-
ralism, which holds that individuals are more themselves in their
most familiar environment [Mbiti 1969]. In-home family therapy
creates an optimum environment for building the therapeutic
relationship. Therapists are afforded a wealth of insight into family functioning in the home environment that they do not have
access to when sessions are conducted in the agency [Akbar
1984]. In-home family therapy also eliminates the problem of
accessibility to services.

The family sessions ideally encompass the entire family system—adolescent, parent(s) or guardian(s), other family members in the household, and any significant others determined
by the family to be essential to the stability, growth, and development of the family. In this intervention, the family is given
the opportunity to define who constitutes the family. Since many
parents may be unavailable during the day, evening and Satur-
day sessions are made available. Family sessions are scheduled
once a week, with additional sessions scheduled as needed.

Family therapy focuses on problem-solving, decision making, awareness and identification of one's feelings/emotions,
improving communication skills and practices, conflict resolution, and appreciating and understanding other family members. These skills are developed within the context of assisting
the family to establish a sense of harmony and of working together as a collective to achieve successful functioning. Family
members learn that every human being has inherent value, and
that it is important to respect each member's individual personality. Through cooperation and shared efforts to maintain
family cohesion [Fraser 1994], the sessions enable the family
members to view themselves as being interconnected and interdependent.

Within the family unit, in-home family therapy seeks to enhance effective parental control and discipline, positive self-
concept and high self-esteem, emotional strengths to resolve
stress, happiness, family ties, parent-child relations, family

cooperation, and abstinence from alcohol and other drugs. As the family unit internalizes the elements of Afrocentricity as a worldview for coping, the family members are then able to assist the adolescent male to seek alternatives to gang involvement and crime; to develop an appreciation for himself, his family, and the community; and to learn how to engage productively in society.

Individual adolescent counseling interfaces with family therapy and the male adolescent after-school groups. The adolescent is given the opportunity, at his own pace, to develop his strengths, capabilities, attitudes, and perceptions. These sessions allow the adolescent to recognize and work on his perceptions of himself as an individual and as a member of a collective family unit, peer group, community, race, and society. The adolescent meets once a week at a regularly scheduled time and location with an African American male therapist. The adolescent selects either home, school, or the agency as the site for counseling. The therapist and youth work toward establishing a relationship of trust so that the adolescent will seek advice and guidance from the therapist rather than from individuals who provide nonconstructive views and philosophies based on their deviant lifestyles.

Individual counseling assists the adolescent to build character, self-esteem, and pride through incorporating the principles of collectivity and spirituality as fundamental values. Adolescents are helped to develop these personal characteristics by becoming aware of their strengths and their ability to achieve goals without engaging in violence or delinquent acts. The adolescent first gains a positive sense of his internal locus of control and self-worth by examining his feelings/emotions. Then, the focus is on strengthening the adolescent's internal locus of control and eliminating gang involvement/crime as behaviors that define self-worth, and on helping the adolescent understand the long-term merits that educational and employment opportunities provide for goal attainment. Furthermore, the youth is afforded the opportunity to explore, become aware of, and understand his feelings/emotions by acknowledging the sources of his anger and learning how to manage his anger constructively.

Second, the adolescent and therapist engage in problem-solving and decision-making skills. The adolescent identifies the choices he has made, defines those that have had positive and negative outcomes for him, and then works with the therapist to use a cognitive and behavioral worldview in making appropriate life choices.

Individual adolescent counseling continues until the adolescent demonstrates attitudinal and behavioral lifestyle changes. Adolescents are able to return to individual counseling without a formal referral if they or a family member express the need. This Afrocentric intervention emphasizes the reciprocal nature of community support of the individual and the individual's support of the community.

Adolescent After-School Groups

As a component of the Rites of Passage program, adolescent after-school groups involve the interactions of African American adolescent males in group sessions to make lifestyle changes by developing constructive interpersonal skills, fostering new relationships, and building positive self-esteem based on personal and cultural strengths. The purpose of these groups, from an Afrocentric perspective, is the capacity of the group to help adolescent African American males develop the skills they need to make a positive transition from adolescence to manhood [Hill 1992], and to help each youth develop a network of peers with similar values to socialize among as he incorporates new and constructive attitudes and behaviors into his lifestyle [Oliver 1989]. Primary attention during group sessions is given to enabling these youths to gain knowledge and positive behaviors that help them eliminate involvement in gangs and the effects of negative peer pressure; correct misperceptions regarding the African American race and culture; discard distorted images of manhood, fatherhood, and male-female relationships; avoid escalating acts of violence and crimes; ignore substance abuse; and give up delinquent behaviors and low educational and occupational aspirations that create disruptive life crises for them and the community [Isaacs 1992].

Each group comprises 10 to 15 adolescents. The groups meet once a week for two hours in the evening and are led by a trained staff person. Included in the group sessions is an understanding of their ethnicity as African Americans. *Nguzo Saba* (n-goo-zoo sah'-bah), the African name for what has been called the Seven Principles [Fraser 1994; Karenga 1965], is used to teach youths the principles of spirituality, culture, family, education, economics, community, and youth activities to help them understand themselves, others, and the world in which they live (these principles are explained later in this article.) Many youths develop an increased sense of unity, identity, and purpose as they understand and begin to incorporate the principles of Nguzo Saba into their worldview [Fraser 1994; Assante 1990; Bennett 1993; Billingsley 1992].

The group sessions are defined by the modules listed below. Youths participate in each module as they progress through the program. The modules support the Afrocentric principles of Nguzo Saba. A high level of knowledge enhancement is achieved through interactive techniques, such as role-playing and ceremonial rituals in each module.

Group module sessions are based on the following topics:
- African American Culture and Heritage
- Principles and Guides for Living
- African American Lifestyles
- Oppression and Racism
- Adolescent Stages of Development
- Male Physical Development
- Female Physical Development
- Birth Control
- Fatherhood/Marriage
- Physical Health
- Diet and Exercise
- HIV/AIDS

- Drugs and Other Harmful Substances
- Entrepreneurial Development
- Win-Win Relationships
- Mediation as a Means to Self-Development and Self-Control

Adolescents receive a certificate for completing each module. Upon completion of all modules, the youths participate in a formal rite of passage ceremony with a celebration consisting of food, music, a Karamu (the Kiswahili name for a celebration), and demonstrations or exhibits of the skills [Hill 1992] they obtained while in the program. Family and members of the adolescents' community are invited to witness the knowledge, attitudes, and skills the youths have learned. The event is planned by the youths with assistance from the group leader as needed. The planning of the event by the youths affords them the opportunity to demonstrate their creativity, and to engage in collective work and responsibility.

Family Enhancement and Empowerment

The Family Enhancement and Empowerment component includes two interventions: Monthly Parent Training seminars and the Semiannual Family Therapy Retreat. This program component is a complementary service to In-Home Family Therapy. The objectives for these interventions are (1) to increase parental competence in developing quality parent-child relationships that strengthen family bonding, and (2) to increase parents' abilities to advocate for their families and communities. The family enhancement and empowerment component focuses on reducing parents' inability to control their children; inadequate parenting skills; inadequate or incorrect knowledge about child and youth development; poor parent-child relationships; weak family ties; poor communication skills; and inadequate individual or group strategies for coping with environmental systems (law enforcement, courts, juvenile justice agencies, schools, health clinics, social welfare agencies, mental health agencies, etc.). Coping with community problems (gangs, drug dealers and users, neighborhood crime, and truancy) is also a part of this component.

The Monthly Parent Training (MPT) seminars are an educational treatment intervention that assists parents (1) to identify common issues of parenting and family life, (2) to develop family support networks, (3) to develop community cohesion, and (4) to enhance parenting skills. The MPT seminars include families who are participating in the In-Home Family Therapy component of the Rites of Passage program. One seminar is held every month for two hours in the evening at a community church family center. The location is selected to help families feel comfortable in a familiar environment and to foster a sense of spirituality. Child care and transportation services are provided, putting an end to obstacles that can often keep entire families from participating.

The MPT seminars include the following educational topics; (1) African American Family in Context, (2) Adolescent Development, (3) Effective Communication, (4) Home Management and Effective Discipline, (5) Health, and (6) Developing Family or Community Businesses. The topics are presented from an Afrocentric worldview, using the principles of Nguzo Saba, to enable the participants to understand that spirituality, culture, family, education, economics, community, and youth activities are critical to the survival of African American children, families, and the race [Fraser 1994; Assante 1990; Bennett 1993; Billingsley 1992]. A variety of training modes are used in the MPT seminars. Audiovisual aids, role-playing, psychodrama, and nonverbal therapeutic techniques are used to encourage families to identify concerns and to practice solution-oriented behavior as the various topics are presented. Family members are provided with written materials at each session, including pamphlets on effective parenting of African American children.

The Semiannual Family Therapy Retreat was developed (1) to enhance bonding between African American families and between members within families, and (2) to enhance the spiritual growth of individuals in an effort to create a sense of community. This intervention emphasizes the Afrocentric belief of tribalism. Tribalism is the belief in being faithful to one's own kind, defined by ethnicity, language, culture, and religion. The identifiable values of tribalism are strong ethnic identity and a belief in self-help, hard work, thrift, education, and the family [Naisbitt 1994]. The activities for the retreat include (1) cooperative recreational groups, (2) educational groups (i.e., business development, community resource development and networking skills), (3) family therapy and self-help groups, and (4) spiritual ceremonies.

The families attending the Semiannual Family Therapy Retreat are composed of family members who participated weekly for six months in the In-Home Family Therapy intervention. The retreats are held on a weekend in the fall and spring of the year in a nonurban location. The retreats include full conference accommodations (lodging, meals, recreation, and meeting rooms). Group transportation is provided for participants wishing to attend. Child care is available during group sessions for families with young children.

In summary, the Rites of Passage program provides individual and collective interventions from an Afrocentric worldview to high-risk adolescent African American males and their families to reduce and/or eliminate negative lifestyle behaviors. The following section describes the life skills adolescent African American males learn to use as long-term behaviors to avoid the juvenile justice system, and to maintain themselves as productive members of their families, communities, race, and society.

Life Skills

Life skills development for adolescent African American males is critical to their successful functioning in society. The Afrocentric worldview provides life skills development in regards to values clarification, education, economics, spirituality, and self-pride. African American adolescent males learn to use the principles of Nguzo Saba to problem-solve effectively and to make the decisions necessary to manage their behavior.

In values clarification, the adolescent is confronted with making choices about the individuals (peers and adults) with whom he will associate. Adolescent African American males learn to rely on the Nguzo Saba's principles of self-determination (Kujichagulia) and creativity (Kuumba) as their worldview in making such decisions. Specifically, the principle of self-determination teaches the adolescent to be committed to defining and developing himself, instead of being defined and developed by others. The principle of creativity teaches the adolescent to be committed to building rather than destroying, to engaging in positive action, and to pursuing a continual search for new and fresh ideas that can improve his life and the lives of others [Fraser 1994; Assante 1990; Bennett 1993; Billingsley 1992]. Essentially, when confronted with the pressures of peers or gangs that wish to recruit him to engage in negative behaviors, the adolescent must use the value base of these principles. The vignette below illustrates values clarification.

> Jamal, a 15-year-old African American male, is a participant in the Rites of Passage program. Jamal is known to the juvenile justice system for handgun violations and car theft. He was referred to the program by the court. One evening, Jamal was asked by his old buddies to take a ride with them. Jamal declined the ride. They began to call him names, inferring he was no longer a man, and one youth pulled a gun on him. He escaped from the youth and ran. During an individual counseling session with his therapist, he discussed the incident. He said that his decision to escape was based on the principles of self-determination and creativity and he was no longer going to allow them [his past buddies] to define who he was. He said it was clear they were planning to rob a store in an African American

neighborhood and wanted him to be the driver. Jamal said he no longer wanted to destroy his people and their communities.

Education is a life skill that is critical to the well-being of adolescent African American males in our society. Often these youths have to make a choice between immediate or delayed gratification of a desire. To incorporate as a life skill the long-term benefits of completing one's education, African American adolescents are encouraged to use as their guide the principle of purpose (Nia). The principle of purpose teaches the adolescent to define his goals and motives in terms of what can best benefit the collective society [Fraser 1994; Assante 1990; Bennett 1993; Billingsley 1992]. The principle of purpose helps the adolescent examine the merits of education in relation to being able to achieve more over a longer period of time. In addition, the adolescent learns that his education can not only improve his life, but the lives of others. This principle also allows the adolescent to assess his education goals and possibly pursue a college or vocational program during high school.

African American adolescent males are encouraged to rely on the principles of collective work and responsibilities (Ujima) and cooperative economics (Ujamaa) to avoid negative economic lifestyles. The principle of collective work and responsibilities provides the adolescent with a sense that people must work together for the common good, even though each person accepts responsibility for both the successes and failures of the group [Fraser 1994; Assante 1990; Bennett 1993; Billingsley 1992]. The adolescent learns from these principles that high economic rewards obtained illegally often lead to failures that the youth must suffer alone.

The youths experience a series of sessions where they are taught in a collective experience the skills of painting, plumbing, and electrical repair. The principle of cooperative economics helps the adolescent to understand that wealth, talents, and resources can be shared for the common good [Fraser 1994;

Assante 1990; Bennett 1993; Billingsley 1992]. The youths learn that the cooperative economic efforts of individuals provide a reciprocal relationship for building better economic foundations and occupational alternatives. From both principles, the adolescent is encouraged to appreciate the importance of being a part of the mainstream job market and the benefits for himself and others.

Youths need to incorporate a sense of spirituality as a part of their life skills. The principle of unity (Umoja) provides the adolescent with a concept for developing his spiritual self, and a sense of togetherness and collective action among family, community, nation, and one's ethnic group [Fraser 1994; Assante 1990; Bennett 1993; Billingsley 1992]. Each session incorporates a unity circle—the holding of each other's hands. During this opening ritual a series of nondenominational spiritual readings are done and each youth is asked to call out the name of a deceased person, either a family member, a friend, or a historical person of African descent. This ritual demonstrates respect and honor for African ancestors. The youths are also reminded that all interactions are sacred [life is a spiritual phenomenon to be lived from a moral perspective] and that they are children of the Creator.

Finally, the principle of faith (Imani) has the potential to provide the adolescent with a sense of self and group pride. The principle of faith provides the adolescent with a belief in African Americans as individuals and as a people with abilities and the right to control their own destinies as a race of people [Fraser 1994; Assante 1990; Bennett 1993; Billingsley 1992]. Program participants are provided with biographies of famous people of African descent. Various problem-solving and decision-making scenarios are created in which the youths are required to think, feel, and behave as one of these historical figures. As African American adolescent males experience these exercises, they can begin to eliminate the negative misperceptions about themselves and their race, and develop a sense of self-pride and a belief that their own personal life has within it the potential to improve.

Conclusion

While no one approach is the answer to the myriad social problems facing African American adolescent males, an Afrocentric approach is a vehicle for helping to reestablish a sense of self-dignity, self-worth, spirituality, and community among this youth population. It is imperative that individuals working with African American adolescent males provide culturally relevant programs and services on a consistent basis to these youths. It is also incumbent upon agencies to employ an array of African American professionals and nonprofessionals to act as racial role models in the delivery of services to African American adolescent males in the juvenile justice system. Finally, policymakers must be made aware continually of the needs of these children and the necessity to fund programs that use an Afrocentric approach. ♦

References

Akbar, N. (1984). Afrocentric social services for liberation. *Journal of Black Studies, 14,* 395–413.

Assante, K. A. *(1988). Afrocentricity.* Trenton, NJ: African World Press.

Bennett, W. J. (1993). *The book of virtues.* New York: Simon & Schuster.

Billingsley, A. (1992). *Climbing Jacob's ladder: The enduring legacy of African American families.* New York: Simon & Schuster.

Daly, A., Jennings, J., Beckett, J. 0., & Leashore, B. R. (1995). Effective coping strategies of African Americans. *Social Work, 40,* 240–248.

Everett, J. E., Chipungu, S. S., & Leashore, B. R. (Eds.). (1991). *Child welfare: An Africentric perspective.* New Brunswick, NJ: Rutgers University Press.

Fraser, G. (1994). *Success runs in our race.* New York: Avon Books.

Harvey, A. R. (1994). Afrocentric model of prevention with African American adolescent males: The MAAT rites of passage program. In J. Rauch (Ed.), *Community-based, family centered services in a changing health care environment: Selected papers from a conference held June 6 & 7, 1994, Baltimore, Maryland* (pp. 115–130). Baltimore, MD: University of Maryland at Baltimore School of Social Work.

Hill, P. (1992). *Coming of age: African American male rites of passage.* Chicago: African American Images.

Isaacs, M. R. (1992). *Violence: The impact of community violence on African American children and families.* Arlington, VA: National Center for Education in Maternal and Child Health.

Karenga, M. (1965). *Kwanzaa: Origin, concepts and practice.* Los Angeles: Kawaida Publications.

Karenga, M. (1987). Towards a sociology of Maatian ethics: Literature and context. In M. Karenga (Ed.), *Reconstructing Kemetic culture: Papers, perspectives, projects.* Los Angeles: University of Sankore Press.

Mbiti, J. (1969). *African religions and philosophy.* New York: Praeger.

Naisbitt, J. (1994). *Global paradox.* New York: William Morrow.

Oliver, W. (1989). Black males and social problems: Prevention through Afrocentric socialization. *Journal of Black Studies, 20*(1), 15–39.

Perkins, U. E. (1986). *Harvesting new generations: The positive development of Black youth.* Chicago: Third World Press.

Pinkett, J. (1993). Spirituality in the African-American community. In L. L. Goddard (Ed.), *An African-centered model of prevention for African-American youth at high risk* (CSAP Technical Report No.6) (pp. 79-86). Rockville, MD: U.S. Department of Health and Human Services.

Schiele, J. H. (1994). Afrocentricity as an alternative world view for equality. *Journal of Progressive Human Services, 5*(1), 5–25.

11
Same-Race Practice: Do We Expect Too Much or Too Little?

Bernadette Jeffrey Fletcher

To add to same-race practice knowledge, this article explores practitioners' perceptions, expectations, and service recommendations for troubled youths age 12 and age 16 along racial, gender, and age dimensions. A random sample of African American members of the National Association of Social Workers rated case analogues in which client characteristics varied by experimental design. The more positively social workers perceived the youths, the higher the social workers' expectations of outcomes after intervention. Social workers' expectations for better outcomes were more forceful than their perceptions of those outcomes. Male social workers' expectations for African American male youths emphasize within-group male hopefulness. Additionally, African American social workers recommend intervention more strongly for Caucasian youths than for African American youths. Practice implications of these findings are discussed.

Bernadette Jeffrey Fletcher, Ph.D., is Assistant Professor, School of Social Work, University of Pittsburgh, Pittsburgh, PA. This article is based on a dissertation study submitted to the faculty at the Graduate School of Social Work in partial fulfillment of the requirements for the degree of doctor of philosophy.

On any given day, three million children or more, in communities throughout this nation, experience situations and conditions that place them in or near crisis. Under this tremendous burden, social workers and child welfare practitioners have the responsibility of responding to children and their families by using a wide array of service interventions in ways that ameliorate distress.

African American clients often struggle against a number of hostile consequences, intended and unintended, resulting from this country's social definitions of race, age, and gender. Surprisingly, race- and gender-related perceptions and expectations remain a pivotal practice concern for workers [Jones et al. 1995; Davis & Gelsomino 1994; Davis & Proctor 1989; Devore & Schlessinger 1996]. When these consequences converge in practice settings, they often tend to produce fractionated, hostile client-worker relationships that hinder helping. Particularly during initial case planning activities and first-time appointments, a client's or worker's race, age, and gender may interact and negatively influence the help [Dana 1993; Davis & Gelsomino 1994; Fletcher 1995; Green 1995; Kavanagh & Kennedy 1992; Lehman & Salovey 1990; Ingram 1986]. To teach social workers how to deliver help in a culturally competent fashion to non-Caucasian clients, generalist practice knowledge emphasizes content deemed relevant to Caucasians during cross-race helping [Lum 1996]. Much less practice knowledge emphasizes content relevant to non-Caucasian social workers during same-race helping, particularly for African Americans.

When working with African American adolescents 12 and 16 years old, it is useful to identify and understand the early behavioral and situational indicators of their need for intervention. Additionally, it is important to examine how the convergence of client and worker characteristics of race, age, and gender may influence pre-intake processes.

A random sample of members of the National Association of Social Workers rated case analogues in which client characteristics varied by experimental design. This article analyzes only the ratings of African American social workers. This analogue study examined the influence of adolescents' race, age, and gender on the social workers' initial perceptions of the adolescents, the social workers' expectations of change for the adolescents after intervention, and how strongly the social workers would recommend an array of mental health interventions for the adolescents.

Same-Race Practice

Dana [1993], Everett et al. [1991], and Green [1995] emphasize the power and importance of a within-group group or *emic* perspective when delivering culturally competent services with diverse client groups. An emic perspective includes a structural understanding of social systems [Gould 1991] as well as highly specific cultural knowledge, self-awareness, and interpretations pertaining to the nature of human and transhuman existence encompassing a group's worldview [Dana 1993; Green 1995]. It enriches social workers' assessments and the planning and delivery of client interventions [Dana 1993; Green 1995]. Traditional social work education that uses only a highly abstract global or *etic* perspective lacks practice robustness in the cross-racial-cultural practice encounter. An emic view is used to guide a worker's observations, categorizations, and recordings of client behaviors before selecting the interventions that will facilitate genuine help giving [Dana 1993].

African Americans, currently this nation's largest non-Caucasian population group, have unique historical and contemporary experiences, despite obvious group heterogeneity. African American social workers, as do other social workers of color, have an emic perspective, relating to their intergroup and extragroup status and have emic assumptions about racism and related matters [Sue 1990]. Boyd-Franklin [1989] believed that for African Americans, the issue of race is almost never neutral and is present on both a conscious and unconscious level. It is a challenge for a worker to manage his or her own experiences of racial incongruities, or to struggle to maintain a judicious use of self when practicing with African American clients [Hunt 1987; Williams & Halgin 1995]. Variability in African American worker-client assumptions about racial identity, however, may also become the context that creates conflicts [Hunt 1987; Williams & Halgin 1995] in same-race practice. For example, when an African American practitioner begins an intervention with an African American client, there may be assumptions of cultural similarity in family background, economic experience, and political ideologies [Williams & Halgin 1995]. If neither displays attitudes, behaviors, or communication styles that confirm those assumptions, the client may become wary of the worker and refuse help. Since African American clients generally expect social workers to become involved with them when giving help and may become suspicious if they sense that the social worker is maintaining strict distances, African American social workers sensitively modulate their practice accordingly [Boyd-Franklin 1989].

According to Franklin [1989], many providers of mental health services lack a degree of credibility and remain suspect in African American communities. He argued that African American adolescents' attitudes toward such services reflect their communities' suspicion. Davis and Gelsomino [1994], mindful that those dynamics hinder helping, described those attitudes as "racial in-group/out-group mistrust." In the past, some have called on the mental health system to reevaluate its interventions with African Americans and develop interventions that are culturally syntonic [Ani 1994; Thomas & Sillen 1972; Tyler et al. 1991; Willie et al. 1973; Willie et al. 1995; Wilson 1993].

Race and Troubled Youths

Currently, practitioners are expressing their concern about the growing distress of African American adolescents, particularly the varying rates of successful outcomes after intervention [Gibbs 1990; Moore 1996]. Today, African Americans under the age of 25 represent about 50% of the entire African American population [Gibbs 1990]. Furthermore, half of these children and adolescents are living in poverty and account for more than one-third of all the poor children and adolescents in this country [Children's Defense Fund 1991]. Because of overwhelming poverty and racism, these children and youths will face serious problems as they age. These problems may ultimately increase their vulnerability to mental illness [Comer 1995]. Their experience of violence and poverty produces stress that increases the likelihood of their suffering, regardless of the presence or absence of pathology in their parents [Billingsley 1992; Willie et al. 1995].

Meyers [1989] noted that certain acting-out behaviors that would be considered clinically meaningful if displayed by Caucasian adolescents appear to be considered normative or clinically insignificant behaviors when displayed by African American adolescents. Furthermore, Gibbs [1990] reported that a number of African American adolescents are purposively directed through the juvenile justice systems rather than being served in mental health systems. The Children's Defense Fund [1991] reported that, African American males in out-of-home care are five times more likely to be in juvenile justice systems than for Caucasian males. Those in the justice system are less likely to receive comprehensive care and their psychosocial problems are likely to be further exacerbated [Gibbs 1990].

The literature reports that, despite similar personal and economic characteristics in cases of troubled adolescents, service delivery differences occur along racial lines [Benedict et al. 1989; Close 1983; Stehno 1982]. In comparison with Caucasian adolescents, African American adolescents have been less likely to receive mental health services, more likely to be placed in the juvenile justice system, and more likely to be in out-of-home care than to be served in their own homes [Benedict et al. 1989; Close 1983; Meyers 1989; Stehno 1982]. This may suggest that many troubled African American adolescents are not receiving mental health and other social services that might prevent crime and incarceration. Though multiple factors may contribute to the fact that African American adolescents are less likely to receive mental health and in-home child welfare services and are more likely to be under the supervision of the juvenile justice system than Caucasian adolescents [Comer & Hill 1985; Cross et al. 1989; Gruber 1980; Stehno 1982], the judgments of social workers who are assessing and recommending services for adolescents often have a significant role. If one considers that judges in the juvenile justice system and practitioners in other systems depend upon the assessments and recommendations of these social workers and child welfare practitioners, then it is easy to understand that social workers' recommendations could factor into this larger framework.

Worker Expectations

Devore and Schlessinger [1996] included as vital preintervention processes the reviewing, synthesizing, and ordering of factual and emotional client information, and the client's condition and route to the agency. This preintervention activity, when understood as information processing, does include both affective (perceptions) and social cognitive (expectations) components. When planning for client services, the influence of client characteristics may well be as important as the presenting problems [Corrigan et al. 1980; Fisher & Miller 1973; Wills 1978; Wodarski 1981].

When the practitioner's perceptions of a client's traits and the practitioner's expectancy of outcomes interact, they can influence the practitioner's recommendations for services [Turk & Salovey 1986]. In a practice situation, the practitioner subjectively pictures a client and makes judgments about a client's situation; this judgment affects outcomes [Lehman & Salovey 1990; Martin et al. 1977]. Lehman and Salovey [1990] found that initial perceptions may influence subsequent judgments and expectations related to intervention. For example, intake summaries affect practitioners' expectations for their client's therapeutic success. As such, in the initial contact, a social worker's perceptions and expectations have significance for the processing of information about a new person or a new situation. Casas [1985] discussed racial/ethnic practitioners' expectations as merely reflections of stereotypes that are found in society at large. Those cultural amplifiers that affect so-called troubled African American adolescents are perhaps the same cultural amplifiers that affect professional African American social workers, paraprofessionals, and child welfare practitioners.

Social Information Processing Theory

Although the social work practice literature acknowledges the social "lenses" such as gender, sexual orientation, culture, and disability through which practitioners view the world, social psychology has begun to apply concepts from social information-processing theory for understanding how those social lenses may directly or indirectly affect social behavior. Information-processing theory offers a social cognitive schema that breaks down how individuals process initial information—decoding, encoding, recalling, and judging—in ways that allow them to function in the world [Milner 1993; Taylor 1993]. In new situations, information-processing organizes what is perceived (decoding), what is remembered of the perceptions (encoding), and how those memories (recalling) are understood (judging) [Taylor 1993]. In direct practice, practitioners' perceptions of clients' traits at the initial point of contact constitute the organized or the initially decoded information. That decoded trait information aids in information-processing by locating a client in a group—racial/gender/age—and then activating frames of reference [Hamilton et al. 1990] (decoding) about characteristics of that group [Dovido et al. 1986; Stangor et al. 1992]. Through the process of interpretation of recalled information and through inference of meaning, expectations mold what people are willing to do [Milner 1993; Taylor 1993].

Using this idea, race, age, and gender can be understood to be social lenses, a specialized social filter, a social cognitive schema through which every initial human interaction—direct or indirect, covert or overt—is viewed, and through which information is processed. People respond to this specialized social filter or social schema prior to social interchange or exchange. In this manner, the social lenses of race, gender, and age mediate human interaction. The lenses are reflexive, simultaneously allowing a view of one's self and others. The lenses combine the external reality of what is seen with the internal reality of what is seen to give meaning to perceptions of others before any decision making [Turk & Salovey 1986].

In practice settings, clients' race may influence social workers' initial perceptions and expectations. Before treatment and at or before intake, the lenses of race and gender may influence initial decisions in such a way that they are based primarily on race. That pre-intake influence may contribute to whether a client gains or is denied initial access to human service systems. This concept will be used to explore the influence of race on initial service planning for troubled African American adolescents.

Methodology and Sample

Study packets were mailed to a disproportionate stratified random sample of social workers who were active members of the National Association of Social Workers (NASW) on June 20, 1992 and living in the United States.

Of the 102,684 social workers who were members of NASW and in direct practice on that date, 6,792 were African American. Of those 6,792 African Americans, 375 were male and 6,417 were female. At the request of the author, NASW provided a sample of 1,500 social workers who indicated their primary practice was in the following 14 selected areas: children and youth; community organization and planning; family services; corrections and criminal; group services to the aged; developmental disabilities and retardation; occupational/ medical/ health care; mental health; public assistance and welfare; school social work; and alcohol/substance abuse. Social workers practicing in these areas were thought to be the most likely to be accustomed to the content in the case analogues (described below). The sample of 1,500 consisted of 375 African American males, and randomly selected samples of 375 each for African American females, Caucasian males, and Caucasian females who indicated their primary practice was in one of the previously selected 14 direct practice areas. From the sample of 1,500, the author randomly selected a list of 960 who were used in the study.

In all, eight of the 960 study packets were undeliverable because of address errors or because the addressee had moved away and left no forwarding address. Of the 952 packets that were delivered, 326 were returned. If respondents did not answer at least one-third of the items on each part of the questionnaire, they were dropped for purposes of statistical analyses. This occurred in four cases. In addition, eight social workers who identified themselves as other than Caucasian or African American, or who did not identify their race at all, were dropped from the analyses. The remaining cases ($N = 314$) were analyzed.

Pearson's chi-square statistic was computed to determine whether the study respondents were significantly different from the sample in race and gender, and chi-squares were computed to determine whether returns were significantly different by race of respondent and race of adolescent. Neither chi-square was significant. Finally, Goodness-of-Fit chi-square was computed for the eight analogue descriptions of adolescents. No statistically significant difference was found between the expected frequency of returns ($n = 39$) for any of the eight descriptions of the analogue adolescent [$\chi^2(7, n = 141) = 1.35, p = .98$]. Using these tests with these data yields no findings that would suggest selection bias.

The findings reported here are based on the combined data for only the 141 African American social workers. Responses were coded for each respondent and data analysis was completed using the Statistical Package for Social Sciences. In the 141 questionnaires' cases that were analyzed, 73 (53%) of the respondents were female and 68 (47%) were male. Women were somewhat more likely to respond to this study than men. The differences, however, were not statistically significant $[\chi^2(1, n = 141) = 2.80, p = .10]$. Slightly under 32% of the social workers practiced in the mental health field. Another 53% practiced either in services for children and youths, family services, medical/health care, and/or school social work. The majority of the respondents (96%) had an M.S.W. degree as their highest credential. None of the study respondents were 70 years old or older. No statistically significant difference was found between the expected frequency of returns ($n = 78.5$) by gender of social worker/adolescent.

The author developed a case analogue describing a troubled adolescent. The analogue read: "Mary [or Mark], a 12- [or 16-] year-old, is a slightly overweight, unkempt Caucasian [or African American] 'troubled adolescent' who has frequent arguments with teachers, parents, and adult neighbors. She [or he] has temper outbursts that have been increasing in frequency and duration over the past six months and has been heard to complain about sleeping poorly. She [or he] has average intelligence but has missed two weeks of school during the last nine weeks. Mary [or Mark] has just become sexually active but it is unclear if she [or he] has a steady boyfriend [or girlfriend]. More recently, she [or he] has been seen in the company of 'rowdy' friends. She [or he] is now being evaluated for counseling and/or other services."

In addition, the author developed three checklists: the Client Adjectives Checklist (CAC), the Social Worker Expectancy Inventory (SWEI), and the Recommended Interventions Checklist (RIC).* Cronbach's alpha for the CAC, SWEI, and RIC were .90, .94, and .90 respectively.

---

* For a detailed explanation of the development of the CAC, SWEI, and RIC, see Fletcher [1995].

TABLE 1

Mean and Standard Deviation of Ratings on the Client Adjectives Checklist by Gender of Respondent and Race, Age, and Gender of Adolescent (N = 141)

	Gender of Respondent			
Adolescent	Female		Male	
	M	SD	M	SD
African American				
16-year-old male	2.32	.76	2.16	.68
12-year-old male	2.53	1.01	2.85	1.26
16-year-old female	2.83	.84	3.00	.99
12-year-old female	2.45	.79	3.15	1.19
Caucasian				
16-year-old male	3.08	.38	2.65	.92
12-year-old male	2.67	.69	3.22	.66
16-year-old female	2.74	.60	2.86	.74
12-year-old female	2.21	.69	2.76	.73

Note: Perceptions were rated on a 6-point scale (1 = *not at all*, 6 = *extremely*). The higher the score, the stronger the recommendation for services. The higher the score, the more favorable the perception.

The Client Adjectives Checklist

The CAC consists of 11 adjectives that describe personal traits. To determine how favorably social workers perceived the personal traits of analogue adolescents, scores on the 11 items that loaded on the CAC were summed and divided by the number of items for which there were ratings. Table 1 displays those mean ratings. The higher the total score, the more positively the client was viewed.

The Social Worker Expectancy Inventory

The SWEI has nine items describing workers' expectancies of adolescents' outcome after intervention. To determine how high social workers' expectations were, scores on the nine items of the SWEI were summed and divided by the number of items for which there were ratings. Table 2 displays those mean ratings. The higher the score, the higher the expectations.

TABLE 2

Mean and Standard Deviation of Ratings on the Social Worker Expectancy Inventory by Gender of Respondent and Race, Age, and Gender of Adolescent (*N* = 141)

| Adolescent | Gender of Respondent | | | |
| | Female | | Male | |
	M	SD	M	SD
African American				
16-year-old male	5.54	.92	6.16	1.55
12-year-old male	5.35	1.62	5.94	.97
16-year-old female	5.10	.76	5.25	1.20
12-year-old female	2.62	.89	5.01	1.04
Caucasian				
16-year-old male	5.63	.76	5.38	1.09
12-year-old male	4.71	1.14	5.21	1.61
16-year-old female	5.01	.73	5.39	1.18
12-year-old female	5.69	1.34	5.02	1.18

Note: Expectations were rated on an 8-point scale (1= *not at all expected*, 8 = *extremely expected*). The higher the score, the higher the expectations.

The Recommended Interventions Checklist

The RIC provides a 20-item index measure of how strongly social workers will recommend interventions on the basis of troubled behaviors related to ego-dynamic problems and characterological problems. To determine the strength of social workers' recommendations for behaviors defined as acting out, scores on the 20 items were summed and divided by the number of items for which there were ratings. Table 3 displays those mean ratings. The higher the score, the stronger the recommendations.

Analysis

A four-factor analysis of variance was used to identify any overall main effect or any interaction effect of gender of social workers and race (Caucasian or African American), age (12 or 16 years old), and gender of adolescents on the perceptions, expectations,

TABLE 3

Mean and Standard Deviation of Ratings on the Recommendation Inventory Checklists by Gender of Respondent and Race, Age, and Gender of Adolescent (*N* = 141)

| | Gender of Respondent | | | |
| Adolescent | Female | | Male | |
	M	SD	M	SD
African American				
16-year-old male	5.33	1.37	5.94	2.16
12-year-old male	5.11	1.61	5.56	1.48
16-year-old female	5.83	1.18	5.03	1.01
12-year-old female	4.69	2.08	5.36	1.33
Caucasian				
16-year-old male	5.78	1.49	5.95	1.00
12-year-old male	5.89	1.54	5.86	.97
16-year-old female	5.35	1.25	5.39	.99
12-year-old female	6.80	.95	6.31	.53

Note: Recommendations were rated on an 8-point scale (1 = *not at all recommend*, 8 = *strongly recommend*). The higher the score, the stronger the recommendation for services.

and recommendations checklist ratings. Table 4 displays the ANOVA summary for social workers' perceptions of analogue adolescents, table 5 displays the ANOVA summary for social workers' expectations for analogue adolescents, and table 6 displays the ANOVA summary for social workers' recommendations for analogue adolescents.

Because two marginal interactions were found between workers' favorable ratings for analogue adolescents, a liberal approach was used. A marginally significant interaction between workers' gender and adolescents' age occurred ($p = .055$). Table 7 displays those ratings. A marginally significant interaction between gender and race of adolescents also occurred ($p = .061$). Table 8 displays those ratings.

Social workers' ratings of expectations of adolescent outcomes were more powerful than their ratings of favorable adolescent traits. There was a positive correlation between measures for

TABLE 4

Analysis of Variance of the Relationship Between Perceptions of Adolescent and Gender of Respondent and Race, Age, and Gender of Adolescent

Source	df	MS	F	P
Social Worker Gender [A]	1	1.463	2.134	.147
Adolescent Age [B]	1	.018	.35	.871
Adolescent Gender [C]	1	.024	.52	.852
Adolescent Race [D]	1	.356	3.77	.472
AxB	1	2.581	1.56	.055
AxC	1	1.070	.03	.214
AxD	1	.022	3.13	.858
BxC	1	2.147	.83	.079
BxD	1	.569	3.59	.364
CxD	1	2.458	.03	.061
AxBxC	1	.023	.11	.855
AxBxD	1	.074	.12	.742
AxCxD	1	.085	.25	.725
BxCxD	1	.170	.49	.619
AxBxCxD	1	.33		.486
Within Term	130	.658		

Note: A = Gender of Social Worker; B = Age of Youth; C = Gender of Youth;
D = Race of Youth

perceptions and expectations ($r = .21$, $p = .016$, $n = 141$). A significant four-way interaction between workers' gender and race, age, and gender of adolescents occurred ($p = .015$). Female social workers held the highest expectations for 12-year-old Caucasian females ($M = 5.69$), and the lowest expectations for 12-year-old African American females ($M = 2.62$). Contrariwise, male social workers held the highest expectations for 16-year-old African American males ($M = 6.16$), and the lowest for 12-year-old females ($M = 5.02$). Additionally, the more positively social workers viewed adolescents, the higher their expectations of adolescent outcomes after intervention ($p = .015$)

Finally, adolescents' race and age interacted significantly ($p = .015$) in workers' recommendations for care. Social workers more strongly recommended intervention for Caucasian adolescents than for African American adolescents. Table 9 displays those ratings.

TABLE 5

Analysis of Variance of the Relationship Between Expectations of Outcomes After Intervention and Gender of Respondent and Race, Age, and Gender of Adolescent

Source	df	MS	F	P
Social Worker Gender [A]	1	7.67	5.67	.019
Adolescent Age [B]	1	8.05	5.95	.016
Adolescent Gender [C]	1	12.28	9.08	.003
Adolescent Race [D]	1	.90	.67	.416
AxB	1	2.30	1.70	.195
AxC	1	.66	.48	.488
AxD	1	7.58	5.60	.020
BxC	1	.70	.52	.471
BxD	1	3.04	2.25	.136
CxD	1	13.55	10.02	.002
AxBxC	1	.31	.23	.632
AxBxD	1	3.47	2.57	.112
AxCxD	1	2.18	1.61	.207
BxCxD	1	7.12	5.27	.024
AxBxCxD	1	8.27	6.12	.015
Within Term	130	1.58		

Note: A = Gender of Social Worker; B = Age of Youth; C = Gender of Youth; D = Race of Youth

Discussion

Expectations and Perceptions

African American social workers' rated their expectations for positive adolescent outcomes higher than their favorable perceptions of adolescents. For African American social workers, expectations represent not only a view of here and now but a look ahead to the future. This may well represent African American social workers' hopefulness that troubled adolescents can move beyond current conditions of distress to future betterment. It implies that if adolescents are given time, they could make a difference for their good. It makes positive assumptions that things will get better. As such, workers' expectations for positive adolescent outcomes after services really connect to the

TABLE 6

**Analysis of Variance of the Relationship Between Strength of
Recommendations for Intervention and Gender of Respondent and Race,
Age, and Gender of Adolescent**

Source	df	MS	F	P
Social Worker Gender [A]	1	.33	.20	.659
Adolescent Age [B]	1	.35	.21	.647
Adolescent Gender [C]	1	.14	.08	.773
Adolescent Race [D]	1	9.95	5.99	.016
AxB	1	.21	.12	.726
AxC	1	1.51	.91	.342
AxD	1	.96	.58	.449
BxC	1	2.47	1.49	.226
BxD	1	6.68	4.02	.047
CxD	1	.77	.46	.498
AxBxC	1	.52	.31	.577
AxBxD	1	2.02	1.22	.272
AxCxD	1	.21	.13	.723
BxCxD	1	2.42	1.46	.230
AxBxCxD	1	1.32	.79	.375
Within Term	130	1.69		

Note: A = Gender of Social Worker; B = Age of Youth; C = Gender of Youth;
D = Race of Youth

social work strengths perspectives [Saleebey 1992]. Social workers' expectations for positive change mutually empower both worker and client during the moment one reaches out and the other responds. According to Weick [1992], when adolescents' or any other persons' positive capacities are supported, they are likely to act on their strengths. This implies that African American workers' expectations can be empowering for adolescents. African American male social workers' expectation ratings for African American males were particularly telling because the ratings emphasized within-group male hopefulness. They gave highest and second-highest ratings for positive adolescent outcomes (for example, better self-confidence, self-maintenance, and interpersonal relationships) for 16-year-old and 12-year-old African American males respectfully. This

TABLE 7

Respondent Favorable Perceptions of Adolescent by Gender of Social Worker and Age of Adolescent (*N* = 141)

	Gender of Social Worker	
Age of Adolescent	*Female*	*Male*
12 years old	2.52	3.03
16 years old	2.70	2.70

Note: Perceptions were rated on a 6-point scale (1 = *not at all*, 6 = *extremely*). The higher the score, the stronger the recommendation for services. The higher the score, the more favorable the perception.

within-group male hopefulness toward African American males is in sharp contrast to society's rather hopeless expectations for them. African American male social workers believed that troubled African American adolescents, with interventions, could and would do better. They expected adolescents to improve in self-knowledge and self-management, in communicating easily with others and in being effectively assertive, in experiencing self-acceptance, in making effective decisions, in withstanding outside pressures, and in accepting criticism. African American male social workers' expectations for Caucasians were higher than their expectations for African American females. Why higher within-group-hopefulness did not include same-race females, however, is unclear. Further study is needed.

African American female social workers' highest expectation ratings for 12-year-old Caucasian females but lowest for 12-year-old African American females may reflect an overall gender-hopefulness that does not extend to within the group. Over the years, gender equity has seemed to be within the reach of Caucasian women but just out of the reach of African American women [Hacker 1992]. Although why African American women's expectation ratings occurred as they did remains unclear, several possible explanations can be made. Some people believe that African American women are lesser beneficiaries of gender equality than Caucasian women. Expectation ratings

TABLE 8

Respondent Favorable Perceptions of Adolescent by Gender and Race of Adolescent (N = 141)

	Gender of Adolescent	
Race of Adolescent	Female	Male
African American	2.83	2.45
Caucasian	2.68	2.86

Note: Perceptions were rated on a 6-point scale (1 = not at all, 6 = extremely). The higher the score, the stronger the recommendation for services. The higher the score, the more favorable the perceptions.

for 12-year-old African American females and 16-year-old African American females may be linked to larger matters related to gender equity for women. Second, women in this study may believe that early acting out in troubled females signals greater limits on their possibilities for beneficial changes. These younger females may have increased vulnerability and potentially succumb to negative experiences such as unwanted pregnancies, violence, and addiction before they have a real chance for living. Also, African American female social workers may be less hopeful that troubled African American female adolescents will fare as well as their African American male counterparts. After considering some of the public negativity that is being directed toward troubled African American female adolescents, some African American social workers may begin to lower their expectations and hopefulness about them.

Social workers' expectations were related to their variable favorable perceptions of adolescents. Social workers viewed an adolescent favorably when he or she possessed likable, reliable, benevolent, empathic, sensitive, sympathetic, optimistic, kind, interesting, warm, and physically attractive traits. Overall, male social workers' ratings of adolescents were somewhat more favorable than female social workers' ratings. This may relate to gender differences in the ways that women view children. Perhaps women were somewhat harder but men somewhat easier

TABLE 9
Recommendations for Interventions by Race and Age of Adolescent

	Age of Adolescent	
Race of Adolescent	12 Years Old	16 Years Old
African American	5.13	5.45
Caucasian	6.08	5.58

Note: Recommendations were rated on an 8-point scales (1 = not at all recommend, 8 = strongly recommend). The higher the score, the stronger the recommendation for services.

in their view of adolescents. As a group, African American social workers' ratings of Caucasian males and African American females were somewhat more favorable than their ratings of Caucasian females and African American males. These ratings, rather than measuring social workers' favorable perceptions of analogue adolescents as individual clients, instead might be linked to African American male workers' recognition of the multiple difficulties facing young African Americans males as a group.

Service Recommendations

Social workers recommended that troubled adolescents receive services for acting-out behaviors. African American service recommendation ratings were stronger for troubled Caucasian adolescents than for African American adolescents. African American social workers' highest service recommendation ratings were made for 12-year-old Caucasians, followed by 16-year-old Caucasians. Troubled 12-year-old African American adolescents received the lowest service recommendation ratings. African American social workers appear to be somewhat wary of intervention with troubled African American adolescents. This is particularly true for the 12 year olds. Although recommendation ratings for African American adolescents became stronger as they aged (from 12 to 16 years of age), ratings for troubled African American adolescents remained lower than those for troubled Caucasian adolescents. This could mean that same-race service planning is a multistep process that includes more than just the types of services that can be offered. For African American social workers, same-race service planning may include an unspoken reluctance surrounding a number of etic issues related to differences in worldview, service delivery trends with African American children, and lingering connections between racism and mental health [Willie et al. 1995].

According to English [1991], ethnic minorities of color, when given an opportunity, will avoid bureaucratic services in favor of resolving their problems themselves. This ethnic minority bias against formal agency-based helpgiving is likely to be shared by all African Americans because it represents the African American legacy of self-help. Social workers know that early formal agency-based intervention with African American children generally destines them to longer stays in child welfare systems and poorer outcomes than Caucasian children. Labeling, irregular use of services, and the diminished opportunities for troubled African American adolescents can create a degree of ambivalence in African American social workers and thereby lessen their willingness to refer adolescents for early intervention.

All social workers have high hopes and great expectations for the children's future. African American male social workers hold a forceful positive same-race within-gender hopefulness that would be especially compelling for troubled African American male adolescents who may be faltering. Although these male social workers may be equally skillful in cross-race and gender helping, it is likely that their positive same-race within-gender hopefulness toward adolescents will more powerfully affect same-race males. Their knowledge and skills make a difference. Troubled adolescents want social workers to be there to help them for their betterment and their future. Unfortunately, few African American male social workers are found in child welfare systems; they are more likely to be employed in justice systems.

Children respond to expectations, whether they are expressed in classrooms, agencies, or at home. One hopeful adult can spark hope in adolescents. When troubled adolescents become hopeful, that hope motivates them to use whatever help and resources come within their reach. Families of hopeful yet troubled adolescents may also become open to intervention and experience a increased willingness to join the social worker in "working out problems." This is what Hunt [1987] identified as the proactive use of the African American experience when pursuing goals. The practice literature confirms that clients often prefer same-race social workers. In child welfare, racial sameness between worker and adolescent can facilitate helpgiving by reducing client suspicion and distrust of agencies when delivering in-home or out-of-home services.

Limitations

The findings of this study are necessarily applicable only to the study sample, but responses are assumed to be comparable to those that African American social workers would make in practice settings. Although the findings are potentially informative, the small sample size affects the accuracy of prediction for the group of African American social workers who are not NASW members. Furthermore, present restrictions in direct practice research on human subjects often forces researchers to explore practice using indirect methods. A qualitative study using participant observation of social workers during their practice with troubled Caucasian and African American adolescents might yield more direct and generalizable results. ♦

References

Anderson, M. L., & Collins, P. H. (1995). *Race, class, and gender: An anthology* (2nd ed.). Belmont, CA: Wadsworth Publishing Company.

Ani, M. (1994). *Yurugu: An African-centered critique of European cultural thought and behavior.* Trenton, NJ: Africa World Press.

Atkinson, D. R., Morten, G., & Sue, D. W. (Eds.). (1993). *Counseling American minorities: A cross-cultural perspective* (4th ed.). Madison, WI: Brown & Benchmark.

Benedict, M. I., White, R. B., Stallings, R., & Cornely, D. A. (1989). Racial differences in health care utilization among children in foster care. *Children and Youth Services Review, 11*, 285–297.

Billingsley, A. (1992). *Climbing Jacob's ladder: The enduring legacy of African American families.* New York: Simon & Schuster.

Boyd-Franklin, N. (1989). *Black families in therapy: A multisystems approach.* New York: Guilford Press.

Casas, M. J. (1985). A reflection on the status of racial/ethnic minority research. *The Counseling Psychologist, 13*, 581–598.

Cheatham, H. E. (1990). Empowering Black families. In H. E. Cheatham & J. B. Stewart, (Eds.), *Black families: Interdisciplinary perspectives.* New Brunswick, NJ: Transaction Publishers.

Children's Defense Fund. (1991). *An opinion maker's guide to children in election year 1992: Leave no child behind.* Washington, DC: Author.

Close, M. M. (1983). Child welfare and people of color: Denial of equal access. *Social Work Research and Abstracts, 16*, 26–33.

Cohen, N. A. (1992). *Child welfare: A multicultural focus.* Boston, MA: Allyn & Bacon.

Comer, J. P. (1995). Racism and African American adolescent development. In C. V. Willie, P. P. Rieker, B. M. Kramer, & B. S. Brown (Eds.), *Mental health, racism, and sexism* (pp. 151–170). Pittsburgh, PA: University of Pittsburgh Press.

Comer, J. P., & Hill, H. (1985). Black children and child psychiatry (special issues). *Journal of American Academy of Child Psychiatry, 24*, 175–181.

Corrigan, J. D., Dell, D., Lewis, K. N., & Schmidt, L. (1980). Counseling as a social influence process: A review. *Journal of Counseling Psychology, 27*, 395–441.

Cross, T. L., Bazron, B. J., Dennis, K W., & Isaacs, M. R. (1989). *Towards a culturally competent system of care. A monograph on effective services for minority children who are severely emotionally disturbed.* Washington, DC: CASSP Technical Assistance Center.

Dana, R. H. (1993). *Multicultural assessment perspectives for professional psychology.* Needham Heights, MA: Allyn & Bacon.

Davis, L. E. & Gelsomino, J. (1994). An assessment of practitioner cross-racial treatment experiences. *Social Work, 39*, 116–123.

Davis, L. E., & Proctor, E. K. (1989). *Race, gender, and class: Guidelines for practice with individuals, families, and groups*. Englewood Cliffs, NJ: Prentice Hall.

Devore, E., & Schlesinger, W. (1996). *Ethnic-sensitive social work practice* (4th ed.). Boston: Allyn & Bacon.

Dovido, J. F., Evans, N., & Tyler, R. B. (1986). Racial stereotypes: The contents of their cognitive representations. *Journal of Experimental Social Psychology, 22*, 22–37.

English, R. A. (1991). Diversity world views among African American families. In J. E. Everett, S. S. Chipungu, & B. R. Leashore (Eds.), *Child welfare: An Africentric perspective* (pp. 19–35). New Brunswick, NJ: Rutgers University Press.

Everett, J. E., Chipungu, S. S., & Leashore, B. R. (Eds.). (1991). *Child welfare: An Africentric perspective*. New Brunswick, NJ: Rutgers University Press.

Fisher, J., & Miller, H. (1973). The effects of client race and social class on clinical judgments. *Clinical Social Work Journal, 1*, 100–109.

Fletcher, B. J. (1995). The influence of race in social work practice with troubled youth. *Dissertation Abstracts International, 95* (1), 521. (University Microfilms No. DAO 72699)

Franklin, A. J. (1989). Therapeutic interventions with Black adolescents. In R. L. Jones (Ed.), *Black adolescents* (pp. 309–337). Berkeley, CA: Cobb & Henry.

Gibbs, J. T. (1990). Mental health issues of Black Americans. In A. R. Stiffman & L. E. Davis (Eds.), *Ethnic issues in adolescent mental health* (pp. 21–52) Newbury Park, CA: Sage.

Gould, K. (1991). Limiting damage is not enough: A minority perspective on child welfare. In J. E. Everett, S. S. Chipungu, & B. R. Leashore (Eds.), *Child welfare: An Africentric perspective* (pp. 58–78). New Brunswick, NJ: Rutgers University Press.

Green, J. W. (1995). *Cultural awareness in the human services: A multi-ethnic approach* (2nd ed.). Needham Heights, MA: Allyn & Bacon.

Gruber, M. L. (1980). Inequality in the social services. *Social Service Review, 37*, 60–76.

Hacker, A. (1992). *Two nations: Black and White, separate, hostile, and unequal*. New York: Ballantine Books.

Hamilton, D. L., Sherman, S. J., & Ruvolo, C. M. (1990). Stereotype-based expectancies: Effects on information-processing and social behavior. *Journal of Social Issues, 46,* 35–60.

Hunt, P. (1987). Black clients: Implications for supervision of trainees, *Psychotherapy,* 24, 114–119.

Ingram, R. E. (Ed.). (1986). *Information-processing approaches to clinical psychology.* Orlando, FL: Academic Press.

Jones, J. F., Stevenson, K. M., Leung, P., Cheung, K-F. M. (1995). *Call to competence: Child protective services training and evaluation.* Eglewood, CO: American Humane Association.

Kavanagh, K. H., & Kennedy, P. H. (1992). *Promoting cultural diversity: Strategies for health care professionals.* Newbury Park, CA: Sage Publications.

Lehman, A. K., & Salovey, P. (1990). Psychotherapist orientation and expectations for liked and disliked patients. *Professional Psychology: Research and Practice, 25,* (351–391).

Lum, D. (1996). *Social work practice and people of color: A process-stage approach* (3rd ed.). Pacific Grove, CA: Brooks/Cole Publishing Company.

Martin, P. J., Sterne, A. L., & Lindsay, C. J. (1977). Causative vs. predictive models of therapists' expectancies: A further evaluation. *Psychological Reports, 40,* 835–839.

Meyers, H. F. (1989). Urban stress and the mental health of Afro-American adolescents: An epidemiologic and conceptual update. In R. L. Jones (Ed.), *Black adolescents* (pp. 123–152). Berkeley, CA: Cobb & Henry.

Milner, J. S. (1993). Social information-processing and physical child abuse. *Clinical Psychology Review, 13,* 275–294.

Moore, C. (1996). *Primary care clinicians and the recognition and management of psychosocial problems among children: Labeling theory revisited* (unpublished dissertation, Pennsylvania State University, University Park, PA).

Saleebey, D. (1992). Introduction: Power in the people. In D. Saleebey (Ed.), *The strengths perspective in social work* (pp. 3–17). New York: Longman.

Stangor, C., Lynch, L., Duan, C., & Glass, B. (1992). Categorization of individuals on the basis of multiple social features. *Journal of Personality and Social Psychology, 62,* 207–218.

Stehno, S. M. (1982). Differential treatment of minority children in service systems. *Social Work, 27*, 39–45.

Sue, D. W. (1990). *Counseling the culturally different: Theory and practice* (2nd ed.). New York: Wiley.

Taylor, J. (1993). *Formulating cultural identity* (unpublished manuscript).

Thomas, A., & Sillen, S. (1972). *Racism and psychiatry.* Secaucus, NJ: Citadel Press.

Turk, D. C., & Salovey, P. (1986). Clinical information processing: Bias inoculation. In R. E. Ingram (Ed.), *Information-processing approaches to clinical psychology* (pp. 306–323). Orlando, FL: Academic Press.

Tyler, F. B., Brome, D. R., & Williams, J. E. (1991). *Ethnic validity, ecology, and psychotherapy: A psychosocial competence model.* New York: Plenum Press.

Weick, A. (1992). Building a strengths perspective for social work. In D. Saleebey (Ed.), *The strengths perspective in social work* (pp. 18–26). New York: Longman.

Williams, S., & Halgin, R. P. (1995). Issues in psychotherapy supervision between the Caucasian supervisor and the Black supervisee. *The Clinical Supervisor, 13*, 39–58.

Willie, C. V., Rieker, P. P., Kramer, B. M., & Brown, B. S. (1995). *Mental health, racism, and sexism.* Pittsburgh, PA: University of Pittsburgh Press.

Willie, C. V., Kramer, B. M., & Brown, B. S. (1973). *Racism and mental health.* Pittsburgh: University of Pittsburgh Press.

Wills, T. A. (1978). Perceptions of clients by professional helpers. *Psychological Bulletin, 85*, 968–1000.

Wilson, A. N. (1993). *The falsification of Afrikan consciousness: Eurocentric history, psychiatry, and politics of white supremacy.* New York: Afrikan InfoSystems.

Wodarski, J. S. (1981). *The role of research in clinical practice: A practical approach for the human services.* Baltimore: University Park Press.

12

Why African American Adoption Agencies Succeed: A New Perspective on Self-Help

Geraldine Jackson-White, Cheryl Davenport Dozier,
J. Toni Oliver, and Lydia Barnwell Gardner

This article traces the history of self-help in the African American community, with emphasis on services and programs for children. The traditions of self-help are very much alive in the African American community, and are manifest in a range of activities. The self-help activities specific to one adoption agency illustrate contemporary models of self-help in the African American community.

Geraldine Jackson-White, Ed.D., and Cheryl Davenport Dozier, D.S.W., are Assistant Professors of Social Work, University of Georgia School of Social Work, Athens, GA. J. Toni Oliver, M.S.W., is Executive Director, ROOTS, Inc., College Park, GA. Lydia Barnwell Gardner, M.S.W., is a recent graduate of the University of Georgia School of Social Work.

A frican American children continue to be disproportionately removed from their families by the child welfare
system and placed in alternate care [Billingsley &
Giovannoni 1972; Leashore et al. 1991]. "African American children are more likely than other children to be reported as neglected, to enter out-of-home care and to have a prolonged duration of care, and they are less likely to secure permanence
through adoption" [Williams 1991: 276]. To say that the plight
of African American children is the result of an African American community that lacks an interest in taking care of its children is a fallacy that has been dispelled by current and historical research [Billingsley & Giovannoni 1972; Gutman 1976; Hill
1977; Martin & Martin 1978; Ross 1978; Williams 1991; Wilson
1991]. For the burden of responsibility to rest with the "client"
(African American children and their families) is to continue to
blame the victim. The focus must be on the institutional practices of agencies and the child welfare system at large.

During the past 20 years, several initiatives were undertaken
to increase the adoptive placement of African American
children [Williams 1991]. These initiatives represented public
and voluntary child welfare agency efforts to reduce the
disproportionate number of African American children in the
child welfare system. Many of these efforts have proven to
be successful in facilitating permanent outcomes for African
American children—some more successful than others [Williams
1991].

This article examines the use of self-help as a means to increase adoption opportunities for African American children.
The history and role of traditional self-help efforts in the African American community related to caregiving of African
American children are also reviewed, with particular attention
to identifying the steps and the activities that occurred in the
beginning stages of one agency's development, to illustrate new
perspectives on self-help.

Traditions of Self-help

The use of formal adoption services are relatively recent for African Americans [Williams 1991]. This is not to suggest that adoption did not take place in the African American community. Hill's [1977] research on the adoption practices of African Americans substantiates that a system of informal adoption has been a historical part of the African American community. This informal system of adoption is consistent with cultural traditions of African Americans in which caring for and protecting children is a value held in high esteem. The strengths of the African American community in providing services and responding to the needs of the children are a consistent theme in the literature on African American adoptions [Billingsley & Giovannoni 1972; Billingsley 1992; Everett et al. 1991; Hill 1977; Ross 1978].

The literature also references self-help efforts that were developed to respond to children's needs for care, protection, and nurturing. Ross [1978] offers an overview of organized efforts of African Americans in providing social welfare services, including child welfare services. Ross' overview substantiates the presence of self-help as a continuing attribute of the African American community. While the literature indicates that the history of self-help in the African American community is ongoing, the strategies and techniques of providing permanence for children differ significantly from Hill's initial assessment [Wilson 1991]. Although challenges and difficulties continue to confront the African American community today, the cultural tradition of self-help, particularly as it relates to responding to the needs of children, also continues to exert its influence.

The tradition of self-help in the African American community is one of the key factors that contribute to the success of contemporary adoption services for African American children. Self-help has a documented history and tradition in African

American communities from the days of enslavement to current times [Billingsley 1992; Ross 1978]. Contemporary self-help
builds upon this history and tradition and can be defined as
efforts undertaken by individuals or groups (social, religious,
professional, community) that use a broad spectrum of strategies and techniques to resolve social/community problems affecting a particular group. Self-help in the African American
community is defined as individual or group efforts that replicate the traditions and culture of African Americans, that is, cultural traditions that incorporate interdependence and a sense
of shared ancestry and history [Ross 1978].

African Americans have traditionally used a variety of self-
help efforts to survive years of oppression, discrimination, and
exclusion. It is important to recognize the resilience and cultural continuity with African traditions that African Americans
bring to their self-help efforts [Billingsley 1992; Ross 1978]. Hill
[1977] described how thousands of children of slave parents
were reared by elderly relatives who served as a major source
of stability and fortitude for many African American families.
This is in keeping with African history and the tradition that
the birth of a child was the concern of the entire community,
especially relatives. Children were highly valued in traditional
African culture, and the concept of an out-of-wedlock child did
not exist because all children were seen as belonging to the community [Turner 1991].

Billingsley [1992] identifies four sets of organizations that
have persisted over time in the African American community,
"the church, the school, the business enterprise, and the voluntary organization." The critical distinguishing characteristics of
these organizations is their connection to African American heritage. These organizations "grow out of the African American
heritage, identify with it, and serve primarily African American people and families" [Billingsley 1992: 73]. It is this distinguishing quality that evokes the uniqueness of self-help in the
African American community. "African Americans have success-

fully exercised economic independence and self-determination with only 'pennies, nickels and dimes' at their disposal" [Burwell 1994: 27]. Escapes to freedom and other survival activities undertaken by African Americans have relied heavily upon the individual and collective resources within their community.

In addition to the significant roles of the extended family and the church, other organizations in the African American community have traditionally responded to the needs of the community. Ross's [1978] overview of the involvement of the African American community in the provision of social welfare services documents the range and depth of organized efforts to provide for the welfare of community members. Educational institutions, civic and social organizations, and individuals have all had a role in self-help efforts. Some self-help efforts included providing benefits for the sick, paying small death claims, and establishing hospitals, orphanages, homes for the aged, kindergartens, day nurseries, and other needed institutions. For the most part, these self-help efforts were culturally appropriate responses based on African tradition. They also represented the African American community's way of providing services that were not available from the wider society. "The Black heritage is a complex of genuine responses by Black people reacting to the need for social welfare services in their own communities" [Ross 1978: 465].

Extended Family

African American families have traditionally relied upon the interdependence of the extended family and kinship groups for maintenance and survival [Gutman 1976; Hill 1977; Wilson 1991]. Hill [1972], in his classic *Strengths of Black Families*, described five major strengths, of which two—adaptability of family roles and strong kinship bond—focus specifically on the role of the extended family in relation to caring for children. African American families have traditionally absorbed or "taken in" children of blood and nonblood relatives on both a temporary and permanent basis. Hill [1972] acknowledged that informal, open adoption among African American families often tightened kinship bonds, since traditionally African American women were reluctant to give up their children for agency-originated closed adoptions. In addition, the flexibility of family roles enabled older children and the elder members of the family to take care of young children. "Informal adoption of Black children in the Black community is a process whereby adult relatives or friends of the family took in children and cared for them when their parents were unable to provide for their needs" [Boyd-Franklin 1989: 52]. The capacity and readiness of African American families to open their homes to children and others in need of specialized care is both a traditional and a current practice [Billingsley & Giovannoni 1972; Hill 1977; Wilson 1991].

The Black Church and Spirituality

The African American church and the spirituality of African Americans have been integral components of self-help efforts. The church is perhaps the most universally recognized institution in the African American community when discussing self-help. Through the church, African Americans used religion as a primary survival mechanism; the church concurrently became one of the most economically independent institutions in the African American community [Billingsley 1992; Hill 1972]. The church has been in the forefront of self-help initiatives in the African American community. "Over the centuries, the church has become the strongest institution in their community. It is prevalent, independent, and has extensive outreach" [Billingsley 1992: 349]. "Historically the [c]hurch is the place where individual families come to form an extended family and act as one unit, whether this involved spiritual worship, political action, or economic development" [Harvey 1985: 19].

Many African Americans who may not be affiliated with a particular church continue to feel greatly connected spiritually to a Creator or a higher power, as evidenced by their beliefs, practice, and reference to faith. Three sources of hope and strength form the basis of a strong religious and spiritual orientation among African Americans: (1) the family as a source of support; (2) faith in God for help in the removal of psychological stresses; and (3) the church as an emotional release of the tensions faced in an oppressive society [Knox 1985].

For families with young children and adolescents, the church fulfills important family functions such as providing role-models and sources of help and support in crises. "Black churches often function as surrogate families for isolated and overburdened single mothers" [Boyd-Franklin 1989: 83]. The majority of institutions for African American children toward the end of the 19th century were established and supported by church organizations [Billingsley & Giovannoni 1972; Hill 1977].

The Child Welfare System and the African American Child

It is important to note that social services for African American children were for the most part provided by organized efforts of community self-help, rather than by governmental entities. Formal governmental child welfare services were not the primary providers of protection to African American children. According to Billingsley and Giovannoni [1972: 213], "the dominant child welfare institutions of the country openly excluded Black children." Adoption as a service from a formal institution was not considered or available for African American children until the end of World War II, when the Social Security Act opened many social services to African Americans. The decades of 1960 and 1970, however, witnessed the emergence of adoption services in the African American community [Williams 1991]. Many of these agencies were developed in response to the equal opportunity and equal access emphasis of the Civil Rights movement. The criteria used by formal adoption agencies for the adoption of Caucasian infants were elitist and screened out many eligible African American families. To make the process more inclusive of African American families, culturally relevant services were essential in all areas, including assessment criteria and processes, community outreach efforts, child and family advocacy services, elimination of fees and provision of subsidies, increases in the employment of African American staff members at all levels, and sensitive, child-specific recruitment [Williams 1991].

Traditional adoption agencies were hard-pressed to find "appropriate" families for adoption of African American children. This was primarily due to their lack of experience in providing services to African American families and acting on the belief that African American families were beset with pathology. They did not recognize the strengths in African American families and often mistakenly identified strengths as pathology. Lack of attention to the traditional roles of single and elderly relatives as caregivers for children in the traditional African American family is an example of this kind of misperception. Many traditional adoption agencies had policies that discriminated against or screened out persons over the age of 40, as well as single parents. As a result, African American children suffered from the child welfare system's inability to work in their best interests and became its victims. The children were subsequently blamed for the system's weaknesses by being labeled "hard-to-place" and the prospective adoptive families "hard-to-reach" [Billingsley & Giovannoni 1972]. Even today, African American children are included in the category of "hard-to-place" children and children with special needs, along with children with disabling conditions, or of school age, or in sibling groups.

The Civil Rights struggle, the passage of the Adoption Assistance and Child Welfare Act of 1980 (P.L. 96–272), and the emergence of voluntary sector pilot adoption programs targeted to African Americans stimulated adoption agencies to rethink their policies and practices to determine the extent to which African American families were being screened out of the adoption process [Billingsley & Giovannoni 1972; Everett 1991; Williams 1991]. Consequently, many agencies began to develop strategies designed to aggressively recruit African American families [Williams 1991].

At the heart of the child welfare system's failure to provide adequate services to African American children is its inability to understand, use, or replicate the manner in which communal identity operates in the natural environment to take care of the community's members [Gould 1991]. Through their various social, civic, fraternal, and religious groups and organizations, African American communities demonstrate communal identity and responsibility. Using these resources to promote family reunification and preservation demonstrates collective responsibility. Collective efforts, self-help, and mutual aid promote the well-being of African American children and families, promote community development, and strengthen the capacity of community groups and organizations to help reunite and preserve African American families [Leashore et al. 1991].

This review of the literature makes clear that self-help efforts in the African American community are pervasive and provides insight into the cultural continuity of the African American heritage as protecting and caring for children. The next section describes the self-help activities undertaken in behalf of one African American adoption agency.

ROOTS... An Example of Community Self-help

ROOTS, Inc., is an African American adoption agency formed to change the adoption outcomes for African American children in the state of Georgia. The formation and continued support of ROOTS are examples of contemporary self-help in the African

American community. The successful ROOTS program is a prototype of African American adoption agencies that have achieved significant success in providing adoptive placements for African American children considered to be "hard-to-place." The ROOTS example can provide contemporary adoption programs with strategies for tapping into resources in the natural environment of African American communities, and elevating outcomes for African American children.

ROOTS grew out of the personal and professional commitment and desire of its founder to respond to the needs of African American children in the child welfare system. Forming an adoption agency is not a simple task. Most adoption agencies that are formed in response to the needs of the children in the custody of a public agency are developed with the support and backing of foundations, well-endowed institutions, or well-established public or private agencies. ROOTS lacked organizational or financial support, and began with the call to respond to African American children by the founder, who also became the executive director. This initiative is an example of the traditions of self-help observed in the literature.

Examples of individual self-help initiatives are seen in the response to ROOTS from members of its board of directors. Board members were selected based on a profile that identified skills, talents, and resources critical for implementation and operation of an agency. In addition, because the intent was to increase adoption opportunities for African American children, individuals from the African American community were identified to serve on the board. Most of the members were unfamiliar with adoption and social services in general. They were asked to serve because of their particular expertise, or because they had influence in the community and access to resources that would benefit the agency. In the start-up phase of ROOTS' operation, individual board members immediately responded by providing direct resources such as office furniture, telephones, and other supplies needed by the agency for basic operation. Board members also obtained other professional services directly or through their access and influence with other individuals within the community who had particular skills.

The board members' responses reflect the tradition of self-help in the African American community to "help their own." The efforts of board members represent the new perspective of self-help in that they all responded by providing those services, products, or contacts that they could personally access through their positions in the community.

The response from board members could be interpreted as typical of persons who agree to serve on a board, but differs in the sense that the responses were unconditional and required nothing other than a request and the ability to fulfill that request or refer the requestor to a source that could meet the request. The ability to meet specific needs or refer to a source that could provide needed services differs from historical self-help. Many of the individuals tapped for ROOTS possess greater personal access and decision-making capabilities than were previously available in African American communities.

In addition to the self-help initiatives of individual board members, the African American community also answered the ancestral call to respond to the needs of children. The first response came from the church. When ROOTS had no place to locate its offices, the church responded with an in-kind offer of office space. Additionally, ROOTS became the focus of one of the ministries of the church, underlying the role of the church in self-help activities.

The community response did not end with the involvement of the church. Once individuals in the business, civic, and social community heard about the efforts of ROOTS, other offers to help were forthcoming. These offers covered a range of professional services including public relations, accounting and bookkeeping services (including audit preparations), printing services, and fund-raising. The response to the fundraising drive clearly demonstrates the continuity of self-help traditions in the

African American community. One example was the general African American community's response to the inclusion of ROOTS in the Black United Fund's (BUF) Charitable Contribution drive. As one of BUF's federated agencies, ROOTS was among the listings of thousands in the Combined Federal Campaign, and received a significantly large number of contributions in its first year on the list. Thus, the continuity of self-help and the communal call to respond and care for children were again demonstrated in the community. The initiatives discussed thus far clearly support the spirit and presence of self-help in the African American community.

ROOTS was able to provide adoption services successfully in its first year of operation primarily because of unconditional support from its board and community supporters. During its first year and a half, ROOTS responded to nearly 300 inquiries about adoption from the African American community, prepared 35 African American families for adoption, and placed 15 children ranging from three to 12 years of age in African American adoptive homes. This was accomplished without any established financial support such as grants or contracts. After the first 10 months of operation, ROOTS did receive a small financial grant from BUF and a very small purchase-of-service contract for recruitment from the public adoption agency. It was not until its second year of operation that ROOTS received contributions from the Combined Federal Campaign. From this demonstration of communal self-help to "make a way out of no way," ROOTS was able to submit a proposal for funding that resulted in the award of a two-year federal grant that supported the acquisition of a full-time paid staff. Community self-help efforts, however, are necessary to provide ongoing support of this agency.

As ROOTS approaches its fourth year of operation, the future looks promising. In order to maintain its operation and expand its services, a formidable fundraising initiative has already been implemented. The fundraising activities will reach out to the entire community. Most importantly, the effort is being spearheaded by members of the African American social, civic, and business community. ROOTS will also continue to pursue grants and contracts with public and private funding sources to help support its operation.

Strategies to Maximize Self-Help Initiatives

The illustrations of self-help activities in behalf of ROOTS suggest that the African American community is indeed willing and able to respond in a variety of ways to the needs of its children. The examples from ROOTS document how natural helping networks among individuals and groups continue to provide solutions to social problems without formal agency intervention.

The experience of ROOTS does not provide generalizable evidence that the same effort can be replicated. It does, however, provide evidence of the availability of critical resources in the African American community and the willingness of individuals and the community to respond. The ROOTS experience points out that the African American community does still engage in self-help activities and that those activities may manifest themselves in nontraditional ways.

One national example of organized institutional self-help that demonstrates continuity of efforts is the National Association of Black Social Workers' (NABSW) "Fists Full of Families" National Adoption Campaign [1996]. Through this campaign, NABSW has created a mechanism for the development of "Local Village Councils." The Local Village Councils, coordinated by local chapters of NABSW, include representatives of the many and varied African American civic, social, and professional organizations that can be helpful in organizing and supporting adoption initiatives. Since the range of organizations may differ in each community, the identification of African American individuals and organizations in each community that have direct access to resources and or influence in accessing resources is vital.

The "Fists Full of Families" campaign outlines strategies and activities for local NABSW chapters to develop networks within their communities for the sole purpose of creating adoption opportunities for African American children. Many of the strategies posed by NABSW, such as identifying and including key individuals and organizations, include many of the activities observed in the formation and development of ROOTS. The key individuals and organizations are not limited to those that have knowledge of adoption or the particular needs of African American children; rather, they are willing to help and they have access to resources. The similarity between the NABSW initiative and the ROOTS initiative is the self-help response to a need that emerges from within the African American community. Both initiatives have a potential for success because they are tapping into the wide range of resources available from the African American community. Consequently, any effort to initiate successful adoption programs within the African American community must recognize and use the resources of organizations and individuals within the African American community.

Conclusion

The definition of self-help in the African American community includes the traditions of interdependence. It generates a response in ways and numbers unparalleled by traditional and formal agencies. ROOTS is but one example of the ongoing self-help efforts concerning adoption currently in operation. In keeping with traditions of taking care of its children, the African American community conducts these self-help efforts without recognition or documentation. The observations cited in this article underline the need for research to verify and quantify the existence of other self-help initiatives in the African American community. This information is needed to diffuse the misperceptions about the "disintegrating" African American community. The experiences of ROOTS affirm the presence of resources and influences within the African American community that have not always been available. Reductions in and elimination of publicly supported programs for adoption of African American children demand that the self-help initiatives discussed in this article be continued and expanded. "We believe that self-help is fundamental to African-American progress in an often, though clearly not always, hostile society. Unfortunately, the future of African-American families depends on how well the black community understands this" [Billingsley 1992: 379].

The experience of ROOTS demonstrates that the African American community understands its need to participate in ongoing self-help efforts and responds accordingly. ♦

References

Billingsley, A., & Giovannoni J. M. (1972). *Children of the storm: Black children and American child welfare*. New York: Harcourt Brace Jovanovich, Inc.

Billingsley, A. (1992). *Climbing Jacob's ladder: The enduring legacy of African-American families*. New York: Simon & Schuster.

Boyd-Franklin, N. (1989). *Black families in therapy: A multisystems approach*. New York: Guilford Press.

Burwell, Y. (1994, Spring). Pennies, nickels & dimes: Raising money to care for our own as American tradition. *Black Caucus, 3*, 27–32.

Everett, J. E. (1991). Introduction: Children in crisis. In J. E. Everett, S. S. Chipungu, & B. R. Leashore (Eds.), *Child welfare: An Africentric perspective* (pp. 1–14). New Brunswick, NJ: Rutgers University Press.

Everett, J. E., Chipungu, S. S., & Leashore, B. R. (Eds.). (1991). *Child welfare: An Africentric perspective*. New Brunswick, NJ: Rutgers University Press.

Gould, K. (1991). Limiting damage is not enough: A minority perspective on child welfare issues. In J. E. Everett, S. S. Chipungu, & B. R. Leashore (Eds.), *Child welfare: An Africentric perspective* (pp. 58–84). New Brunswick, NJ: Rutgers University Press.

Gutman, H. (1976). *The Black family in slavery and freedom, 1720-1925*. New York: Pantheon Books.

Harvey, A. (1985). Traditional African culture as the basis for the Afro-American church in America: The foundation of the Black family in America. In A. Harvey (Ed.), *The Black family: An Afro-centric perspective* (pp. 1–21). New York: United Church of Christ.

Hill, R. B. (1972). *The strengths of Black families.* (2nd ed.). New York: National Urban League.

Hill, R. B. (1977). *Informal adoption among Black families.* Washington, DC: National Urban League.

Knox, D. (1985). Spirituality: A tool in the assessment and treatment of Black alcoholics. In F. L. Brisbane & M. Womble (Eds.), *Treatment of Black alcoholics* (pp. 31–44). New York: Haworth Press, Inc.

Leashore, B. R., McMurray, H. L., & Bailey, B. C. (1991). Reuniting and preserving African American families. In J. E. Everett, S. S. Chipungu, & B. R. Leashore (Eds.), *Child welfare: An Africentric perspective* (pp. 245–265). New Brunswick, NJ: Rutgers University Press.

Martin, E. P., & Martin, J. M. (1978). *The Black extended family.* Chicago: University of Chicago Press.

National Association of Black Social Workers. (1996, April). Developing local village councils. In J. T. Oliver & K. Assem (Co-Chairs), *A fist full of families.* Institute conducted at the 28th annual meeting of the National Association of Black Social Workers, Houston, TX.

Ross, E. L. (1978). *Black heritage in social welfare 1860–1930.* Metuchen, NJ: Scarecrow Press, Inc.

Turner, R. (1991). Affirming consciousness: The Africentric perspective. In J. E. Everett, S. S. Chipungu, & B. R. Leashore (Eds.), *Child welfare: An Africentric perspective* (pp. 36–57). New Brunswick, NJ: Rutgers University Press.

Williams, C. (1991). Expanding the options in the quest for permanence. In J. E. Everett, S. S. Chipungu, & B. R. Leashore (Eds.), *Child welfare: An Africentric perspective* (pp. 266–289). New Brunswick, NJ: Rutgers University Press.

Wilson, M. N. (1991). The context of the African American family. In J. E. Everett, S. S. Chipungu, & B. R. Leashore (Eds.), *Child Welfare: An Africentric perspective* (pp. 85–118). New Brunswick, NJ: Rutgers University Press.

13
Cultural Competence in Child Welfare: What Is It? How Do We Achieve It? What Happens Without It?

Anna R. McPhatter

The overrepresentation of minority children in the child welfare system is well-documented. Providing culturally relevant and effective medical and psychosocial services in the field, while an enduring goal, still remains elusive. This article asserts that before significant progress toward achieving these goals can be made, what constitutes cultural competence must be elucidated. A Cultural Competence Attainment Model, comprising a grounded knowledge base, affective dimensions, and cumulative skill proficiency, is described for use by child welfare practitioners. The effects of cultural incompetence are also addressed.

Anna R. McPhatter, Ph.D., LCSW, is Chair and Associate Professor, Department of Social Work and Mental Health, Morgan State University, Baltimore, MD.

The overrepresentation of racially and culturally diverse children and families in the child welfare system is well-established. In the general population, four times as many African American children as Caucasian children become wards of the state; the former also spend a longer time in the child welfare system [Everett et al. 1991; Edelman 1987]. Nationally, 26% of the children entering out-of-home care are African American and 10% are Latino [National Center on Child Abuse and Neglect 1992]. Moreover, in a number of jurisdictions and states, the percentage of African American children in the out-of-home care system is staggering. These figures range from a high of 87.5% in the District of Columbia to over 45% percent in Illinois, New Jersey, South Carolina, Louisiana, Georgia, and Mississippi. Latino children are overrepresented in several states as well; they comprise 45% of the children in New Mexico, 31% in Texas, 29% in California, 25% in Arizona, and over 15% in Connecticut, New Jersey, Massachusetts, and New York [Children's Defense Fund 1994].

It is also well-established that the professionals who provide health and social services to these children are predominantly Caucasian. For well over a decade, a variety of efforts have been undertaken to enhance the ability of child welfare practitioners to respond to the needs of children and families of color in ways that are culturally congruent and effective. These efforts have been largely sporadic, with an emphasis on raising awareness and sensitivity. Additional efforts have sought to increase knowledge and understanding about the unique aspects of the history and culture of specific groups, primarily African Americans and Latino Americans. These efforts, however, have not addressed culturally effective practice in a comprehensive and sustained manner, and have been inadequate.

Cultural competence in child welfare practice has become a buzz phrase in dire need of elucidation if we are to move beyond the fragmented approaches that have characterized previous efforts. This article seeks to advance the conceptual

understanding of what child welfare practitioners have identified as a goal—cultural competence. A comprehensive model
for achieving cultural competence in child welfare is presented
and implications of cultural incompetence are discussed. The
underlying assumption of this model is that children and families should be provided with health care and psychosocial services that are culturally acceptable and that support the integrity and strengths of their culture. Child welfare practitioners
have an obligation to provide culturally congruent interventions
if they are to achieve, in actuality, the goal of preserving the
best interests of children, families, and communities.

Literature Review

Social demographers project that in less than two decades, racial and ethnic minorities will become the numerical majority
in the U.S. [Sue et al. 1992]. Motivated by long-term profit pro-
jections, corporate America has taken seriously the inevitable
racial and cultural diversity of the future labor force and is in-
vesting tremendous resources in preparing for this eventuality.
It recognizes that productivity in the workplace is greatly enhanced by the extent to which people engage effectively in cross-
cultural interactions. Social work, health, and other human services would do well to emulate the commitment of corporations
to achieve a genuine level of cross-cultural competence, not-
withstanding the corporations' motivation for doing so.

For nearly two decades, the social work profession has de-
creed the importance of cultural diversity in student enrollment,
faculty, and curricula. Schools of social work are required to
demonstrate throughout their curricula that students are being
prepared to serve a culturally diverse client population. Despite
this ongoing mandate, born of ethical obligation, there is reason to believe that the demonstration has been substantially
ineffective. McMahon and Allen-Meares [1992: 533] concluded
from a content analysis of recent social work literature that most

of the social work literature on practice with minorities is "naive and superficial." Moreover, the authors believed that those who publish in the predominant social work literature have a powerful influence on framing practice knowledge. Similarly, Diggs [1992] found in a large study ($N = 200$) of graduate social work educators that (1) when schools did not make the inclusion of ethnic and cultural content in the curriculum a priority and did not provide pertinent resources, the content rarely appeared; and (2) two-thirds of the educators in her study described the lack of knowledge and competence to teach diversity content as their most problematic teaching concern. These educators described textbook content as inadequate and superficial. The educators themselves were not generally knowledgeable of even classic works on diversity such as Norton's work [1978] on the "dual perspective" in social work. Many of these same social work educators (70%), while believing that cross-cultural practice required different skills, could not identify what the different skills were. Another disturbing trend found by Diggs was the tendency of social work educators to repeatedly use the same content on diversity in each social work course, effectively thwarting the development of knowledge at an advanced or content-specific level. These transmitters of the profession's most fundamental education process openly admitted that they had not been educated and trained in their own social work preparation to deliver multiculural content and did not feel confident or competent to do so in their courses.

Social work is not alone in its inability to meet the complex challenge of cultural competence despite its avowals to do so. Sue et al. [1992] indicate that despite continued efforts by the counseling profession to press for multicultural competencies, the Association for Multicultural Counseling and Development is still trying to justify the need. They note that the American Psychological Association and a number of government-sponsored conferences have identified the serious lack and/or inadequacy of training programs that deal with racial, ethnic, and cultural matters. In fact, in its code of ethics, the American Psychological Association [1992] requires mental health professionals to be aware of differences due to race, ethnicity, language, socioeconomic status, gender, and national origin. Violation of this principle may be considered unethical and may present a cause for action for unfair discriminatory practice. Kavanagh and Kennedy [1992], in *Promoting Cultural Diversity: Strategies for Health Care Professionals,* make it clear that culturally relevant health care is a right, not an option, and that health care professionals are obliged to pursue competence in this area as painstakingly as they do in clinical training or other specialities.

All of these exhortations and descriptions are reminders of just how essential it is for practitioners in child welfare to move beyond the obvious identification of the need for culturally competent practice. Commitment to cultural competence at this point demands an advanced level of activity, that is, critical discourse on what constitutes cultural competence and a thoughtful delineation of the path one must traverse to achieve it. What follows is an effort to stimulate this badly needed initiative.

The Child Welfare Challenge

There is a clear imperative in child welfare to provide services that deal effectively with the oftentimes life-threatening conditions that face children and families. Social work educators as well as child welfare practitioners often assume that competence with racially, culturally, and ethnically distinct groups can be achieved through short-term—and often one-shot—workshops or classes. This assumption reflects a short-sighted, simplistic view of a complex process. Restructuring one's worldview and developing a sound base of knowledge and skills are long-term professional endeavors.

The first step toward achieving cultural competence is understanding and accepting the reality that openness to long-term, ongoing, and persistent development is required. As in all professional development, there is no ideal completion. Sue et al. [1992: 75] describes the culturally skilled counselor as "one who is in the process of actively developing and practicing appropriate, relevant, and sensitive intervention strategies and skills in working with his or her culturally different clients." Thus, any serious initiative to work effectively with diverse client populations begins with this premise.

As variably expressed by others [Devore & Schlesinger 1996; Green 1995; McAdoo 1993; Sue et al. 1992; Logan et al. 1990], preparation for serving ethnically and culturally diverse populations effectively must be pursued on a three-level—yet highly integrated—front. A unimodal focus on raising awareness or sensitivity is necessary but not sufficient. Neither is it acceptable to believe that increasing one's level of cognitive understanding of culturally different groups is all one needs to do. The literature gives much support to the idea that behavioral change does not necessarily follow knowledge about social phenomena. For example, the perennial battle against HIV—the deadly virus that causes AIDS—has raged for several years now around the goal of bridging the gap between information and high-risk behavior, with only marginally positive results.

Over the course of more than 20 years of teaching and practice in the field of child welfare, it is clear to this author that a comprehensive model for achieving cultural competence is sorely needed. It is from my own work in child welfare that the following model evolved as a response to demands from the field. The discussion begins with definitions of several concepts critical to understanding the model.

Cultural Competence Defined

The study and description of culture is massive. Most pertinent to this discussion is Green's [1982: 6–7] description of *culture* as "those elements of a people's history, tradition, values, and social organization that become implicitly or explicitly meaningful to the participants…in cross-cultural encounters." *Culture*, then, connotes worldview, behavioral styles and inclinations, and thinking patterns that present and can be anticipated in inter-personal interactions across social boundaries. It is precisely the different ways in which culture becomes manifest that are piv-otal in this discussion. It is one's culture that distinguishes and brings meaning to social events, necessitating knowledge of readily observable distinctions as well as less discernible nu-ances between and among groups.

As used in this context, *competence* refers to an ability or a capacity equal to the requirement, that is, responding effectively to the purpose or goal. Further, Green [1995: 52] asserts that the competent practitioner is able to conduct her or his "professional work in a way that is congruent with the behavior and expecta-tions that members of a distinctive culture recognizes as appro-priate among themselves." Dana et al. [1992: 221] likewise de-scribe *cultural competence* as "an ability to provide services that are perceived as legitimate for problems experienced by cultur-ally diverse persons." Cultural competence denotes the ability to transform knowledge and cultural awareness into health and/or psychosocial interventions that support and sustain healthy client-system functioning within the appropriate cultural con-text. This definition compels one to ask, "What purpose is served by providing services in any other context?" Unfortunately, much of what occurs in child welfare practice falls far short of meeting the foregoing criteria.

The Cultural Competence Attainment Model

The proposed model assumes that (a) achieving competence in any sphere is developmental and (b) learning may take place in any or all of one's thinking, feeling, sensing, and behaving di-mensions. In this regard, the model is holistic, circular, and in-terconnected, as shown in figure 1. The components of the model are an Enlightened Consciousness, a Grounded Knowledge Base,

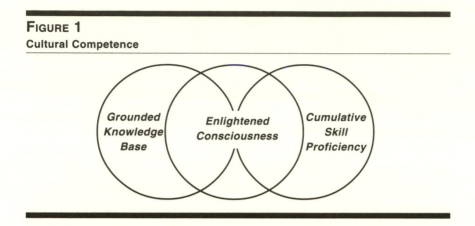

FIGURE 1
Cultural Competence

and Cumulative Skill Proficiency. Although each component represents a substantive goal unto itself, none is sufficient alone to produce competent cross-cultural practice. Each dimension must be embraced as an essential part of a mutually influencing whole. This fact is precisely why earlier professional declarations of becoming "culturally sensitive," brief overviews of ethnic group history, or cursory cross-cultural communication techniques have not evolved into a level of competence that effectively encompasses the needs of culturally diverse child welfare clients. Focus in one area must not exclude substantive endeavor in the other areas. Each dimension of the model will be discussed separately, but the reader is cautioned not to presume that proficiency in one area takes precedence or priority over the others.

Enlightened Consciousness

Enlightened consciousness involves a fundamental process of reorienting one's primary worldview. It often requires a radical restructuring of a well-entrenched belief system that perceives oneself and one's culture, including values and ways of behavior, as not only preferred but clearly superior to another's. The ultimate goal of this shift in mind-set is to create a belief in, and acceptance of, others on the basis of equality solely because of a sense of shared humanity. Much of what people have become through socialization, formal and informal education, cultural transmission, and so on, contradicts the real essence of equality between and among us. This is particularly evident in century-old traditions and beliefs fueled by declarations of "unbiased scientific research" that support the superiority of European Americans and everything derived therefrom. Altering one's worldview is often a frightening effort because it forces one to challenge the very foundation on which one's personhood stands, even when it is clear that this foundation is substantially out of line with reality.

This essential transformation begins with a shifting of consciousness and awareness of just how endemic and narrow one's socialization has been. Individuals who have grown up in environments in which most of the people with whom they interact are racially, ethnically, and culturally similar to themselves have had a monocultural early socialization. They will likely experience a great deal of peeling away and restructuring in this process of enlightened consciousness. Monoculturally oriented individuals experience a great deal of personal and professional discomfort when interacting with people significantly different from themselves. In the real world of practice, such individuals often exhibit nervousness and insecurity with culturally different clients and may resort to superficial small talk with culturally different professionals. It is quite common in situations where an African American professional might expect engagement in substantive dialogue on pertinent issues with Caucasian professionals for the latter to resort to commenting on clothing styles, the weather, and other frivolous matters. This behavior occurs frequently even with professionals who share common education, training, and experiences. The discomfort is often driven by a fear of offending, a lack of a fundamental understanding of the other's culture, or by the meaning attached to specific events or behaviors. As an example, a nationally regarded social work educator expressed his extreme discomfort with how to refer to people of African descent, making a joke about whether to call them Negro, Black, Afro-American, or "just what" (to use his precise words). His discomfort came across as offensive to African Americans in a situation where it clearly was not the intent. An awareness and understanding of the often dissimilar worldview of people of African descent may very well have prevented the perceived trivializing comment about an aspect of identity that is so meaningful.

Enlightened consciousness also has attitudinal and affective dimensions. The restructuring of worldview requires a critical review of what individuals believe is reality. When awareness, sensitivity, and genuine acceptance toward culturally different others are internalized, our whole affective demeanor moves closer to one of openness to engagement. The reality of a multicultural society is accepted, and the struggle to maintain the superiority/inferiority dichotomy eases. We acknowledge the shortcomings of our education and socialization, we express the need to expand our knowledge and understanding of others, and we make a steadfast commitment to do the work necessary to move from the comfort of a monocultural existence to a bicultural and, ultimately, a multicultural existence.

It should be apparent that this dynamic process cannot even begin in short-term or brief overtures into another's world. It must be a sustained effort motivated by a true desire to become accepting and comfortable in personal cross-cultural interactions and effective in providing services to clients whose cultural realities differ markedly from one's own. This work requires immersion experiences through what Green [1995] refers to as participant observation using cultural guides. Genuine efforts to increase knowledge and awareness of others are often met with positive responses from professionals and clients alike, especially when attitudes of condescension and voyeurism are resolved. Professionals and clients of color willingly engage in a teaching/learning process that is approached from a position of equality and shared meaning. African American professionals often experience and describe resentment when approached and expected by colleagues to be teachers in unidirectional ways. Too often, they are requested to share content and material on diversity without accompanying offers to share resources or demonstrated effort to obtain information through normal pursuits. This failure is often viewed as a less than genuine commitment to expand one's knowledge base absent clear and sustained previous work to do so.

Exploring the uniqueness of one's own culture, and identifying and embracing both positive and negatively perceived aspects, increases one's ability to approach these aspects in the cultures of others. A state of enlightened consciousness enables one to connect with culturally different others at a new level of excitement and joy. Blockades and walls erected to separate begin to crumble, making way for a lifelong journey toward the attainment of cultural competence.

Grounded Knowledge Base

We are all burdened with the Eurocentric bias that is the foundation of our formal and informal education. The very nature of the education process, as well as the content that is selected and presented, is flawed in ways that make it extremely tedious to dissect and dismantle its stronghold. The formal education process begins with the highly questionable—if not false notion—that science is neutral and lacks bias. History, mythology, values, culture, scientific methodology—all shape the basic essence of knowledge building. The bias is so deeply entrenched that it is often difficult for the most adept among us to engage the misinformation in a productive way. A *grounded knowledge base* begins with the premise that everything must be exposed to a process of critical analysis. This is emphatically true because the selection of content to which we are introduced has so thoroughly excluded perspectives that both challenge and broaden the Eurocentric worldview. The theory and practice wisdom that form the basis of social work practice demand considerable and ongoing critique, in addition to teaching future social workers how to develop this mode of inquiry.

Examples of major weaknesses and gaps in the knowledge base passed on to others in the profession of social work are numerous. For example, contributions of African Americans and other people of color to the social welfare systems rarely, if ever, are included in the knowledge base. Further, most of us were introduced to mainstream developmental theories—Freud, Erikson, Kohlberg, and so on—in human behavior courses, and completed this education exchange without knowing that these conceptualizations of normal life-course development describe women and culturally different people as deficient and abnormal. Theorists who describe normal adult development as career attainment, heterosexual marriage, childbearing, and managing a household exclude the developmental experiences of a substantial number of people. Unfortunately, in this educational scenario, alternative theoretical perspectives are either not available or seldom get presented.

The pursuit of a grounded knowledge base demands creative use of a wide range of sources of information that includes other disciplines, related subject matter, and nonmainstream works. Communities of color, key informants, and traditional and nontraditional economic, religious, and social institutions are dynamic laboratories for relevant knowledge building and must be seen as valuable resources.

In the field of child welfare, developing an essential knowledge base is an expansive endeavor. A number of areas, however, are absolutely critical to enhancing competence with ethnically and culturally diverse people. No list would ever be considered complete or comprehensive, but the following essentials are believed to be foundational components for every child welfare worker actively engaged in becoming culturally competent.

1.   Knowledge of the history, culture, traditions and customs, preferred language or primary dialect, value orientation,

religious and spiritual orientations, art, music, and folk or
other healing beliefs of the groups for which the worker carries out professional responsibilities is required. While it is
frequently necessary in cognitive processes to rely on generalizations, practitioners must discern important differences
in culture and practice between and among groups typically
categorized as monolithic. Further, the worker's exploration
of her or his own ethnic or cultural group is essential because the value and meaning others hold about the culture
will likely emerge from it.

2. Child welfare workers need intimate familiarity about so-
    cial problems and issues that have different impacts on mi-
    nority group members. These conditions are, most especially,
    sustained patterns of socioeconomic disadvantage because
    of poverty, unemployment, or truncated education; morbid-
    ity and mortality; health and psychosocial risk factors such
    as substance abuse; and increasing rates of interpersonal and
    community violence. It is fundamentally important that
    workers understand the dynamics that sustain these prob-
    lems, as well as their origin and etiology, so that interven-
    tions may be appropriately targeted.

3. Because children and families live in and relate to neighbor-
    hoods and communities in deeply interlocking ways, work-
    ers must include neighborhoods and communities as vital
    aspects of their practice domain. Neighborhood and com-
    munity profiles, including, for example, sociodemographic
    information and a comprehensive knowledge of neighbor-
    hood needs and resources, are essential. Formal, civic, and
    informal resources are important. Workers often fail to use
    valuable resources offered by churches, religious institutions,
    and other community-based programs that have a long his-
    tory of prominence in communities of color.

4. Practitioners must demonstrate a firm understanding of the
    dynamics of oppression, racism, sexism, classism, and other
    forms of discrimination that shadow and defame culturally

different clients irreparably. It is also critical to understand
the process by which clients internalize oppression, how that
process is manifested, and how it compounds an already
overburdened reality. Persons with an enlightened consciousness no longer engage in the futile process of denying
the historical and current existence of oppression; they no
longer make excuses or try to justify the fear and hatred that
fuel it. Instead, they acknowledge the need to develop stra-
tegic and persistent responses to thwart and eliminate individual and institutional mechanisms that maintain oppression, and busy themselves doing so. These efforts require
knowledge of advocacy and individual and community
empowerment as child welfare professionals form real collaborations with families and communities.

5. Child welfare workers should have knowledge of the formal child welfare system, its history, the contributions made
by people of color to the development of services for children and families, the current issues facing child welfare (including funding and policy shifts), and, most especially, the
obstacles to providing effective services to culturally diverse
clients. Workers must clearly understand minority group
perceptions and feelings about the larger social welfare system generally, and specifically, their own perceptions and
feelings concerning the child welfare system. Consumers of
social and child welfare services have a long history of receiving degrading and humiliating experiences within these
systems and harbor great fear and distrust of the system. In
fact, social workers are generally held in extremely poor regard in communities of color, where the negative experiences
of members are transmitted over time. Recent focus groups
of child welfare clients conducted by the author in an east-
ern city confirmed just how negatively perceived these institutions are. Workers must be able to engage clients
empathically and with sensitivity concerning these very real
perceptions, and most importantly, must stop citing the un-

derstandable resistance offered by clients as something inherently deficient in the client when inappropriate interventions fail.

6. Workers must be well-versed regarding the diversity of family structure and the often overlooked functionality of diverse family forms among families of color. Billingsley [1992] provides an exhaustive and informed description of the great variation in African American families and an unparalleled discourse on the remarkable strategies these families have used to survive and to excel over time.

7. Knowledge about family functioning is a broad and expansive area fraught with ambiguity concerning indicators of what constitutes optimal functioning or its opposite, dysfunctioning, within families. Assessing family functioning is even more problematic when one lacks knowledge about culturally proscribed and prescribed behavior. Child-rearing practices, including methods of discipline, nurturing, and meeting physical and psychosocial needs of children; responses to illness and health; and racial socialization are all areas where culturally competent practitioners must be adept. The imprecise nature of the ways in which the profession assesses risk for children and what genuinely constitutes neglect and abuse demand that we approach these areas solidly grounded in community and cultural norms. The use of corporal punishment in many African American families, for example, is an area where great care and understanding must be exercised. Coping strategies and survival behaviors of people of color demonstrate great variance, and lacking knowledge that an immersion experience provides puts practitioners at an extreme disadvantage when seeking to discover "what works." Martin and Martin [1995] portray dynamically how African Americans use blues and spirituals as a way of defining a problem through "moanin;" engage a problem-solving process through "mournin," which includes collective empathy, emotional catharsis, in-

culcation of hope and faith, and facing reality objectively;
and express through "mornin," finally seeing the light and
achieving hoped-for dreams most typically through the connection and intervention of a sovereign God. It is knowledge of these diverse cultural processes and the ability to
validate and support them that increases the effectiveness
of child welfare practice with culturally different clients.

8. Knowledge of child welfare interventions is enhanced by
incorporating alternative theoretical and practice perspectives that are culturally relevant. One must be constantly
alert to the possibility of alternative explanations for behavior and events. For example, what is often described as ma-
nipulative behavior may be reframed as problem-solving
efforts in need of support and skill development. Chestang
[1972], in a seminal work on character development in a
hostile environment, describes an effective dual response
wherein a balance is sought between a perennial belief in
the goodness of people and the reality of threats posed by
them. Workers who recognize and understand the dynamics of hostile environments for people of color do not ask
them to give up a major survival and adaptive strategy before they are on firm footing with other more effective alternatives.

9. Child welfare practitioners must value and build on the
longstanding informal foster/adoption/kinship care practices that are characteristic in families of color. Because family preservation, family reunification, and family support
interventions are pursued within a cultural milieu, they represent new challenges for practitioners. Many of the models
being implemented in various parts of the U.S. are built on
theoretical and practice perspectives that are incongruent
with minority families' belief systems. For example, many
ethnic and cultural groups use faith and the belief in a higher
power to resolve difficult and seemingly elusive problems,
whereas professionals often minimize or dismiss the legiti-

macy of this practice. In this regard, it seems obvious that cultural context must form the basis of intervention choices and strategies with clients of color. Short-term and intense interventions must be measured in the context of the oftentimes longstanding risk factors such as poverty and unemployment that clients have little control over and are not likely to resolve in an arbitrary time, despite their best efforts.

10. Concepts related to strengths and resilience must be incorporated into explanations of behavior and approaches to intervention. The ability to identify assets in a family beset by overwhelming liabilities often produces the pivotal turning point toward successful interventions with culturally different clients. Although a great deal of effort has been made by child welfare practitioners to incorporate a strengths perspective in work with families, many of the models that make up the landscape of practice continue to overemphasize deficits, making it difficult to help clients glean a sense of hope for positive change. This point is especially pertinent due to the unrelenting negative images of people of color portrayed in our society.

A grounded knowledge base must significantly expand the social work and child welfare knowledge base as currently constructed. To become culturally competent, workers must engage in persistent and thoughtful analysis of the cultural implications of the most basic and fundamental theoretical constructs and practice approaches. The search for cultural relevance must be put to the test unapolegetically and used in ways that continually enrich this critical knowledge base.

Cumulative Skill Proficiency

Enlightened consciousness and a grounded knowledge base are the bricks and cement that build *cumulative skill proficiency*. *Cumulative* connotes the process nature of skill development and suggests that the practitioner who is committed to becoming culturally effective recognizes the building and constructing nature of this effort. *Skill proficiency* is not a haphazard process; it is focused, systematic, reflective, and evaluative. Continuing to use skills because we were trained that way or because we lack alternative skill proficiency is out of sync with the goal of achieving cultural competence.

One of the most crucial skills for a culturally competent practitioner is the ability to engage a culturally different client's reality in an accepting, genuine, nonoffensive manner. Practitioners who give equal value to others' worldview are more able to engage clients in ways that put them at ease quickly and successfully. People of color are adept at reading the slightest nuance or cue that carries even the most carefully concealed message of disapproval, discomfort, or nonacceptance because of one's race, culture, or ethnicity. A description of a worker as "she's alright" by a client of color in reference to a cross-cultural interaction is usually a response to an accurate reading of the worker's skill at entering a dissimilar cultural milieu. Acquiring such a fundamentally important skill can only take place through consistent practice motivated by an authentic goal to be real with others.

Prevailing practice principles are clear about the importance of developing rapport and trust with clients. Cultural differences, by their very existence, complicate the bridging of what often appear as gulfs. An inferior knowledge base, coupled with a skewed view of our multicultural reality, doom the best efforts to connect with clients in productive work. In clinical practice, for example, it is futile to expect people of color, given their contravening history with the Caucasian world, to immediately trust the intentions of Caucasian workers or to honestly disclose deeply personal and threatening information about themselves or their families. Closing this cultural gap is the professional responsibility of the culturally competent practitioner.

Assessment and intervention skills in a broad sense form the child welfare practitioner's armamentarium, and grow out of the critical knowledge base above. In assessment, the very questions we pursue are determined by worldview and practice theory [McPhatter 1991]. Our beliefs about why people experience unusual problems in living and how change occurs guide assessment and intervention processes. The areas we pursue in assessment must be informed by substantial understanding of the client's cultural reality or the result is often distorted, confused, and unhelpful.

Given the longstanding institutional and environmental structures that have a negative impact on people of color, the culturally competent worker must be able to intervene skillfully at every level—organizational, community, social, economic, and political. Intervening swiftly and effectively to remove organizational or community obstacles to the benefit of clients sends powerful messages to clients of color about the worker's skill and commitment, with invaluable outcome. This is especially true if Caucasian workers correctly identify and confront issues of racism and discrimination, a battle that people of color often feel they fight alone.

Practitioners who do not view macro issues as their domain, given their import to minority clients, function in a vacuum and will not achieve even minimal levels of effectiveness in their work with culturally different clients. Knowledge of organizational and structural dynamics and related intervention skills are critical for effective work with clients of color. Early and successful interventions by workers in behalf of clients with court systems, social welfare agencies, and health care and other service providers often convince clients of color of the worker's trustworthiness, thus easing the way for more intra/interpersonal interactions.

Cross-cultural communication skills are also a must. Use of professional jargon with clients and equating the lack of a command of standard English with a lack of intelligence are frequent errors made by child welfare workers. Culturally incompetent workers more often than not walk away from interactions with clients with a distorted and incomplete view because the workers know so little about the language and dialects used by the clients. For example, how often do workers know to interpret a reference to "my raise" as describing a parent; "keep it on the down low" as hold in confidence; or "running it" as manipulating or getting over on someone. The fact that language and accompanying meaning change so frequently among some cultural groups emphasizes the importance of frequent and ongoing connections within the cultural environment of clients.

Proficiency in practice skills with culturally diverse groups is an important component for measuring successful outcome. Effective cross-cultural communication results in increased accuracy in assessment of problem areas, leading to appropriate and strategically targeted interventions. If we clearly grasp culturally expressed intrapsychic and behavioral dynamics, opportunities for effective resolution increase exponentially.

The Consequences of Cultural Incompetence

The current level of cultural incompetence can persist only at vast detriment to children, families, communities, the child welfare system, and society as a whole. Policymakers, administrators, planners, and organizers design culturally irrelevant programs and services in sync with perceptions and agendas that are not only incongruent with the realities and needs of culturally diverse populations, but also often exacerbate the very problems they aim to ease. The cost of this business-as-usual approach to child welfare concerns is incalculable. The socioeconomic, personal, familial, and community problems we now face are increasing in complexity each day. Burnout and worker turnover add to these complexities. Programs and practice interventions born outside of the appropriate cultural context pursue erroneous targets, squander scarce resources, and help few. Child welfare agencies continue in disarray and uncertainty about real visions and ways of reaching them. Caucasian professionals, professionals of color, and culturally diverse clients are estranged from one another; they are anxious, angry, and bitter as they seek targets for their confusion and sense of failure. Cultural incompetence does absolutely nothing to rescue the neediest of our children and families from the tragic futures they face. Professionals cannot model or emulate what they do not understand and do not know how to practice.

What are the benefits of an authentic commitment to achieving cultural competence? In the short run, efforts at enlightened consciousness help free us from ignorance, and truth is aired. The effort helps us to regard, respect, and value each other. The real payoff is the realization that we are more effective in our efforts and more energized toward goal attainment when we are not constantly trying to protect our fears, trying to say or do the politically correct thing, and trying to avoid the most frightening prospect—being thought of as a bigot. We begin to develop a foundation of trust at the core of which is equality, resulting in more creative solutions to difficult problems. Culturally competent practitioners provide culturally relevant services to people. We ask and listen to what culturally diverse people say about their needs and we attend and respond to their views about how to approach resolution.

The Challenge

The process of becoming culturally competent begins with an honest assessment of one's level of functioning with culturally different others. This challenge requires a level of honesty and forthrightness that eludes most. Practitioners and educators alike consistently perceive themselves to be considerably more effective in their cross-cultural work than they, in fact, are. It is these faulty perceptions that get in the way of the real work that must be done to achieve the level of effectiveness that children and families of color have every right to expect. The questions below, honestly approached, are designed to assist in the initiation of that appraisal.

1. How much personal/social time do I spend with people who are culturally similar to or different from me?
2. When I am with culturally different people, do I reflect my own cultural preferences or do I spend the time openly learning about the unique aspects of another person's culture?
3. How comfortable am I in immersion experiences, especially when I am in a numerical minority? What feelings and behaviors do I experience or exhibit in this situation?
4. How much time do I spend engaged in cross-cultural professional exchanges? Is this time spent in superficial, cordial activity, or do I undertake the risk of engaging in serious discourse that may divulge my fears and lack of knowledge?
5. How much work have I actually done to increase my knowledge and understanding of culturally and ethnically distinct groups? Does this work include only an occasional workshop in which I am required to participate? What are my deficiencies and gaps in knowledge about important cultural issues?
6. What is my commitment to becoming culturally competent? What personal and professional sacrifices am I willing to make in the short term for the long-term benefit of all children and families?
7. To what extent have I nondefensively extended myself in approaching professional colleagues with the goal of bridging cultural differences?
8. Am I willing to discontinue representing myself as knowledgeable and as having expertise in areas of cultural diversity that I have not actually achieved?
9. If I am unwilling to commit to a path leading to cultural competence, will I take the moral and ethical high ground and discontinue providing services to people I am unwilling to learn about?◆

References

American Psychological Association. (1992). *Ethical principles of psychologists and code of conduct*. Washington, DC: Author.

Billingsley, A. (1992). *Climbing Jacob's Ladder: The enduring legacy of African American families*. New York: Simon and Schuster.

Chestang, L. (1972). Character development in a hostile environment. *Occasional Paper No. 3*. Chicago: University of Chicago.

Children's Defense Fund. (1994). *The state of America's children*. Washington, DC: Author.

Dana, R. H., Behn, J. D., & Gonwa, T. (1992). A checklist for the examination of cultural competence in social service agencies. *Research on Social Work Practice, 2*, 220–233.

Devore, W., & Schlesinger, E. G. (1996). *Ethnic sensitive social work practice* (4th ed.). Boston: Allyn and Bacon.

Diggs, C. H. (1992). *Ethnic minority content in graduate social work education: Faculty views and experiences* (unpublished dissertation, University of Texas, Austin).

Edelman, M. W. (1987). *Families in peril: An agenda for social change*. Cambridge, MA: Harvard University Press.

Everett, J. E., Chipungu, S. S., & Leashore, B. R. (Eds.). (1991). *Child welfare: An Africentric perspective*. New Brunswick, NJ: Rutgers University Press.

Green, J. W. (1982). *Cultural awareness in the human services*. Englewood Cliffs, NJ: Prentice-Hall.

Green, J. W. (1995). *Cultural awareness in the human services: A multi-ethnic approach*. Boston: Allyn and Bacon.

Kavanagh, K. H., & Kennedy, P. H. (1992). *Promoting cultural diversity: Strategies for health care professionals*. Newbury Park, CA: Sage Publications.

Logan, S. M. L., Freeman, E. M., & McRoy, R. G. (1990). *Social work practice with Black families: A culturally specific perspective*. New York: Longman.

Martin, E. P,. & Martin, J. M. (1995). *Social work and the Black experience*. Washington, DC: NASW Press.

McAdoo, H. P. (Ed.). (1993). *Family ethnicity: Strength in diversity*. Newberry Park, CA: Sage Publications.

McMahon, A., & Allen-Meares, P. (1992). Is social work racist? A content analysis of recent literature. *Social Work, 37,* 533–538.

McPhatter, A. R. (1991) Assessment revisited: A comprehensive model for assessing family dynamics. *Families in Society, 72,* 11–22.

National Center on Child Abuse and Neglect. (1994). *Child maltreatment 1992: Reports from the states to the National Center on Child Abuse and Neglect.* Washington, DC: U.S. Government Printing Office.

Norton, D. G. (1978). *The dual perspective: Inclusion of ethnic minority content in the social work curriculum.* New York: Council on Social Work Education.

Sue, D. W., Arrendondo, P., & McDavis, R. J. (1992). Multicultural counseling competencies and standards: A call to the profession. *Journal of Multicultural Counseling, 20,* 64–88.